THE FRENCH PRESS IN THE AGE OF ENLIGHTENMENT

"This book is well written, well conceived, and based on both original sources and a mastery of secondary literature. It will make a substantial contribution to our knowledge of eighteenth-century France . . . It does not simply summarize the monographic literature, it goes well beyond previous scholarship . . . This volume will become the standard work for many years on the French press in the Age of the Enlightenment."

Professor Gary Kates, Trinity University

The ideas of the Enlightenment and belligerent royal officials critically influenced the French Revolution, but how did an entire generation learn about such ideas prior to the Revolution? Jack R. Censer's achievement in this volume is to marshal a vast literature in order to provide a coherent and original interpretation of the role of the French Press in the dissemination of social and political ideas in the years leading up to the Revolution. Censer also explores the relationship between journalists and government officials and unearths a range of sophisticated censorship techniques employed by the government to keep Bad News off the front pages.

In a field dominated by specialized studies but few generalizations, *The French Press in the Age of Enlightenment* provides a bold synthesis regarding the periodical press from mid-century to the Revolution.

Jack R. Censer is Professor of History at George Mason University. His most recent publications include *The French Revolution and Intellectual History* (1989), and he is series editor of *Rewriting Histories*.

THE FRENCH PRESS IN THE AGE OF ENLIGHTENMENT

Jack R. Censer

London and New York

First published 1994
by Routledge
11 New Fetter Lane, London EC4P 4EE

Simultaneously published in the USA and Canada
by Routledge
29 West 35th Street, New York, NY 10001

© 1994 Jack R. Censer

Typeset in 10 on 12 point Palatino by
Computerset, Harmondsworth, Middlesex
Printed and bound in Great Britain by
T.J. Press (Padstow) Ltd, Padstow, Cornwall

British Library Cataloguing in Publication Data
A catalogue record for this book is available from the British Library

Library of Congress Cataloging in Publication Data
Censer, Jack Richard.
The French Press in the Age of Enlightenment/Jack R. Censer.
p. cm.
Includes bibliographical references and index.
1. Press—France—History—18th century. I. Title.
PN5176.C46   1994
074'.09'033—dc20   93–44377

ISBN 0-415-09730-4

To Jane

CONTENTS

TABLES

ACKNOWLEDGEMENTS

Projects long in the making incur many debts, too great to be sys-tematically recorded and paid here. In fact, many assisted me just by listening to or tolerating my ruminations. The very existence of the supportive network of dix-huitièmistes in America, my French historian colleagues in the Baltimore/Washington area, those American historians of France with whom I shared time abroad, and finally that growing coterie of Frenchmen willing to listen to Americans interested in their history all contributed mightily to the completion of this project. Fund-ing institutes – the Max Planck Institut für Geschichte, the American Philosophical Association, the National Endowment for the Humanities, and the American Council of Learned Societies–all played a critical role. At the very beginning of this work, in 1978–79, I spent an extremely fruitful year as a Mellon Fellow at the University of Pittsburgh. My academic home, George Mason University, provided great assistance.

I should like to mention specifically a few individuals among the many who helped. Robert Forster, Seymour Drescher, Dan Resnick, Joe Klaits, Robert Darnton, Steve Kaplan, Daniel Roche, and Sheila Levine listened to versions of this project. Nina Gelbart and Keith Baker have been close friends and influences for years. Don Sutherland, Tim Tackett, and Hans Erich Bödeker helped me talk through problems in French history in general; and Betty Eisenstein has been a constant source of good ideas and information. Shaul Bakhash and Tony LaVopa provided enormously helpful sounding boards for my poorly formed ideas. In my own depart-ment, Roy Rosenzweig and Marion Deshmukh were very encouraging and supportive. The encouragement from my editor at Routledge, Claire L'Enfant, proved essential. And Tina Raheem was both typist and friend.

Lynn Hunt and Claude Labrosse read the entire draft and offered excellent suggestions. Pierre Rétat did the same and also was instrumen-tal in facilitating a French response to my work. Gary Kates provided a very thorough reading of the manuscript and gave large doses of friend-ship and encouragement along the way. Lenard Berlanstein and Jim

ACKNOWLEDGEMENTS

Turner have read almost everything I have written over the last twenty years and assisted both intellectually and personally. This work owes a great deal to Jeremy Popkin, whose own research proved essential for this study. In addition, he gave a very, very thorough and thoughtful evaluation of this book in manuscript. But, most important, the intellectual debates that we have had for over a score of years forced me to sharpen my arguments and think in ways that were very valuable but not necessarily congenial to me. To all those who assisted me, I offer a grateful thank-you and, of course, relieve you from all the errors and infelicities still remaining.

To my family, I cannot say enough. To my encouraging parents, I am sorry that you did not live to see this book completed. Although this project began before my children Marjorie and Joel were born, they lived with it through many stages and have given me the needed perspective to keep plowing through it. They really helped even when, or especially when, they kept me from my work. With good cheer, strength, and innumerable intellectual contributions, Jane Turner Censer made this book possible. Every line benefited from her attention. It simply never could have been accomplished without her.

INTRODUCTION: THE PERIODICAL PRESS

By the second half of the eighteenth century, the French language periodical press had become a very substantial enterprise with dozens of competing publications. Various characteristics distinguished it from the larger world of print: above all, the government recognized its different characteristics and accorded it its own regimen of regulation.[1] The press's periodicity also provided a particular sort of challenge to state authority. Critics, indeed, considered periodicals a single group, often assailing it – rather contradictorily – for useless polemics as well as for dryness.[2] Forced to develop a different work schedule for the periodical, printers came to recognize the medium as especially problematic.[3] Editors too came to regard periodicals as a genre, remaining in journalism even if they seldom idealized such a career. Some publishers specialized in the periodical, and norms governing proper reporting began, hesitantly, to be articulated.[4]

A common-sense definition of "a periodical," that would capture contemporary opinion on this subject, might specify it as a printed publication available on announced dates, at least once a trimester, designed to serve a broad, at least regional, reading public.[5] In addition, these organs must have published something that their audience would have seen as current news; whatever the subject, contributing to the present remained critical. Otherwise, they were simply volumes in a series. "French periodicals" include, for this study, the considerable Francophone press, published beyond the nation's borders but intended to a substantial degree for a French audience.

Such a definition excludes, in particular, specialized magazines intended for particular interests, professions or organizations, such as periodicals that were exclusively composed of price lists, ship arrivals and departures, or technical, scientific or artistic materials, as well as manuscript newsletters whose price and small number of copies allowed only limited circulation. Excluding such newsletters may seem arbitrary, but this genre possessed an entirely different milieu and purpose than its printed relatives.[6] In general, the manuscript newssheet was far more

1

elitist and far more focused on clandestine information. Other relatives of the press excluded from this study include annual almanacs and pamphlets whose subjects competed with periodicals but whose infrequent periodicity, among other characteristics, made them rather different creations.

To delineate what this book or this extended essay – as a general survey of the French periodical from 1745 to the revolutionary crisis early in 1787[7] – can contribute to our knowledge of the press requires some review of the literature. The historiography of the press already consists, not only of countless monographic investigations, but also of a number of general histories.[8] Perhaps the greatest synthesis, that by Eugène Hatin in the mid-nineteenth century, set the pattern for all the other overall accounts by providing individual treatments of many journals. In effect, his and other general histories consisted of serial biographies of periodicals.[9] For many publications, they fulfilled this goal very well, although gaps in information about some papers made their findings uneven. Of course, such biographies could hardly be melded into an overall picture of the press for the late Old Regime. But such studies comprised the best and the bulk of the work up through the last general history edited by Claude Bellanger and others in 1969.

In large part originating in France under the leadership of Pierre Rétat, Jean Sgard and Claude Labrosse, more studies have likely been published since 1969 than in that long period from 1789 to 1969. Broader waves of scholarship have also been responsible for this surge. Among the many influences was a shift in the historiography of the French Revolution and the Enlightenment. As social history propelled researchers to examine the ideas of those outside the intellectual elite, historians turned to the press to see how journalists presented politics and culture to a wider public. Scholars interested in literature simultaneously invaded the history of the press as their interest in different types of genres mounted. More recently, as historians became concerned with discourses, the press appeared a good place to explore the general resonance of particular sets of ideas. Scholars have taken soundings of eighteenth-century feminism and misogyny in the pages of the press.[10]

The more recent studies differ significantly from their forerunners. This new research has greatly deepened our knowledge. First, scholars have seriously investigated the content of journals. While Hatin relied largely on journalists' published promises for content, we now have content analyses. Second, historians of the press have charted new areas in the milieus that produced and regulated the press. Important investigations have taken place about such topics as the role of the government, business practices, expectations of readers, the backgrounds of journalists, and availability of information. Finally, some scholars trained in the study of literature have addressed the press, not so much as a carrier of ideas, but as a system of communication. How were ideas transported through the press compared with other media?[11] Furthermore, many of these new analyses have attained a level of detail and nuance previously unmatched. Expanding onto virgin turf, such research has mapped the press with unprecedented sophistication.

But what new and old share is a great fragmentation in understanding. While previous works reported the field without much effort at synthesis, recent studies seem to excavate an increasingly deeper trench with little reference to one another. Even the best work seldom tends to utilize the findings of nearby scholarship.

In this study, I hope first and foremost to create a general interpretation and reverse the growing incoherence of the field by providing overall treatments of selected areas. By outlining the general contours of the press and its contents, this book supersedes several past general histories composed of juxtaposed press biographies. Yet the complexities of these new areas of investigation have also made summary difficult; in their own ways they provide pictures as partial as those of Hatin and others. Overall, I plan to use and supplement not only all earlier work, but to direct it toward a synthesis.

Producing a general interpretation while retaining the subjects and techniques of generations of scholars, especially the most recent, requires significant compromises. First, the treatment of many topics had to be limited. Generalized coverage of a myriad of areas – some of which require very painstaking approaches – is beyond the competence of a single scholar, and perhaps even a team. Yet even for the subjects selected, other choices and strategies had to be made. No general account could meet the current high standards regarding the necessary level of detail and nuance. Yet simply to report various evidence about periodicals would end up like Hatin and his successors. To circumvent this problem, this essay relies on two approaches. Most chapters employ a few carefully chosen case studies to take advantage of the detailed research of others. For other questions, it has been possible to explore evidence concerning many periodicals and extrapolate the conclusions. Essentially, to reach a sophisticated level of general understanding, this book relies on generalizing from limited information. Even though this technique can partly overcome past problems – and, I hope, sustain the high level of recent scholarship found in monographs – it demands the reader's indulgence for adventurous extensions from details to generalizations. Such an approach holds yet another seeming drawback since its reliance on specific cases may omit some of the best known journals and journalists. Fortunately, the older general histories as well as the newly published *Dictionnaire des journaux* (Paris, 1991), provide much information on these well known cases.

3

With such compromises, this admittedly limited synthetic picture can reduce the fragmentation already described. By providing a bird's-eye view, this book should provide a focus, or at least a target, for future research. In any case, this extended essay – for that is what it is – by establishing a general interpretation can build the framework to allow concentrated studies of journals and thus can facilitate more rapid advances in this important subfield. Despite the considerable achievements of the work of Hatin and others, the history of the press has been little integrated into the general interpretation of the Old Regime and the coming of the Revolution. In part, this stems from a lack of generalizations about the press – a gap this study attempts to fill. At the same time this process ought to encourage further the incorporation of the periodical into general interpretations of eighteenth-century France.

Twin goals – drawing the first overall picture of the press and relating it to broader historiography – provide the impetus for this study. What then are the areas selected for synthesis? The first half of the book addresses the point of view expressed in three main genres: the political press, the advertisers, and the literary/philosophical press.[12] The remainder of the work concerns the milieu. While many subjects might have been selected, the justification for the choice here of the journalistic community, the role of the central government, and the audience is that these three factors seem the most significant in understanding the press's perspective. Moreover, historians have addressed all three (as well as content) on their own merit.

Informing the selection of the particular areas of concentration were broader historical contentions beyond the history of the press. Central to motivating this work is the interest, already noted among many scholars of the press, in the ideas debated and available in the eighteenth century. This concern not only led here to focusing on content, but also to exploring the implications of the findings. More precisely, whenever scholars have weighed the political opinions circulating in eighteenth-century France, they have employed a crude continuum ranging from the values of absolutism at one end to those of the Revolution at the other. This approach is problematic because over the century the king became less and less an absolutist himself. Nonetheless, the monarchy, even if not the monarch, still rested on the foundation of divine right; and it remains reasonable to take this as one end of the spectrum.

Specifically, this overview contributes to mapping the range of political ideas by showing a mixed picture of how periodicals understood the monarchy. The first half of Chapter 1 on the newspaper reveals that the coverage of events arrived late and appeared rather indistinct, depriving these periodicals of an opportunity to inject much of a system of timely accountability into politics. As the century came to its climactic end, this situation ameliorated but without substantive change. The remainder of the chapter indicates that, with regard to the more open expression of attitudes, newspapers could contribute though perhaps in rather unexpected ways. Direct criticism of the crown emerged in the press of the 1750s and 1760s, but this critique largely withered in the later decades until the series of crises leading directly into the Revolution were underway. And there was praise for the government's foreign policy. Although an ideological challenge indirectly emerged in the 1770s and 1780s through newspaper coverage of the democratic revolutions, this material could not compensate for the decline in direct criticism. No individual publication broke out of this pattern. While some historians have found the political press merely an organ of the monarchy,[13] others (and I too in an earlier work) have portrayed the press as becoming increasingly bold.[14] Some scholars have even seen the Revolution developing in the pages of the Old Regime papers. This chapter reaches a more nuanced and diachronic assessment than the extremes, as it shows both the extent and the transformation of the press's criticisms.

In contributing to understanding the problematic nature of the press, Chapter 2 on the provincial papers and Chapter 3 on the literary and philosophical press provide the same kind of balanced treatment. Although generally viewed as the least challenging, the provincial press in my account validates a vision of society that questioned traditional arrangements. Still, its somewhat oblique criticisms of society would only indirectly trouble the crown. These affiches thus created some but not extensive difficulties for the monarchy. The literary–philosophical press, discussed in Chapter 3, screened out the majority of the most radical ideas and eschewed direct involvement with the Encyclopédistes and other intellectuals. Yet these periodicals still broadly supported sentimentalism à la Rousseau and Diderot and the High Enlightenment minus its attacks on Church and state.[15] These two intellectual movements were not particularly controversial after mid-century; yet contemporaries believed them to be the antithesis of Old Regime religion, and to a lesser extent, the Old Regime government. Nonetheless, the monarchy endeavored to sidestep even this. As Daniel Roche has shown, the crown tried hard to associate itself with this part of the intellectual outpouring of the century.[16] Although monarchial supporters such as Voltaire considered this effort successful, most people disagreed. Thus, the press's support for sentimentalism and a muted High Enlightenment provided something of an attack against monarchy.

In sum, the first three chapters give a similar portrayal of the periodical and dispute those scholars who claim too little and those who claim too much for the press. This work also adds to the broader debate on the availability of different notions. It reminds us, contrary to common scholarly perception, that the eighteenth century was not simply the crossroads for a maelstrom of unsettling political beliefs. Of course, the press was not totally quiescent politically and was more charged regarding Church and traditional society. Finally, while this study evidently also rejects the direct causal link between an aggressive press and the Revolution, still the press can tell us much about the causes of the Revolution. The conclusion explores this topic and relates it to the historiography of Old Regime and the Revolution.

The second part of this book focuses on the concerns of press history by explaining the contours of the periodicals' context; yet it too contributes to a range of issues of more general concern. Chapter 4 on the journalists adds depth to our understanding of recruitment into the middle ranges of intellectual life. Although historians have tried to comprehend governmental efforts to regulate the printed word, they have never produced a detailed chronological account concerning any medium, much less the periodical. Chapter 5 accomplishes that task and in so doing can cast much light on other literary forms as well as on periodicals. For example, patterns of governmental activity and laxity may explain the rhythm of court cases explored by Sarah Maza.[17] This chapter also provides insights applicable to efforts to reform copyright laws. More important, the limits and strengths of royal authority become evident. Finally, Chapter 6 contributes to the history of reading. Little is known in this area, so every accretion possesses value. This one adds greatly to the hypothesis advanced by Robert Darnton that associates the Old Regime with "intensive" instead of "extensive reading".[18] While not quite paralleling Darnton's, the categories of Chapter 6 argue that the papers expected a critical reader. Such a reader gives force to Darnton's conjecture.

Any investigation of the sort intended here necessitates some preliminary outline of the numbers, growth, and divisions in the press. One way of approaching this subject is to categorize and count published periodicals. Of course, this method indicates nothing about circulation but provides general dimensions over time. Sorting through over one thousand Francophone titles that appeared from 1745 to the Revolution poses still other problems. Simply counting these titles proves problematic because it places the most important and ephemeral publications on an equal footing, vastly overvaluing the latter and potentially overrepresenting their significance. In order to provide some general idea of the size of the press, this book attempts a compromise approach by counting for its purposes those journals – evidently only those published for France, even if they served other countries – that lasted at least three years.[19] Focusing on such periodicals presumes that reasonably successful periodicals that acquired some following are considered. By relying on relatively stable periodicals, this strategy can identify and categorize the journals' primary subject matter. Of course, this criterion still undervalues the most successful periodicals, excluding even a handful of extremely popular literary journals that lasted less than three years.[20] Other difficulties plagued the process of counting, but their effects likely proved negligible.[21]

Such considerations, however, sound an alert that any figures must only be considered suggestive. Yet even when one uses different parameters to define the press, the results tend strongly in the same direction, encouraging a belief in the reliability of the means employed here. First, as all commentators have pointed out, the press experienced substantial, reasonably steady growth throughout the century (shown in Table Intro-1).[22]

Table Intro-1 Numbers of periodicals available to the reading public in France

Date	Number
1745	15
1750	21
1755	25
1760	37
1765	37
1770	50
1775	68
1780	73
1785	82

N.B. This table and the others of this section report on the periodicals that lasted three or more years.

Although any given periodical covered many subjects, it seems reasonable to break down these publications into three major categories: political, literary–philosophical and affiches. The first category with its emphasis on formal politics appears clear, but the others demand clarification. A large number of periodicals ranged over the intellectual world and discussed a panoply of questions from science to literature. Readers of the eighteenth century saw no clear demarcations. People jumbled issues together as did these publications. From these practices emerges a large catch-all classification of literary–philosophical periodicals. The affiches, which began only after the mid-eighteenth century, were a special genre that concentrated on advertising. Generally published in the provinces, they had specific regional bases and also carried news of that area. Exceptions to this pattern were the two published in Paris. The first, the *Affiches de province*, was the forerunner of all the local sheets and was clearly intended for national distribution. The other, the *Petites Affiches*, covered the Paris basin, but because of the economic supremacy of the metropolis likely also found readers all over the country. In it, some advertisements surely aimed at a nation of purchasers.

Many of these periodicals trespassed beyond their field, but most remained primarily in one or another area. In order to count the different genres, (as in the following tables of this section), I sorted combination journals according to the kind of news on which primarily they concentrated. This practice distorted the number of different kinds to a very limited extent. In a later section of this chapter which considers circulation figures for each genre, these assignments could have had significance, at least for particular genres if not for any overall total. Important exceptions are discussed at appropriate times.

Although the press grew throughout the last half-century of the Old Regime, Table Intro-2 indicates that the increase was unevenly distributed across the various categories.

Table Intro-2 Total of papers appearing in given years

Years	Politics	Literary–Philosophical	Affiches
1745	5	9	1
1750	5	14	2
1755	5	16	3
1760	12	19	6
1765	12	17	8
1770	12	22	16
1775	13	31	24
1780	18	28	27
1785	19	39	34

Masked behind the steady increase of the century were some major variations. Numbers in the category of politics jumped sharply after 1755 and again in the last decade of the Old Regime. The affiches came to exist in this latter period and account for a substantial part of all the growth of the decades preceding the Revolution. If one breaks these numbers down by the locations of the periodicals, other patterns emerge (see Table Intro-3).

Table Intro-3 Availability of the periodical press by genre and location

Years	Political papers		Literary–Philosophical	
	France	Foreign	France	Foreign
1745	1	4	5	4
1750	1	4	6	8
1755	1	4	11	5
1760	1	9	16	3
1765	1	9	13	4
1770	1	11	16	6
1775	3	10	23	8
1780	3	15	19	9
1785	3	16	23	6

One major point illustrated by this table is that most philosophical papers were published inside France. Consequently, an explanation for what was occurring within France could go far toward explaining the rise and stagnation of the literary press in general. When Malesherbes assumed office as head of the censorship in 1751, he encouraged, as Chapter 5 discusses more fully below, the system for allowing French literary and philosophical journals to publish, and many seem to have taken advantage of the opportunity.[23] The surge of extraterritorial journals by 1750 might explain Malesherbes's move. Perhaps it was a saturation of the market or perhaps a weariness with the battles between the philosophes and their detractors that led to weakened growth after 1760. After another leap after 1770, the subsequent stagnation clearly stemmed from the efforts of the press tsar Charles-Joseph Panckoucke to absorb as many competitors as possible.[24]

While the Parisian scene illuminates trends in philosophical journals, the extraterritorial press does the same for political newspapers. The first problem is to explain an initial lack of growth, followed by their surge in the 1760s. Until the late 1750s the government allowed entry to only five foreign periodicals, and one attracted so few subscribers (the *Avant-Coureur* of Frankfurt with less than 10) that it was not counted here. But after 1759, a new policy emerged that tolerated the entrance of gazettes from outside the borders.[25] Another increase occurred in the late 1770s, when the political press grew in France while remaining stable abroad. In this case, demand rose because of the American revolutionary war and seems to have been met in part by a relaxed policy that allowed Panckoucke to produce officially foreign but actually domestic political journals.[26] Finally once it became possible to license local affiches, an ever rising number of publishers availed themselves of the possibility. Whatever the ebb and flow, clearly a substantial number of publications spread across Old Regime France.

While counting and sorting the periodicals produces at least a sense of the opportunities for eighteenth-century readers, the size and power of this press become more apparent with the addition of circulation figures (see Appendix I for the circulation statistics used here that lack specific citation). Such data possess the inevitable limit of juxtaposing numbers for dailies, bi-weeklies, weeklies, and other periodicities. Even more speculative are the reflections on the size of the audience that conclude each section.

While new affiches rapidly appeared as the century drew to a close, their circulation always remained small, with a maximum of no more than a few hundred. Still there were many titles available, two dozen by 1775 and almost three dozen a decade later. These myriad journals must have produced several thousand issues weekly. The popular *Journal de Paris*, a hybrid of sorts, was, indeed, somewhat an affiches, though not predominantly so. Had it been included here, obviously the circulation of this category would have soared. The practice of sharing copies, including those available in reading rooms, also expanded readership. In some cases, as the name "affiches" suggests, these papers must have been posted for general and unrestricted inspection.

The number of titles in the literary–philosophical press climbed more slowly than the affiches, but still expanded from about ten to nearly forty durable efforts. And while their circulation could be as small as the affiches, they could range above two thousand. The *Journal de Paris* provided an important addition, perhaps because of its livelier, less ponderous approach and its daily publication schedule.[27] The *Journal de Paris* meant the growth in total circulation of this genre likely exceeded the general growth in titles. Perhaps at mid-century there were a few thousand while toward the end the numbers climbed into the low tens of thousands. Nuancing this projection was the uncertain fate of the foreign press (see note 21 for more discussion) with its disproportionately high representation in the early period. At the least, home consumption was substantial for these foreign journals. Moreover, the periodicals based in France were far more likely to be exported than other varieties. All these considerations surely lowered French distribution, particularly early in the 1740s. But this evaluation proceeds without reference to more ephemeral publications, lasting less than three years, whose presence in this genre was particularly substantial. Their addition, one might hypothesize, might raise overall numbers of issues and show a somewhat altered pattern of evolution. Possibly also adding to this circulation might have been the *Mercure de France*, which after 1778 came to focus on politics and so for 1780 and 1785 is counted among that genre. The *Mercure* actually belongs there because the great bulk of its subscriptions did not arrive until the addition of a political section.[28] But whatever the actual numbers in circulation, sharing greatly amplified readership. Because of the relatively high cost of the literary–philosophical press and the fact that its news was less perishable, its potential for being read and reread was quite high.

The political press grew in titles at about the same rate as the philosophical press and its increase in circulation is far more certain. Work by Gilles Feyel allows us to ascertain precisely the early distribution in France of the foreign produced gazettes (see Table Intro-4). In the 1740s this number at most just topped 3,500. At the same time, the *Gazette de France*, the lone domestic journal, had a maximum of 8,800. In addition, the high cost the government imposed on the most controversial titles made counterfeiting both profitable and seemingly common.[29] Sharing too would have been stimulated. No period after this early one has such clear statistics. It is probable however, that the early 1750s witnessed a decline as peace never attracted as many readers as war. Although the data are clearly insufficient, an advance in subscriptions must have occurred with the Seven Years War in 1754 and the change in government policy in the late 1750s which permitted entrance to several periodicals. Allowing prices to descend with this relatively free circulation for the foreign press surely achieved results.[30] Such efforts undermined many pirated editions[31] and probably sharing too, but still increases would seem to have been well above the levels of the 1740s. Most probably, circulation and readership sagged at the end of the war until the American Revolution. In this period, the number of titles surged once again and the known circulation figures are very high. Gilles Feyel has estimated the number of foreign periodicals in France at 14,000[32] while the domestic newspapers generated close to 30,000 in this period. Briefly, the wildly successful, but relatively shortlived *Annales politiques* by Simon-Nicolas-Henri Linguet augmented these figures in the early 1780s by as much as 20,000! Once again, all these numbers ought to be elevated because readers shared copies, though relatively low prices probably discouraged this practice as well as further reducing counterfeiting. In sum, then, legal circulation was approximately four times what it had been in the 1740s even if actual readership had increased by a smaller factor. Following the war another fall in readership occurred, although its dimensions remain unclear.

Table Intro-4 Approximate legal diffusion in France of foreign gazettes

		At Paris			At Avignon[a]	At Lille
	TOTAL	Gazette d'Utrecht	Gazette d'Amsterdam	Gazette de Bruxelles		
1740		140–50				
1742	563	73	450	28	1,211	
1743	622				1,375	
1744	631				1,769	
1745	643				2,153	
1746	649			40–50	2,305	
1747	620	137	465		2,482	
1748	565				2,353	
1749	420				1,281	
1753	320					80

[a]Combined circulation for a counterfeit *Gazette d'Amsterdam* and the *Courrier d'Avignon*.
Source: Gilles Feyel, "La Diffusion des gazettes étrangères en France et la révolution postale des années 1750," in Henri Duranton, Claude Labrosse, and Pierre Rétat, *Les Gazettes européennes de langue française (XVIIe-XVIIIe siècles)* (St.-Etienne, 1992), pp. 81–99.

Overall then, what may be said of all the genres combined? To advance anything at all requires setting aside, at least for the moment, all but the most important caveats developed in the preceding discussion. Of course, what then follows is quite tentative. In the 1740s there were approximately 15 long-term periodicals with perhaps a French circulation of over 15,000, depending especially on the level of pirating, a subject in need of more illumination. At the peak in the 1780s, over 80 periodicals, seemingly not amplified by extensive counterfeiting, had an approximate circulation of over 60,000 copies, and temporarily, while Linguet flourished, of many more. Except for Linguet this estimate compares closely with that of Gilles Feyel who simply skips this writer and in addition does not reveal any basis, outside of the political press, for his estimate.[33] Furthermore as the analysis here has repeatedly suggested, multiple readers consumed each copy, although this practice varied among genres and circumstances. Feyel has used a factor of approximately four to six readers for each issue, suggesting an audience of 240,000 to 360,000.[34] Arriving at an estimate of our current state of knowledge seems difficult. Nonetheless, one may be certain that the last forty years of the Old Regime witnessed an explosion in both periodicals and readers to create a very substantial subject for this study.

Part I

CONTENT

1

THE POLITICAL PRESS

The French political press originated in 1631 and was launched in earnest when Théophraste Renaudot, under the aegis of Cardinal Richelieu, founded the *Gazette de France*. Closely tied to the government, this newspaper from its inception depended on and reflected royal policy. While handbills, fliers, and manuscript materials abounded, the government squashed any effort to begin alternatives because it had guaranteed a monopoly to Renaudot.[1] Nonetheless, within fifteen years new Francophone organs established themselves across the border to take advantage of the French market and address other French-language readers throughout Europe.

By the middle of the eighteenth century, this system had evolved into the continuing *Gazette de France* and several other extraterritorial papers, though only a few were allowed to enter France. An alteration of policy in the late 1750s opened the borders to a dozen or more periodicals.[2] Most important among them were one in Germany (*Courrier du Bas-Rhin*), another in Avignon, and four based in Dutch cities – The Hague, Amsterdam, Leiden, and Utrecht.[3] Along with the *Gazette de France*, this press generally shared a somber style and comprehensive coverage. A few other political magazines with relatively low periodicities existed, and they have been dropped in this analysis. Focus remains on these gazettes, all similar. Whatever their similarities in appearance, all extraterritorial papers enjoyed an independence from France totally unavailable to the *Gazette*, though they too differed widely among themselves. Interest in this sort of publication continued right up to the Revolution, as Pierre Le Brun founded his *Journal général de l'Europe* in Liège in 1785.[4] Indeed, several of these publications managed to continue well after 1789.[5]

If one focuses upon the entire period of this study, 1745 to early 1787, the *Gazette de France* and its relatives provided the lion's share of political information to contemporary readers. But throughout this period there were papers that varied from this approach, including a few adventurers who tried to publish the equivalent of the gossipy *nouvelles à la main*.[6]

After 1770, however, some really important innovations appeared. Beginning in 1772, the government accepted a proposal by the press tsar Charles-Joseph Panckoucke to publish under its general guidance a paper – the *Journal de Genève* – that would in theory have a foreign provenance but actually a French base. Two years later he added a literary section to this paper, also using it within another paper he founded, the *Journal de Bruxelles*. At first the latter had its own political reporting, but by 1778 the political sections of both papers had become identical. In the same year, the *Mercure de France* added the political portion of the Brussels sheet to its pages.[7] These two French organs differed from other newspapers because they were clearly – at least to twentieth century observers – papers produced in France that nonetheless claimed a foreign origin. Even though their copy might approach the foreign papers, the government held more direct promises of conformity. One other feature separated them from their major competitors. They appeared more like a magazine, with fewer and longer articles than their predecessors.

Other papers with links to the government emerged to compete with the *Gazette de France*, foreign gazettes, and the "Brussels" and "Geneva" hybrids with their revised formats. In the middle 1770s, the foreign minister, Count de Vergennes, to further his policy of supporting the American revolutionaries against the British, helped set up and subsidized the *Affaires de l'Angleterre et de l'Amérique*. In addition, the *Courrier de l'Europe*, which began its life like other foreign gazettes, also became a much more controlled organ. Their mixture of independence and dependence may have been roughly equivalent to Panckoucke's journals, though here, as we shall see, the government systematically played a dangerous game by allowing news that, though favorable at the level of foreign policy, promulgated democratic ideas. From its inception in 1776, the *Affaires de l'Angleterre et de l'Amérique* also distinguished itself by a far more analytic style than that of any other political paper.[8] This overall strategy had been tried from the middle 1750s but without major effect.[9]

Another, and in this case, completely different, political periodical was the *Annales littéraires et politiques*, begun in 1777 by Simon-Nicolas-Henri Linguet. In a sense this paper resembles the foreign gazettes because it was a privately-run journal published abroad. But that vastly overstates the comparison. Like the *Affaires de l'Angleterre et de l'Amérique*, the *Annales* was a journal with a focus, in this case the opinions of Linguet. And his views were possibly the most extreme published prior to the Revolution.[10]

This panoply of print organs competed for the French public's attention. As the introductory chapter argued, the main question about this press is assessing how problematic was it in its own time. The conclusion will address its role in the Revolution. Generally, in the case of politics during the Old Regime, royal self-justifications about the monarchy's claim to rule according to divine right marked the conservative end of the spectrum. More difficult to determine is the polar opposite where many opinions contested. But at the least it may be said that contemporaries, while never envisioning a revolution, scorned, and some even vilified, both sitting kings of the last half of the eighteenth century.[11] While some scholars have placed the press close to the conservative pole,[12] the few who have offered alternatives have tended to discern an evolution toward radicalism.[13]

To address the political meaning of the press, one may begin by asking how clearly did it allow the audience to perceive the political world? Here the focus is, for obvious reasons, on French readers. Did they feel close to the action or far removed from vague images? Did they sense great distance or high magnification of the details and the overall situation? The point is to measure how distant they felt from political activity, not to measure the accuracy or competency of the press. While the latter topic is an important one that other scholars may wish to consider, the appearance of politics provides a reliable index to the "feel" or texture of the press as experienced by contemporaries. The emphasis in this book on the contemporary readers' understanding further reinforces this concern. A second question, worthy of attention for similar reasons, is the political viewpoint available in the press. Narrowing, and thus sharpening, the focus leads to studying the audience's understanding of the French government, surely the most significant question for French people. Concentrating on France does not mean assessing only French news because foreign news also held implications for France. And readers, knowing that the press was at least somewhat controlled, would have read the entire paper with an awareness of what they could learn about their own land through a variety of portals. Considering the perspective on France obviously contributes to assessing how troubling was the press. But the first question is important too because, as the conclusion to this chapter will further discuss, the clarity of the news holds implications about time that could contest monarchial prerogatives.

To understand the nature of the coverage, one might logically begin with the *Gazette de France* but, as will become evident, this newspaper so resembled its foreign doubles that first examining them turns out to be an acceptable strategy. For these extraterritorial gazettes, the basic unit of reporting was the event, understood here as an occurrence or series of occurrences happening over a short period and linked together in the minds of contemporaries. Thus, the news consisted mainly of events, for example, battles rather than military campaigns, or royal visits rather than complete accounts of perambulations.

In the foreign press, most events received only terse coverage. So short were these that contemporaries could only have seen them as cryptic. Even those then deemed significant, still were encapsulated in mere summaries. This lack of detail likewise made the subjects in any one of these news items fuzzy, indistinct, and indeed difficult to grasp.

Other problems further plagued these brief entries making the subjects described even fuzzier to readers. In part, so foggy a picture emerged because of the structure of the Old Regime newspaper, which was mainly organized into separate sections of news from major capitals. Each section housed a series of reports, usually written in the first person plural, about the concerns of that city. Thus, the reader of a pre-revolutionary paper would confront news items which usually seemed to describe occurrences from the point of view of the residents of different cities. As such, these articles generally emanated from a source distant from the readers, who were left to speculate on what the writer might have left out of any given article. This approach was clearly less appealing to the subscribers than one that somehow suggested a shared outlook with them.

Further increasing the reader's tendency to sense that news items issued from hostile or at least unsympathetic sources were the frequent contradictory reports. Differences of fact or interpretation emerged from one issue of a paper to the next or even in different parts of a single issue. Views of the same subject varied a great deal. Because many differences stemmed from the coverage of the same event in the reports of several cities, these contradictions reinforced a perception of the newspaper as an accumulation of many biases alien to the reader.

Certain discrepancies among stories – especially when different national origins were not involved – might have estranged readers from events in an entirely different way. Such divergence portrayed the world as complex, if not confused. In this fashion the world receded from the reader. And the general skimpiness of coverage only reinforced this confusion.

Encouraging such separation between reader and event was a rather strange geographical divide between the subscriber and the event. Because these newspapers were produced beyond the frontier, the French reader often perused a newspaper from a distant place. Even stories from France were transmitted across the border and then back into France. All of this movement could not have encouraged readers to feel close to the source. News always seemed to come from far away.

Chronological gaps reinforced the geographical distance. Given the structure of the press and the slowness of the mails, readers often learned of an event *two* weeks after its occurrence, although the very efficient *Gazette de Leyde* could often shave off a few days. And sometimes the gap was far greater. This chronological distance could often be exacerbated if the news source transmitted the material in batches. Even if these mailings were separated by only a day or two, the vagaries of the postal service combined with the weekly publication of most papers could divide reports over several weeks, creating an impression of chronological disjointedness.[14]

If readers felt distant from the news in the paper they perused, editors claimed no greater proximity. The latter constantly blamed delays on correspondents or on the post, both of whom editors felt powerless to control. One need only scan the papers to find editors claiming that they were at the mercy of their sources. And, to explain their often contradictory reports, the editors frequently averred that they too were mystified and had simply published what they had received. Not only did editors accept their distance from the events covered, they also associated their position with that of their readers. In demeanor and in appeals, editors linked themselves to their readers.[15]

But could perusing several periodicals overcome this distance? Certainly the geographic and chronological gap would remain the same. And the contradictions that led to doubts and feelings of alienation from the narrator would in almost all cases increase. Nothing would seem to alleviate the impression that editors were far removed from politics. Only in some small matters could readers increase mastery over events. Insofar as the papers relied on different sources, the audience might experience an overlapping coverage that would encourage them to believe their knowledge was greater. But most readers would find the overall effect to be much the same as reading their initial newspaper.

In some cases, foreign periodicals gave an event more than a paragraph or two. Some coverage ran on for several paragraphs while, for some events considered especially significant, reporting achieved even greater dimensions. This essay considers these last exceptions because, even though a minority, these far larger reports may have proved the most lucid. Although in these cases the extraterritorial papers could provide quite substantial material, they nevertheless did not overcome all of their customary limits. Indeed, some of these treatments seemed afflicted by virtually all the problems of the shorter reports though others offered much improved coverage.

Most of the variation regarding larger reports may be illustrated by comparing the effort of the *Courrier d'Avignon* with that of the *Gazette de Leyde* regarding the Gordon Riots, a great anti-Catholic explosion in London from June 2 to June 9, 1780. In the Avignon paper, news began to appear in the June 20 edition. A very skimpy, undated report formed one paragraph of the twice weekly paper's eight pages. This initial story from London seemed to refer only to the opening day of the conflagration. But the next issue, June 23, included a complete account, more than one full page, dated June 20, that chronicled the tumultuous week. The following issue, published June 27, contained a report of June 11, illuminating further details. This one and one-half column piece (three-fourths of a page) focused on the fate of Lord George Gordon and the crowd and printed verbatim the British royal proclamation which provided the monarchical version of events. The June 30 *Courrier* mainly retracted much of the previous issue's report. But in this edition of the paper, the editors also tried to explain their contradictory coverage. The *Courrier* of July 4 and July 7 added further detail in short reports. The riots then disappeared from the paper, although occasional reports trickled in about the fate of Lord George Gordon and about parliamentary debates on new measures designed to reduce popular activity.

Despite reporting that lasted over three weeks and often occupied significant space in the *Courrier*, readers likely saw this event as transpiring at considerable distance. First, the perspective on the riots was obviously not their own. The narrator of the stories appeared to readers, regardless of the reality, as an Englishman on the scene, engaged in the swirl of events. The other significant voice appearing in the *Courrier's* reports was that of official royal pronouncements. But what most clearly marks these stories as emanating from another viewpoint is how the paper handled conflicting reports. The edition of the *Courrier* for June 27 reported that because of the dire situation, the king had suspended the laws and ordered military action. The result was 500 dead and 17 hanged. The next edition of the paper retracted this story and asserted that the laws had not been suspended. To explain the discrepancy, the editors claimed that during the heat of battle, commentators from different points of view provided varying accounts. Now, posited the editors, they had found a reliable source. This agonizing over credibility reveals that the paper was trying to assert itself over the competing versions. However, both the contradiction itself and the initial explanation about bias emerging in troubled situations were likely to reinforce the readers' perception that the *Courrier* mainly spoke the political language of those about whom it reported.

Of course, such open grappling with these contradictions not only revealed the distance of subscribers but that of editors as well. And the newspapermen gave other direct testimony on their remove from events. From the very beginning of the Gordon Riots, the *Courrier's* writers accepted their dependence on distant correspondents. Indeed, the first article emphasized: "The English papers have stated. . . ." But it is in the precise language of the issue of June 30, which attempted to explain the contradictory reporting about the suspension of laws, that we can appreciate best the relationship of the editor to the news. The *Courrier* noted:

> We have had too much confidence in our correspondents who were private individuals: these have noted that martial law was not

proclaimed: now a very reliable paper has asserted the reverse and we have not been able to do more than give faith to this last version. Now the retraction of this newspaper has finally enlightened us along with the June 9th proclamation of the king, which shows absolutely that the seditious will be brought to trial following the regular legal procedures. Thus, the 500 held and the 17 killed without benefit of trial, are two errors that must be rejected; although these errors have come to us in a way that we had to believe was surely authentic.

Publishing this retraction revealed to the public, in this case as in so many others, how remote the *Courrier* was from its sources. Furthermore, such a frank admission seemed also to bespeak a candor reserved for equals. Indirectly, it would appear, the editors associated themselves with their readers.

The most evident characteristic of these news items was the limited detail available. The Gordon Riots obviously formed an extraordinarily complex affair, but the configuration of the coverage made it appear the story of a simple uprising and its powerful repression. The characters rarely come into focus, and the most detailed accounts were royal justifications whose purpose naturally lay in reducing the rioters to a blind force and the action of the troops to a simple extension of monarchical authority. As such, the reports mentioned very few individuals and allowed most actions to seem collective. Not only did a generalized, rather faceless picture emerge, but the lack of detail verged on the extraordinary. For the entirety of June 2, a day of much violence with numerous participants, the *Courrier* offered: "On the second, the populace attacked the members of Parliament so vigorously that they were forced back into chambers. . . . The furor of the rioters concentrated particularly against Arbuthnam." Finally, the manner in which the succeeding reports corrected one another introduced, in addition to the other problems it created, uncertainty about the material in the press. Two hundred years later, the reader can clearly determine which was the final report on the Gordon Riots, but contemporaries could not. Consequently, subscribers became accustomed to the possibility that the knowledge they held might be at best highly provisional.

Alienated by the foreign narrations whose stories were not very precise, readers also found themselves chronologically removed from the event. The *Courrier* first published news of the riots 18 days after they had begun; and given the vagaries of the mails, most subscribers learned about the struggle three weeks after its initial outbreak. News trickled in during five additional editions, so that even over a month after the authorities had quelled the rebellion, readers were still treated to corrections and amplifications. Receiving reports so late, of course, distanced readers.

While the effort of the *Courrier d'Avignon* overcame precious few of the customary difficulties, leaving readers much to ponder, the approach of the *Gazette de Leyde* to the same event revealed a much more coherent – but not impeccable – level of reporting. Even more than the Avignonese paper, the newspaper of Leiden expanded its coverage. The first report covering the earliest events of June 2 appeared in the June 13 issue with some two and one-half pages of coverage in type even smaller than that employed by the *Courrier*. This type, just short of microscopic (92 characters in a five inch line with nine lines per column inch), allowed an immense amount of material on every page (8 x 11 inches). The next issue of the twice weekly *Gazette de Leyde* (June 16) picked up the story of June 2 and carried it forward three days, consuming almost six more pages. Most of the remainder of the next three days were reported in the June 20 issue in yet another six pages. On a final three-quarter page in the June 27 edition of the *Gazette de Leyde* appeared the finale of the Gordon Riots. In that issue and subsequent ones, Leiden editors extensively covered the political fallout from political contestation that exceeded any violence experienced in England since its revolution almost a century and a half earlier.

Obviously, the sheer weight of the *Gazette*'s coverage overcame the brevity plaguing most accounts. Moreover, unlike the *Courrier d'Avignon*, which, despite additional space, simply could not provide enough detail to make the participants come into focus, the *Gazette de Leyde* inundated readers with material. Parliamentary debate received serious attention; royal edicts were printed in full; and a precise narrative of the street battles was included.

Yet all this elaborate information created a new and different challenge. In other cases, a lack of knowledge defeated readers. Having solved this problem, the *Gazette de Leyde* created, rather predictably it must be allowed, another – that of a bewildering welter of facts. To be certain, the story did not lack organization. First, the paper arranged the material into a chronological narrative which, in and of itself, gave some order. Yet problems emerged in the narration. Because the story was divided over several issues of the paper, each beginning proved quite abrupt. Several days transpired between issues, so each of them probably required readers to refresh their knowledge from previous issues. Whenever that was impossible, befuddlement must have ensued. Readers had to work on building familiarity; it was not provided for them. The editors, indeed, recognized the problem and referred back and forward in the text but the following example reveals their limits. The journalists appeared on their way to making a special effort in the June 20 issue (whose report had a June 13 London dateline), when they announced:

From the ninth of this month, everything began to return to order; and today June 13, tranquility has been perfectly established. It's a precis of the awful scene that we have seen pass before our eyes: As for particularities, they are so numerous that in order to satisfy the Public, we will follow the dates in an abridged account which follows.

Such language would appear to promise a summary of events, but what the paper actually did was far less. Noting rapidly, "After the disorder of June 2 and the three following days (*which were reviewed in our last two sheets*)," the *Gazette* began exactly the same very detailed voyage through the story.

Even if the narrative had been better structured, the density of information would have proven an obstacle. It appears that some explanatory framework to organize the data could solve this problem. Building an argument into the description, with paragraphs organized around such statements, likely would have sufficed. And the reports in the *Gazette de Leyde* gave some direct indications of an argument. The most explicit statement came on the second page of the entire account. "Since the second of this month the Capital has been the theater of a tumult, whose cause the sanest part of the population detested." But the *Gazette* published no other obvious indications of an arrangement for the facts.

Oddly, the failure to provide necessary explanations occurred even when the paper evidently held a particular point of view. The Leiden journalists showed the Gordon riots as an explosion originating in the "vile" classes, misled by one articulate, misguided aristocrat. Opposing these twin evils were the king, the nobility, and the bourgeoisie who stood up to the threat. A twentieth-century reader would perhaps find this viewpoint thin and would wonder what motivated the actions of the "vile." But for contemporaries unruliness was likely intertwined in their conception of this class of people, so the argument advanced already contained enough explanation.[16] Whatever the completeness of this explication, that it emerged only from a close reading of the text, makes it even more difficult to understand the *Gazette*'s unwillingness to organize the evidence.

The failure to insert keys to understanding pertained not only to the overall thrust of the story on the Gordon riots but also to subparts. In particular, comprehending much of the parliamentary debate required the knowledge that many of the protagonists belonged to two opposed parties, but only once in the story was the "Opposition" mentioned. Although most readers likely understood the basic structure of English politics, they probably could only identify the most important members on each side.[17] Some of the debate must have appeared incoherent or at least confusing.

Discontinuities in the narrative and a paucity of explanation undermined but surely did not cancel out the wealth of data in the *Gazette de Leyde*. However, the long reports in this journal feature some of the other problems typical of short reports. For one, the gap between the on-scene reporters on one hand, and both editors and readers on the other, persisted as if the articles continued to be written as reports from involved Englishmen, not unbiased observers. An alien voice, routed through Leiden, surely distanced readers from events. Furthermore, despite the excellent connections of the *Gazette de Leyde* to London and its much greater proximity than the *Courrier* staff, it still took 20 days to complete reporting.[18] Yet on one very important point, reliability, the Leiden newspaper achieved much, for it did not avow ignorance or withdraw information. In this case, the paper published a long, complicated story without retractions, surely inspiring trust in its account.

The overall standard achieved by the *Gazette de Leyde*, demarcates, more or less, the upper limit of reporting in the foreign gazettes. A different assemblage of strengths and weaknesses appeared in other reports, but long stories, even at best, indicated a general difficulty in managing the wealth of information. And, because of this problem, the weaknesses in most long accounts, like those in the brief stories, proved difficult to overcome even for those reading more than one paper. Only in the circumstances in which the stories greatly overlapped – and this did occur – would a subscriber, simply by repeating the effort of sorting through the information, gain by scanning multiple accounts.

Of course, exceptions existed to this assessment of the gazettes' coverage of events. Even when the difficulties of insufficient or unmanageable detail were overcome, other problems – such as the geographical gap – could intervene, and hardly any coverage avoided all problems. Still, some reporting was far better than others, bringing events into relatively sharp focus. In addition, though unusual, the equivalent of editorial remarks intruded here and there. In an extraordinary example in what was otherwise a most cautious paper, the *Courrier d'Avignon* entirely devoted the first edition of each new year to reviewing the past year, with opinion organizing the description. Despite all such occasions, the overwhelming circumstance was one of distance for readers. In the end, the lack of directions – either by way of summary or opinion – must have led to a generally befuddled understanding.

The *Gazette de France* treated events largely as did the other gazettes.[19] Even more rarely than the others did this paper provide detailed accounts, and its coverage seldom broke out of the cursory summary. On the positive side, this newspaper, as a governmental organ, possessed coherence and consistency regarding French news. Furthermore, there was nothing tentative and hesitant, as chronological and geographical remove were foreshortened. Nonetheless, the *Gazette de France* largely dissipated its advantage in domestic reports because relatively little of it related to anything except the most innocuous happenings. Information was well presented but was of little use. Readers surely sensed this was not taking them close to events. Only in the case of military battles was this tendency largely overcome, though these too remained bogged down in detail. Still such reports were much more certain and constitute a large exception. But overall, the *Gazette de France* did not make readers feel any closer to events than the rest of the papers.

Why the *Gazette de France* and the other gazettes processed events in such a manner is worth some speculation. Perhaps the general format in the press reproduced, at least vaguely, the way information arrived in editorial offices. Why correspondents would then have sent either snippets or at best mountains of unorganized detail remains elusive as well, but in this they acted much as wire services would in following centuries. One might guess that the major exception to simply presenting the correspondence submitted would be the *Gazette de France* whose major news – foreign reports – largely came from the office of foreign affairs, so news had a French, not foreign, origin. Yet the *Gazette de France* also followed the usual format. Perhaps, the *Gazette de France* put in an alien voice to distance itself from official sources or to appear like the other, privately owned, journals that apparently lay outside governmental control. If this logic holds, the *Gazette de France*'s approach depended on the others, and so to them one must turn.

What remains the most mystifying is the willingness of the press to reveal so clearly its distance from the news.[20] Would not the use of neutral, authoritative tones have been more desirable? Quite likely the press's strategy was no pose, but simple acceptance of how it received news. This may have been desirable to insulate it from reprisals by the authorities. Newspapers may have cited their correspondents and admitted problems to evade recriminations from the French government or others that could pressure officials where the paper published. Yet another reason involves the gazettes' relationship to their audience. These periodicals proclaimed a communal identification with their readers and may have wished to present themselves as transparent filters, not as channels altering the flow of information.[21] By adopting such a strategy, they may have accepted their position, conceding a lack of clarity.[22]

Whatever the reasons, the gazettes – both foreign and domestic – stuck with this approach. Even when the state captured the *Courrier de l'Europe* and made it into a propaganda arm, the format remained basically unaltered. But the new political periodicals – Panckoucke's journals and their contemporaries – adopted new strategies of reportage.

At first glance, Panckoucke's *Journal de Bruxelles* and the *Journal de Genève* share much with the vast bulk of reporting in the gazettes. The majority of the articles were brief, like those in the previously discussed political papers.[23] On the whole, Panckoucke's papers contained fewer short and more long pieces. While these extended discussions continued to emerge in an alien voice and to accept chronological and geographical distance,[24] they seldom introduced internal contradictions and, most important, handled details far more coherently than even most of the best gazette reports. In this last area, they improved upon their siblings in part purely through format. Both the Brussels and Geneva papers abandoned microscopic, irregular type for a more regular, more widely spaced presentation. This in itself made the more voluminous accounts more accessible. In addition, the editors' use of explanatory remarks to organize the story often cut their coverage into fewer, more manageable parts; and they employed human interest materials to make the entire business easier to follow.[25]

An example which clearly illuminates the increased ability of Panckoucke's periodicals to master detail is the coverage of the Gordon riots in the *Journal de Bruxelles*. By this point the Brussels paper, though apparently available separately,[26] was mainly distributed as the political half of the weekly *Mercure de France*, formerly an exclusively literary journal. The first mention of the riots appeared in eleven pages of the June 24, 1780 edition which described the entire riot. In the following issue of July 1, the staff considered the aftermath as well as various other newly available materials in a six-page discussion. From this division of the story, in this case assisted by the reduced publication schedule of one issue per week, readers could understand what they read even if they had only that issue available. They would not need to refer forward and backward to other dates.

In addition to providing a narrative without problematic breaks, the *Journal de Bruxelles* printed an account that was far easier to follow. Although affected by some of the same tendency to treat events as a series of occurrences, this story did possess clear unmistakable introductions for each of the two weeks' coverage. Interestingly, the *Journal de Bruxelles* interpreted the Gordon riots largely as had the *Gazette de Leyde* but from the very first provided a much clearer statement of its viewpoint:

> The excesses caused by the fanaticism of the *peuple*, whipped up by Lord Gordon . . . created alarm everywhere. Conceivably the Lord did not believe that the Protestant Association would produce the fatal effects that it did; but his good faith is no excuse. . . . When one assembles such a numerous crowd, it is difficult that it not include a bad element and that it not yield itself to excesses. Those who have read the resolutions of the Protestant Association . . . are not surprised to see what happened.

The introduction continued by giving a brief synopsis of the Gordon riots and concluded "this event, which is inconceivable in this century and ought to make all quiver by revealing the continued existence of fanaticism, in spite of the Enlightenment and its spirit of tolerance, merits being known in all its details. . . ." These opening remarks effectively set up what followed, framing the narrative which resonated with the themes first struck though including few explicit guideposts.

Also making the article easier to follow was a less dense prose. Individual events received more attention, reducing the swirl of information that in the gazettes seemed to impede, not improve, comprehension. Also making the story more penetrable was the insertion of personal stories which must have piqued curiosity and further enhanced the reading. For example, the *Journal de Bruxelles* reported:

> A knight, Philip Jennings Clerke, testified at the House of Commons about what happened to him on the sixth. In a moment when the populace swirled around him, he had seen Lord Gordon pass in a carriage and had begged him for asylum. Scarcely was he seated beside him than the seditious took away the horses and led the Lord down several streets. Clerke, desperate at participating in such a dangerous triumphal march, waved his arms, cried, swore to let him get down, but the *peuple* made fun of his cries and he could not set his feet on the ground until the conclusion of the promenade.

Such anecdotes, along with a more prolix treatment, provided an account with more readable writing.

The increase in long stories and the better strategy for handling voluminous information made the political events seem clearer to readers. Doubtless, as the interpretation appeared more and more clear-cut, not simply buried in the welter of facts, some readers thought themselves separated from events by a layer of analysis. But outweighing this feeling of distance, even for these skeptics, was surely the satisfaction of understanding.

Other journals that appeared toward the end of the Old Regime took still different approaches toward the news. The *Affaires de l'Angleterre et de l'Amérique* divided its reports into two sections. In one portion the political periodical explained the American Revolution – its basic subject – through the chronological arrangement of documents. The second part of the *Affaires* consisted of a series of letters from a British banker who served as narrator. By using epistles, the paper hoped to, and probably did, direct readers toward an interpretation without exactly seeming to. Cleverly, through this veiled form of editorials the *Affaires* allowed readers to consider themselves well-informed.[27] In any case, the pro-American tack of this periodical was unlikely to create much cynicism as its cause was so popular.[28] But one should also be reminded that this was a foreign journal with foreign news and a heavy dose of unedited documents; perhaps a great improvement over the gazettes, it still generated a feeling of distance.

No periodical was so distinctive as the *Annales politiques* by Linguet. While it too was produced abroad, it came much closer to events, if only because it held France in its field of vision. While most other political papers scarcely embraced open interpretation of events and only the *Affaires* cautiously experimented with a kind of editorializing as a regular feature, Linguet produced a paper packed with commentary. He mentioned specific events only as spring boards to launch volleys of opinion. Not at all reticent, Linguet commented broadly upon the general state of affairs, providing a basic context for understanding the passing events. Certain features characterized Linguet's writing: he marshalled suspicion, employed paradoxes, exploited personalities in the crudest way, and relied upon slogans. All these together created a very emotional appeal. Beyond this, as Jeremy Popkin has pointed out, Linguet manipulated time in a new way. According to Popkin, ". . . time moved forward in a succession of terrifying lurches, and every crisis brought Europe to the edge of apocalyptic disaster. But each disaster brought with it at least the possibility of a millenarian redemption." Linguet himself found the eighteenth century, ". . . more full of bizarre occurrences, completely contradictory to the ordinary cause of events. . . ." This use of time, coupled with other stylistic techniques and a thorough explanation of the world, might thrust readers into an exciting pace of politics. Unlike the puzzled reader studying the gazette to make sense of a faraway world, Linguet's reader would find the world swirling all about him.[29] And some surely did. Nonetheless, the unexpected nature of many of the journalist's assertions, including, for example, a defense of slavery, simultaneously lessened the believability of others. Eighteenth-century readers surely were titillated by the *Annales politiques*, but they may have enjoyed the provocation of his remarks without believing they understood more specific information about politics.

Though one might doubt how much information the conscientious reader believed when he read the *Annales politiques*, such newer periodicals appeared to provide more insight to readers than the gazettes generally could. Panckoucke's publications, whose circulation was quite large,[30] played a special role in enhancing the available level of magnification. Understanding this improvement, as well as the original limits, makes clearer the situation facing readers.

Finally, one should examine quickly the different styles of coverage between the Old Regime and the revolutionary press in order to help evaluate, in the conclusion of this chapter, how problematic reporting was.[31] After 1789 the press assumed many forms, making comparisons difficult. But for the purposes of this analysis, one can concentrate upon the most important genre during the first years of the Revolution – those papers combining a discussion of events with political opinion. And to simplify matters, one can primarily contrast these papers with the gazettes which for most of the Old Regime provided the predominant form for political news.

28

The structure of the revolutionary press would have reduced comparatively the chronological gap, for both the principal location of the press and its main subject were Paris. Consequently, journalists were instantly on the scene of events. In addition, while weekly papers continued, dailies also flourished. The latter's frequent publication gave subscribers "fresh" news. The one gap remaining was the time required for distribution of papers through the postal system. But since most Old Regime journals had to come across the border, surely even this time must have been somewhat reduced. One week rather than two must have become a more normal period intervening between event and subscriber.

Likewise, the geographical gap was closed. The end of censorship allowed free coverage of French news.[32] Furthermore, revolutionary events made France central in the press throughout Europe. And since the revolutionary newspapers used in my analysis badly wanted to influence politics, discussing the homeland was central. For all these reasons, French men and women who read papers during the revolutionary period would have found the news from places not so distant and not so foreign as in the Old Regime newspaper.

In contrast to earlier journals, the revolutionary press generally covered events without contradictions and in much greater length. The political opinions that animated these papers eliminated almost all internal disagreements. And their reporting went into far greater detail. Although short reports that must have seemed elliptical persisted, a giant leap forward in specificity occurred. In part, this sprang from the ability of many journalists to view personally what they were reporting. In addition, revolutionary newspapers covered fewer subjects. Not only did they virtually ignore foreign news, but they also concentrated on fewer incidents each week. Individual papers rode their own hobby horses. Finally, they tended to put together central stories each week that were long, detailed, and very specific.[33] Editors employed a raft of strategies to organize these materials, strategies which inevitably inserted the editor between the subject and the reader. But this distancing of the event, because it simultaneously organized the report, generally remained a minor problem. Only when newspapers gave focus to materials by using opinions alien to readers could their ordering prove problematic. Yet the polarization of opinion meant this was a common part of the revolutionary press that needs broader consideration.

The special problem of the revolutionary audience was that it routinely confronted a domestic voice that could be alien. Because founders of these periodicals intended to influence opinion, they inserted their own strong views into most columns. While Linguet and to some extent the *Affaires de l'Angleterre et de l'Amérique* pursued that approach in the Old Regime, it became common only after 1789. Of course, the editor's was not the only voice heard. Journalists also reproduced documents from various sources, and the papers frequently reported events in unemotional tones intended to show that a neutral, unbiased observer was on the scene. Such diction told readers that objective truth was available. Thus subscribers had to negotiate their path between the evident opinion of the journalist and the narration of seemingly absolute fact.

These twin approaches – detachment and commitment – were present from the very beginning of the revolutionary press. In the prospectuses issued in 1789, editors promised impartiality, clarity, honesty, and accuracy. Simultaneously, they also mentioned instructing and educating audiences. They glorified the staff of writers by describing their skills and the careful recruitment involved.[34] The prospectus of *Le Solitaire* even argued that it deserved attention because the editor's solitary existence allowed time for careful, fair presentation of material. Yet, offered the journalist, from this perspective he could provide an informed scrutiny of the National Assembly and a questioning of each member about his activities. The journalist then proclaimed that he would inform the representatives what they needed "to fear and the obstacles they must avoid. . . . What remains yet to be done despite all their enemies and all their obstacles. . . ."

The gradual change of perspective within the prospectus of *Le Solitaire*, which began calmly but ended strongly assertive, perhaps indicates that revolutionary readers would not have seen this dichotomy very clearly. The skimpy evidence as yet uncovered about readership suggests that subscribers tended to purchase journals reflecting their own point of view.[35] For individuals who accepted the opinions they read, the mixture of editorializing and a factual approach would have been neither so obvious nor so peculiar. It is likely, then, that the propagandistic side of the revolutionary press would not have made readers feel distanced from events.

An example which illuminates most of these points regarding the revolutionary press is the *Révolutions de Paris*'s coverage of the suppression of mutineers at Nancy on August 30–31, 1790 . This weekly paper deserves attention because it was the most popular revolutionary paper.[36] Also common was the intensity of its coverage of the Nancy incident – the brutal repression by the Marquis de Bouillé of a mutiny by soldiers who, imbued with revolutionary principles, wanted to change military practice. The paper often focused on a single dominant event, covered it very closely for one or two issues, and then moved on to new ground.[37] One aspect of this affair – its location far from Paris – unfortunately makes this coverage a little atypical. However, as will become apparent, this anomaly, which skews the coverage somewhat from the revolutionary pattern previously described, still does not undermine the comparative differences with the Old Regime press.

30

The news of Bouillé's assault on the troops at Nancy first appeared in the issue for the week of September 5th. The paper devoted 22 of its 48 pages to it. After loudly lamenting the deaths among the troops, the *Révolutions de Paris* provided the background to the bloody days and then, while promising more definitive reports later, printed Bouillé's justification. In addition, the paper covered the reaction in Paris, particularly at the National Assembly. The next week's issue devoted only four pages to Nancy. These reports described the event and the number of deaths but primarily complained that conflicting reports made determining the truth difficult. However, promised the *Révolutions de Paris*, its next issue would print what actually occurred. And on September 19, like clockwork, the newspaper devoted 19 pages to its version of events and to condemnations of those responsible.

Readers of the *Révolutions de Paris* had to wait almost three weeks for the paper to complete its analysis of the Nancy affair. Compared with other coverage in the Revolution, this was an exceptionally long wait brought on, at least in part, by the paper's weekly schedule of publication and its distance from the confrontation. Despite such relatively slow coverage, readers remained no further from this event than was normal for the Old Regime press. And their sense of closeness was surely amplified by much greater geographical proximity.

What principally took readers much nearer to these events, however, was the volume of copy prepared. The accounts of the background to and the actual developments at Nancy were extremely detailed as the *Révolutions de Paris* wound its way through personal motives and actions. Moreover, the *Révolutions de Paris* managed to refer to – and sometimes even print – competing versions of the event without introducing confusion. Because the writers of the paper always treated the alternative visions skeptically and contrasted these with authoritative reports, little doubt would exist in a reader's mind about where the paper believed the truth lay. Finally, one might note that extending the story over three issues and adding to it along the way might have produced uncertainty about whether future changes would follow. However the *Révolutions* would seem to have counteracted this by promising in the first and second issues more material and then by relating with certainty the story in the third issue. Such prompt delivery might well have convinced readers not to expect future revisions.

For the most part, the voice in which the attack was described may have brought readers closer to the events. The lion's share of the coverage was communicated in a dispassionate tone which must have seemed that of a judicious judge, not a prejudiced polemicist. Furthermore, the paper was careful not simply to ascribe its version to one or more authorities. If it had, the journalistic voice might have appeared overcome by its sources as had been the case with Old Regime newspapers. Instead, noted the *Révolutions*, it created its rendition of events by carefully weighing and logically evaluating the evidence.

But even if most of the story was calmly told, the journalists peppered the story with moral lessons. For example, the very first news from Nancy began: "French blood has been shed. The torch of civil war is lighted. . . . The disastrous truths would destroy our courage and strength, if the danger that menaced the nation did not still our profound grief." And in the final account of the attack, the paper exclaimed:

> . . . we dare to accuse M. de Bouillé, we denounce him to the French people, not as guilty of treason to the nation . . . but of treason to humanity. It's up to the patriot writers, it's up to us, it's up to public opinion to render justice for the crimes that the law cannot touch. It's to this fear inspiring and just tribunal and to public opinion that we yield this ferocious general, who . . . has neglected nothing to shed the blood of his brothers and comrades. . . .

Because some of these declamations appeared to issue from the French people, they potentially would not have intervened between readers and events. But generally, such outbursts punctuated the overall account as an unrestrained outburst by an enraged journalist. Such striking statements of the independent journalist competed rather unselfconsciously with the calm tone otherwise dominant.

For the reader who accepted the *Révolutions de Paris*'s point of view, the existence of this second histrionic language might not have induced skepticism about the veracity of the paper. Those who differed would certainly have been troubled by this ideological voice. Nonetheless, all the other characteristics of the reporting would have certainly made the repression at Nancy reasonably clear to the revolutionary reader.

But what of the readers who perused a number of papers? Those – probably the majority – who simply consulted several like-minded periodicals, surely would have grown more certain of events as chronological and geographic propinquity as well as clarity and calm would have been reinforced by a commonality of opinion. But there were some who consumed papers with competing visions. Indeed, Jeremy Popkin cites a case of a marquis who made every effort to read conflicting papers.[38] Of course, geographical and chronological distance would not have been greater. And the various papers would have simply expanded some stories. But the comparative perspective gained by reading such papers would have revealed that even the ostensibly dispassionate accounts in the paper were quite politicized. Consequently, both the certainty of accounts would have been shaken and the voice of the journalists would have appeared more audibly. Both of these effects would have surely distanced readers somewhat from events. But this point should not be overemphasized, for the editorial voices were still

French with identifiable ideological alliances, and readers could sort through the accounts.

Comparing the revolutionary papers which mixed opinions and news with the Old Regime gazettes for their ability to bring readers close to their political subjects yields an interesting insight. Clearly the later papers surpassed the gazettes in virtually every way, except that the revolutionaries peppered their papers with opinion. Yet this opinion offered little distraction to most readers, and the revolutionaries were far better at bringing their audience close to the action. Their edge over Panckoucke's journals, though reduced, persisted for the same reasons. Theirs was a somewhat closer race with the *Affaires de l'Angleterre et de l'Amérique*, which as the title implies, did not focus upon France. This latter paper lacked the immediacy of the Revolution. As Jeremy Popkin has argued, the *Annales politiques* possessed much in common with the revolutionary newspapers,[39] but Linguet's palpable wrath would have generated even more skepticism than the revolutionaries'. Nor could any one Old Regime paper compensate for all the others' deficiencies. The most important factor giving the advantage in reporting to the revolutionary paper was its immediacy; its main liability might have been the penetration of ideology into its pages. But the audience was so politicized that it likely did not care about this filter. In the particular circumstances between 1789 and 1792 this problem proved less consequential and guaranteed readers would find the revolutionary press observed politics more keenly than earlier papers.

Although images provided in the Old Regime press were not as clear as those published after 1789, they were improving. Political implications of this may best be understood after reviewing the image of the French government that the newspapers elaborated from mid-century to the Revolution. But this message is not easy to grasp. Establishing the contemporary meaning of any text is challenging, but special problems engage a scholar interested in the political press. While an apt selection of particular cases narrows the field of vision, the massive amount of copy still remains daunting. Furthermore, the great range of interlocking subjects complicate understanding any particular country covered in the press.

Another problem plaguing this analysis, particularly with the foreign gazettes, is that in the absence of editorials, the succession of fuzzy or complicated accounts of events seem to make difficult the emergence of any viewpoint. But it did occur. Even the most mundane description held implications. In addition, the press did communicate, as revealed by the *Courrier*'s printing of the royal version of the Gordon Riots, coherent interpretations and sometimes blatant opinions. The total tilt in all these provided an angle of vision, even if they rarely mounted up for a substantial and clear view of an event. Lacking editorial direction, this viewpoint was not forcefully presented but was reasonably clear. The emergence of general perspectives should have sharpened images for readers by establishing categories to assist the audience. Nonetheless, such assistance was meager indeed as subscribers basically perused a newspaper that communicated an overall impression far better than it could specific details.

With all these difficulties in mind, one can commence with how the monarch's own *Gazette de France* treated the government.[40] Although this periodical stylistically shared much with the other gazettes, its unique role within the press as the representative of the royal viewpoint probably encouraged a certain distinctiveness. This paper presented events that appeared blurry, though less so than others. To understand the *Gazette*'s approach, it is necessary first to examine domestic, then foreign affairs.

When directly covering France, the editors tried to bolster the image of the monarchy and monarch, by emphasizing the king in his ceremonial and familial role. The other institutions of state and prominent individuals appeared only as they circulated through the royal domain. The mysteries of state, a term referring to monarchical habits whose actual practices were reserved to the king and shrouded from the public, remained absolutely safe in the hands of the *Gazette*. Other news, such as that regarding cultural developments, circulated in the paper; but this material, which was both disparate and lacked editorial comment, little challenged the supremacy of the monarchy.

In its coverage of France's foreign policy, however, this government organ produced a more mixed picture. As a paper of record, the *Gazette de France* presented reports that accorded generally with how the unfettered educated elite would have interpreted events. As such, the domestic and military failures of France's allies and the successes of her enemies would eventually surface. And this general truthfulness emerged for France's own military ventures. In this way, royal policies received a more direct criticism than on domestic matters. But one should not overemphasize this negative reporting because the government also occasionally imposed a certain propagandistic angle, or more often simply omitted problems which would then only slowly appear in a rather distorted manner later. Moreover, many events reinforced French policy and the *Gazette* swiftly and ably reported them. A more definitive conclusion about this coverage requires greater in depth research, but an impressionistic survey suggests that the *Gazette* generally backed royal foreign policy but without the same certainty as in its specifically French coverage. Indeed, so much was this the case that during periods when the news was clearly better, the reports still varied along an axis of optimism, unlike the greater certainties in domestic reportage.[41]

Nonetheless, in presenting the domestic political structures of other countries, the *Gazette de France* over the course of the century developed a somewhat challenging coverage of France. To explore this evolution requires examining the *Gazette*'s reporting. In the forties and early fifties the *Gazette*'s approach to the affairs of other countries emphasized the role of the primary political authority. And when the countries covered were monarchies, personal rule and intervention into daily affairs received attention. All this resembled reporting on France. By the end of the Old Regime, the paper reported, at least obliquely, many more conflicts and stressed the activity of competing elites rather than the rulers themselves. The image of monarchial control had partly given way to that of governmental conflict. Perhaps this point may be demonstrated by contrasting two issues of the *Gazette* – one from 1751, the other some thirty years later in 1782.

In 1751 the *Gazette de France* published a twelve-page weekly edition. No different than usual was that of July 24. Of the sixty-three news bulletins on foreign matters in this issue, one covered armed conflict, and the remainder of the articles related the internal political situations of many countries in Europe – including Scandinavia, German and Italian principalities, Great Britain, and Spain. Regardless of the country described, the only significant place for political contestation implicitly lay within the ruling elite since the *Gazette* reported not only on sovereigns but on ministers, diets, parliaments, and significant personages at court. This coverage paid no attention to problems between these elites and the rulers but tacitly recognized divided authority.

Whatever potential tensions implicit in the *Gazette*'s pattern of reporting tended to be nullified by the enthusiasm the paper manifested toward each country's leader. Twenty-seven of the sixty-three articles exclusively described the sovereign and consort, and the attitudes expressed supplemented this volume of attention. While the *Gazette* routinely noted the intermediate bodies and courtiers, it only concentrated on the rulers of state. The leading article in the July 24 issue described the resolution and diligence shown by the Swedish king in rebuilding fire-ravaged Stockholm. Even more significant, these encomiums merely reinforced the yet stronger plaudits of the preceding week's description of the actual fire. The *Gazette* noted that "the wind was blowing directly on the port, the storehouses, and artillery depot; it is only by the presence of the Monarch and by the admirable dispositions that His Majesty ordered, that these depots, so precious to the defense of the state, have been saved." The *Gazette* focused on other monarchs in the July 24 issue by similarly indicating their intervention as crucial.

By the 1780s this newspaper published four pages twice weekly in far smaller print. Appearing no different than others, the November 19, 1782 copy included material from Warsaw, Madrid, Vienna, Naples, London,

The Hague, and Versailles. The physical change over thirty years proved less than the alterations in content.

The largest change in emphasis in the later *Gazette* did not lie in its coverage of conflict between the ruling elite and the population at large. Only one of the twenty-two articles really concentrated on such a problem – that was Irish resistance to the draft. Since France and England were still at war, the *Gazette*'s reporting of the Irish military problem must be viewed in that context rather than as any general policy of chronicling social tension. Both the democratic revolutions and local, more "social" insurgencies scarcely received notice in this paper. For example, the aspect of the American Revolution stressed was the war, not the democratic changes.

The coverage of the politically constituted entities did, however, undergo a significant change. Only four articles directly concerned the monarch. Now, the *Gazette*'s portrayal of the elite showed a variety of elements without any one preeminent. For the most part articles simply recounted how various officials and courtiers performed their political and social duties. An aimlessness seemed to have replaced the strong royal leadership reported thirty years earlier. But this disintegration of leadership even seemed to manifest itself quite openly by suggesting limits to sovereign authority. The lead story of November 19 about the manifesto promulgated by the Polish Grand Chancellor before a meeting of the Diet provides an excellent example. Instead of leading, the Chancellor was pleading. Rather than commanding, the official "strongly recommended," "reiterated," and "wished." Of course, Polish officials must have always approached the Diet that way, but this case was hardly unique in the *Gazette* at this time. Still the general view put forward by the paper was that of shared authority.

A wide reading in the *Gazette* of the late 1740s and early 1750s as well as the late 1770s and early 1780s, though inevitably impressionistic, further validates this pattern. To be certain, military campaigns in both periods, despite the appearance of officers and generals, seem most often implicitly to focus reporting on kings. Those were, after all, emanations of royal power. But, moving from that constant, one sees the pattern described above. During the earlier period, even the reports of internal crises kept the king's government in the center. The London reports of the *Gazette de France* stated: "As contraband is always proceeding despite the measures taken by the government, and since the Isle of Man, by its location, contributes much to illicit commerce, the Government would like to unite this island with Great Britain."[42] But more common were reports of uprisings, especially in European colonies, where accounts of rioting often concluded by announcing the resumption of order.[43] Implicit in the phraseology of these reports was a government with a single leader. And the *Gazette*'s emphasis on the sovereign's leadership remained great; it even presented George III, the constitutional monarch of England, as an absolutist.[44]

An examination of the last few years of the *Gazette* further confirms the pattern of change from earlier tendencies. The *Gazette* continued to take little interest in societal conflict and revolutions and to focus on the elite and struggles within it. However, important exceptions can be found. Under the influence of Vergennes, some positive reporting of the Americans and their revolution filtered into the paper. But this only exceptionally was the case. The text of the Declaration of Independence, for example, was never printed.[45] Nonetheless, to a small extent, these favorable mentions overcame the generally spare reporting of such matters. Sometimes the paper came to treat monarchs less as free agents and instead to describe their actions as responses to unavoidable moral dicta. Rulers thus behaved according to ethical constraints.[46] While such occasional coverage did not overturn the *Gazette*'s view of Old Regime governance as the rule of competing bodies, it did modify even further the paper's emphasis on personal rule. Such articles encouraged an entirely different notion of government – as an organism whose goal was serving society instead of simply providing positions for its functionaries.

This transformation in the *Gazette*'s portrayal of internal politics occurred seamlessly over time. Gradually the paper paid less and less attention to monarchial authority and gave more and more space to competition, at least with the other constituted powers. This was the case when it encountered the democratic revolutions at the end of the century. The new view, not of subordinate political organs and individuals, but of monarchy primarily characterized the change. Indeed, one simply finds fewer items about the sovereign. By the end of the century a new notion of the monarch as an agent subordinate to moral considerations was beginning to emerge.[47]

The *Gazette*'s representation of the monarchy posed difficulties, at least in theory, for the French state. Describing other governments facing internal contestation might or might not reflect badly on the French government. How well reports indicated alternate structures worked might have influenced reactions. But overall, envisioning foreign countries as functioning while consisting of competing bodies undermined the view of France that the royal government was endeavoring to advance, even though in practice the Bourbons operated more flexibly. The public, though considering limited alternatives, already believed in contestation with the crown and was only too willing to accept that vision. Juxtaposing these articles about foreign power struggles next to those on France permitted readers to use the first to deny the latter as unrealistic.

To be certain, the contrast between the coverage of French and foreign governments late in the Old Regime provided at most an indirect critique. Probably, it was the mildness of the problem that allowed the government to tolerate an implicitly positive view of alternate political structures. Probably, this new reporting mainly reflected a shift in structures or understanding about these structures.[48] Thus, even in the *Gazette*, clearly identified with the government, problematic news seeped out. Although the *Gazette* overwhelmingly bolstered the French government's position, challenges still appeared, here and to some extent in the reporting of foreign policy. It should be no surprise that the extraterritorial gazettes posed even greater difficulties.

Two case studies of the competitors stationed across the frontier allow some general understanding of the foreign political press. Because of a large number of factors – none more important than the relative influence of the French state – these gazettes held a variety of opinions on the neighboring colossus. The strategy here is to examine, in some detail, the reporting of two different periodicals, one among the most, the other the least, adventurous in their presentation of France.

Least pointed was the *Courrier d'Avignon*, which published in a Papal enclave surrounded by France. Founded in 1733, it generally appeared bi-weekly in a four-page edition with sporadic supplements until its demise in 1794. It was priced at 18 livres annually. A local writer, François Morénas had originally begun the newspaper with the Giroud family, Avignon publishers. Various events in 1742 had allowed the Girouds to gain complete control, but by 1750 after other positions in and out of publishing, Morénas was again editing the *Courrier* for them. This arrangement lasted until 1768 when the French, in a dispute with the Pope over Gallicanism, occupied Avignon. The Bourbon monarchy, which usually allowed only one news journal, the *Gazette de France*, to publish within its borders, outlawed the *Courrier*. Morénas immediately requested and received the right to continue the newspaper from Monaco, another Papal territory. In late 1774 when the French evacuated Avignon, Morénas had just died. Even though anonymous editors successfully maintained the *Courrier de Monaco* for six months in 1775, Bourbon officials had always perceived Monaco as a temporary solution and insisted that the *Courrier* resume in Avignon. Joachim Le Blanc, an important French official then working in Avignon, received the privilege to publish in 1775. At his death in 1782 his wife assumed control and operated it through the Revolution. Le Blanc first hired abbé Roubaud to edit the periodical, and in the spring of 1776 turned to Jean-Baptiste Artaud who lasted until 1783. Sabin Tournal, who would achieve fame in the Revolution, became his successor.[49]

The Bourbon invasion of Avignon and the forced relocation of its newspaper reveal clearly the ultimate and exceptional power the French possessed over both city and *Courrier*. The French also added active intervention to their presence. To promote their own policies, French authorities occasionally intervened in news reporting. On the whole, they seem to have limited themselves to minor adjustments, but from time to time they sought to influence the news more strongly. In addition to such sporadic coercive measures, the French issued a stream of propaganda defining their own view of politics.[50]

Despite this restrictive environment, the *Courrier* depicted a structure of domestic politics outside France that went well beyond that in the *Gazette* and yielded a stronger critique.[51] There was not so much change in how traditional bodies functioned, sharing or monopolizing authority. But as democratic movements emerged, the *Courrier* treated them dispassionately, often favorably, describing a world with many choices. Although the *Courrier* likewise omitted, or downplayed, rioters (as in London in 1781), differentiating them from revolutionaries, this coverage admitted the existence not only of conflicting elites but also of political upheavals.[52] Simply the greater contrast to static absolutism made this coverage more challenging than that in the *Gazette de France*. All this provided the possibility of contemplating absolutism critically; coverage of large scale changes allowed contemplating big alternatives.

Largely by sustained reporting of potential aspersions on France's friends or achievements of her enemies, the *Courrier d'Avignon* also embarked on an approach toward France's foreign affairs that differed from the *Gazette de France*. Not inevitably but generally the former was more aggressive than the latter. A good example of the Avignon paper treating matters contrary to French governmental interests was the coverage with a London dateline of English politics from mid-1778 to late 1780. In this period, the French were at war with their traditional rival; yet the *Courrier* praised the English authorities and downplayed any opposition to them. The paper persisted in praising George III explicitly and implicitly for his performance as chief executive, his paternal relationship with Parliament and the people, and his position in a brilliant court.[53] It admiringly chronicled the king's activities as commander-in-chief of the military forces. One report noted that the royal example inspired the war effort of the entire nation.[54] This and similar encomiums reflected the *Courrier*'s favorable view of the English war effort in a way far more sustained than the *Gazette* would ever embark upon in its reticent admissions of contradictions to French foreign policy.

While such an example indicates the way that the *Courrier* commonly pursued a line relatively independent of French interests, it would be misleading to regard the treatment of foreign affairs as uniformly or even generally inimical to France. Unfortunately, the extremely painstaking research necessary to reach a firm conclusion on this subject simply does not exist. But a careful reading produces a chronology that begins with some very positive reports in the mid-1740s, and with France's enemies in the War of Austrian Succession receiving hostile scrutiny. From the end of the war until the resumption of hostilities in Europe in the mid-1750s, the *Courrier's* coverage apparently rendered few judgments on France's foreign policy. But treatment of the Seven Years War, a very difficult conflict for the Bourbon government, proved far less favorable. Instead of the support during the last war came a muddled coverage – with a mixture of good and bad news – that surely often displeased authorities in Versailles. For the next ten years, with peace more or less the order of the day, the *Courrier d'Avignon's* coverage also appears fairly directionless, but with many silences. The golden period, though, was the American Revolution, despite some kind words for England from the London section of the paper. An avalanche of praise for the Bourbons outweighed this substantial endorsement of Hanoverian policy. This firm advocacy of French foreign policy endured almost to the mid-1780s when the treatment of other problems in Europe reduced the positive edge.

Although much of the foreign analysis remains so nuanced that a systematic analysis might alter assessments, one important aspect appears clear enough. After a long period from the late 1740s whose coverage could be described at its most positive as mixed, the *Courrier d'Avignon* gave French affairs a sustained endorsement qualitatively stronger then earlier. Yet, as repeatedly mentioned, the paper also focused in this period on subjects directly opposed to Bourbon interests. An overview of this treatment of French policy during the American Revolution can both resolve this tension and describe the outer limit of the *Courrier's* pro-French reports.

The route outlined above to explain both the most positive reporting of France's foreign affairs as well as the contradictions to this may be shortened by simply comprehending the image of France's main antagonist during the American Revolution. So important in foreign policy considerations was England that examining its coverage illuminates that of the entire range of France's foreign endeavors. First, as earlier noted, the *Courrier* did publish material problematic for France's vision of foreign affairs through reports from London that favorably chronicled the English government from mid-1778 to 1780. As an addendum to that, one might note that through editorial comments and careful attention to particular successes for the prime minister, the paper singled out Lord North for praise, with one report particularly sympathetic. After describing an attack by George Fox that condemned the entire North ministry, the periodical portrayed the conclusion of the debate:

This bloody diatribe was finished with nothing resolved. The minister constitutionally obliged to listen to all sorts of indignities, Lord N – – – H responded sensitively to the many reproaches. He is accused of having betrayed his country and having accumulated emoluments and offices. He offers to resign what the king has given him. Attacked for his love for his family, he sheds tears at the memory of the death of the son that he has just lost; numerous legislators, thinking that a good father cannot be dishonest, defend him.[55]

To a society brimming with a new sentimentality, such phrases translated into a strong endorsement of North.

But much of the paper was given over to a vision of England that was gratifying for French foreign endeavors. Contradicting the positive assessments, which also predominated in reports on England in the years preceding the Boston Tea Party, were many negative accounts. From 1774 to 1778 and again after 1780 the *Courrier* published assaults on the English government from various English provenances. While the king fared reasonably well, the ministers received strong criticism. In the earlier period the *Courrier d'Avignon* adopted a strong antiwar stand, a position directly contradicting the British executive's policy. Before the outbreak of hostilities, the paper had merely urged compromise with the Americans.[56] Once the Revolution erupted, the periodical pointed out English war atrocities. One article in effect labeled English actions criminal, describing a soldier who preferred to resign his commission rather than "adopt the horrible alternative of stifling his humane impulses and bathing his hands in the blood of his relatives, his comrades, and his compatriots."[57] The *Courrier d'Avignon* also concentrated on military defeats. Even a review of an English military success was likely to point out the temporary and inconclusive nature of that victory.[58]

British reports also applauded the motives of the colonists and thus impugned the motives of the ministers who tried to suppress such noble people. In its view, the Americans possessed wisdom, moderation, and firmness.[59] Although such positions might also tarnish the monarch's image, the paper's direct criticism of ministers made them appear the principal target.[60]

Continued support for French policies came from the London reports in the *Courrier d'Avignon* which openly accused the ministers of carrying out poor policies and immoral plans in violation of historic liberties: such misguided movements against freedom must come to grief. The journal attacked an array of ministerial efforts, including proposals for reorganizing the East India Company.[61] But its criticism focused mainly on their "tyrannical," "despotic," and "arbitrary" actions against the Americans.[62] Their efforts, which were designed to reduce the Americans to "slavery", would end in nothing and lead the nation to the loss of its "blood" and "treasure."[63] The newspaper linked the attack on Americans' freedom to a similar assault on the just liberties of Englishmen.[64] Another article assailed the ministry for failing to allow the king to receive the rightful complaints of the City of London in a suitably decorous manner: such errors might lead to a loss of confidence in the Crown and difficulty for the succession of the royal line.[65] Such a threat contained some criticism of George III, but the *Courrier*, at least on the surface, fired its salvos at the cabinet officers standing between it and the throne.

Not all these criticisms focused on areas of direct conflict with France, but attacking the government on practically any point justified Gallic policy. And after 1780, the *Courrier d'Avignon's* coverage resumed the severe diatribes against the ministry. The paper saw the chief failing of the ministers in their role in the armed struggle, accusing them of persisting in the war against all reason, ruthlessly seeking to dominate all Europe, and misleading the nation about the chances for peace.[66] A new tone characterized the paper's coverage of the cabinet. It began to scrutinize the cabinet's activities far more closely, and its reports consistently revealed a group of men motivated by opportunism and necessity rather than political principle.[67] The *Courrier* reiterated the belief that greed led the ministers to their evil deeds.[68] The fall of the North ministry in March 1782 (reported on April 12) strongly reinforced this criticism, since it suggested the fate that might befall inadequate ministers.

Not only did England's very own reports tend to castigate her but the *Courrier* contained far more negative views with American and Continental datelines. Most of the reports that issued from America between 1774 and 1778 clamored for English resistance and decried the executive. They brutally assaulted the motives and character of both the monarch and his advisers.[69] Only a single report sought to justify the king, and none admired the ministers.[70] The reports dramatically proclaimed a belief in popular sovereignty in England, reflecting the thinking of many Americans who wished to justify both their own behavior and radical activities in London that might benefit the rebellion.[71] As American news about England tapered off in 1778, reports supposedly penned on the Continent began to appear. These reports intemperately assailed George III and his advisers. According to the columns, the king and his ministers set out to dominate the seas to secure their economic and political preeminence. France and her allies had confronted the oppressor simply to preserve the freedom of the seas. Suffering great losses in war and much disruption at home, England was unable to realize her goals. No polite praise for an adversary muted this attack.[72] Nor did these reports view either Parliament or the opposition party positively. The overall picture, which portrayed English politics as corrupt, domineering royalism, reflected the prevalent European opinion that England's bellicosity sprang from the greed and cynicism of George III and his ministers.[73]

Analyzing England gives texture and resolution to the points made regarding foreign reporting. First, this case shows the complicated messages available. This specific examination makes comprehensible how the *Courrier d'Avignon* could be more critical than the *Gazette de France*. Yet, without exactly mimicking the *Gazette*, the *Courrier* could treat French foreign policy positively by lambasting England and did so impressively, though not unqualifiedly, in the years preceding the Revolution.

To examine the *Courrier d'Avignon's* view of French domestic politics can best be accomplished by first considering the *Gazette de Leyde*, a periodical at the other end of the spectrum of gazettes. Using this paper poses a difficulty since from before 1745 up to the late 1750s the French government successfully forbade its legal circulation. Nonetheless, this periodical, though among the most radical, generally resembled others of its type closely enough to justify it as a reasonable selection. Moreover its extraordinary importance over the full period provides important comparisons.

Among the most adventurous papers, the *Gazette de Leyde* held many valuable resources that encouraged independence. True, it possessed some weaknesses, common to publications of its type. The French government tried hard to fetter sources even among the most independent press in order to restrict access to news. As Jeremy Popkin's scholarship has revealed, even when the French government could not actually bury damaging material, it tried to limit the problem by subsidizing and thus controlling Pascal Boyer who ran a Paris news bureau that provided items to the non-French journals during the 1780s.[74] Conversely, all the publications in Holland could count on a home environment that was willing to tolerate critical reporting. And the local government, unlike the pliant Papal authorities, had far less desire to assist the exercise of Bourbon hegemony.

The *Gazette de Leyde* held additional particular advantages. Founded before 1677 by the French Huguenot family, the De la Fonts, the *Gazette de Leyde* or as it was formally known, the *Nouvelles ordinaires de divers endroits*, lasted over a century until 1811 with a brief suppression in 1798. By the end of the eighteenth century, subscribers received the newspaper, normally eight closely printed pages, twice weekly at a cost of 36 livres annually, much higher than either the *Courrier d'Avignon* or the *Gazette de France*. Another Protestant family, the Luzacs, had bought the paper as a family business in 1738. Etienne Luzac acted as publisher until 1772, when his nephew Jean assumed control. Under their aegis, the *Gazette de Leyde* became the most informative Francophone newspaper of its day.[75]

Although ultimately dependent on their subscribers, the Luzacs probably possessed a considerable freedom. The diversity of the audience of the *Gazette de Leyde*,[76] spread throughout Europe, surely insulated the paper to some degree. The fragmented nature of the Leiden paper's potential readership must have given editors substantial leeway in setting policy.

Not only were fewer outside forces brought to bear on the Leiden than the Avignon journalists, but the former also appeared much more likely to resist them. First, the publishers, the Luzac clan, ran the paper and doubtless possessed a great commitment to it, not only as a business. Perhaps, a sense of purpose among these Dutch Protestants made them less profit-minded and more concerned about their paper's content. The *Gazette*'s last publisher during the Old Regime, Jean Luzac, specifically believed in liberty in the abstract and the American Revolution in particular, and helped John Adams gain Dutch recognition of America. He also aided Polish and later Dutch freedom movements. A man with such commitments would likely wish his paper to illustrate his own point of view. And other Luzacs surely had resolved to use their paper to forward a particular perspective, at least within the constraints of the format that characterized the gazettes.[77]

For such reasons the *Gazette de Leyde* enjoyed more independence than the *Courrier d'Avignon* and virtually all the other extraterritorial gazettes. This freedom made its reports quite adventurous, second only, among political papers, to the *Courrier du Bas-Rhin*. But the main question is not the source of its liberty but its content.

Luzac's coverage of the structure of foreign countries' political systems was at least as problematic for the Versailles government as that of the competing paper in Avignon. His paper treated politics as consisting both of contestations among formal bodies and revolts from below. Although the *Gazette de Leyde* generally omitted or deprecated social upheavals, as with the Gordon Riots, the Luzacs went beyond the *Courrier d'Avignon* by systematically favoring democratic rebellions that downplayed social upheaval and seemed largely to concentrate on political change.[78] In taking this position, the *Gazette de Leyde* confronted, on theoretical grounds to be sure, royal absolutism.

Likewise the *Gazette de Leyde* seems to have followed the broad outline of the *Courrier*'s treatment of French foreign policy. But the Leiden newssheet likely went further than its more constricted relative. Still unclear is the overall balance of reports. Nonetheless during the Seven Years War (whose coverage lasted actually from the mid-1750s to the mid-1760s), the *Gazette de Leyde* could portray French folly far more explicitly than its Avignon cousin. In fact, French authorities, who worried about the Dutch gazettes, found the Leiden paper similar, but still the most troublesome.[79] This negative coverage made the positive treatment of French foreign policy during the American Revolution[80] an even greater improvement than this subject had experienced in the *Courrier*.

But the relative independence of the gazettes in general, and the *Gazette de Leyde* in particular, permitted the latter to consider French domestic news in a manner completely beyond that of the *Gazette de France*. Yet for reasons that will be discussed at greater length in later chapters, this difference was not always the case. To deepen our understanding of these different periods, one might compare the *Gazette*'s very bold announcement of Maupeou's reorganization of the judiciary in 1771 with issues from 1782, while Vergennes was repressing reporting. Because the Leiden periodical tended to treat France very tersely during periods when it reported only calm, one must survey several numbers of the paper in such a period. Thus, to contrast with the paper concerning the Maupeou crisis, I selected four consecutive issues, published between July 9 and July 19, 1782.

The *Gazette de Leyde* included twenty brief articles on France during the first half of July, which together showed a smoothly functioning government. To be sure, the paper mentioned a tax increase and the Paris parlement's remonstrance. Yet, according to the *Gazette*, the principal problem with this tax was that the judiciary did not wish it to be extended more than three years beyond the war with England. Such coverage scarcely hinted at the determined resistance of the magistrates. Another article suggested divisiveness in France when it reported on a council of war, held in Brest, that because of conflicting information, was unable to determine the fate of the Indian fleet. Nonetheless, such problematic reports contrasted with the general tenor of the remaining seventeen bulletins. These discussed municipalities donating cannons to the King, the presentation of individuals at court, the travels of the royal family, the construction and departure of ships, and the capture of enemy vessels. One release typified this genre. The issue of July 19 noted: "Since the departure of M. the count d'Artois, the royal family has dispersed: the King remains alone at Versailles; the Queen and Madame Elizabeth occupy the Trianon; Monsieur, Madame, and Madame Countess d'Artois have returned to Brunoy where they plan to rest a month; the Aunts of the King are at Bellevue and will return from there to their property of Louvois." Such reports on the daily life of royalty both presumed and proclaimed its importance.

In sharp distinction to such reports in 1782 was the issue of the *Gazette de Leyde* of March 15, 1771. True, this issue was exceptional, even less restrained than usual. Yet its value lies in providing somewhat of an outer limit both stylistically and substantively. Although the paper concentrated on only four separate questions regarding France, such reports occupied about 65% of the *Gazette*'s eight pages. One article paralleled the newspaper's pattern on those other occasions when the press lapsed into virtual silence. The Leiden paper, indeed, dutifully noted the Marquis of Noailles's leave taking from the King and the royal family in order to assume the position of ambassador to The Hague. Yet the remainder of the paper revealed a France wracked by controversy. One article discussed parlementary resistance to ministerial pressure for taxes; another revealed difficulties in the army. But not surprisingly, the Maupeou reforms and the response to them provided the centerpiece of the problems. In fact, the editors devoted 60% of the March 15 issue to this subject including reports clarifying the position of the government and the reactions to it from parlements in Bordeaux and Besançon as well as from the Paris Chambre des Comptes and from an anonymous writer.

These reports on the Maupeou coup also reveal that the Luzacs wished to accomplish more than simply to show France as a society in conflict. Of course, such reporting pointed out restrictions on absolutist monarchy. But through the arrangement of the story, the paper indicated that not only were the Bourbons not as dominant as they might wish, they ought not to be so powerful. The *Gazette* introduced its account by labeling the alterations as a "total change in the form of administration." The paper then summarized these changes and a large part of the decree that authorized them. However, the one page of the paper devoted to this material was dwarfed by the reporting of objections. The many complaints took a variety of tacks, but almost all labeled the Maupeou reforms as radical, immoderate, and disruptive to the peace of the nation. Typical of these objections was the discussion of the Besançon Parlement, which begged the King to "continue to reign by love, by justice, and by observation of the rules and forms wisely established, in consequence to abolish even from memory an edict destructive of *French* liberty, and to remove himself from the authors of counsels as contrary to his interests and his glory as pernicious for his People, and to reestablish his Parlement of Paris, &c." Selecting and publishing many of these reports placed the *Gazette de Leyde* firmly alongside those who wished to limit monarchial authority.

For the most part an aggressive tone permeated the pages of the *Gazette de Leyde*. At the least in this period readers saw a France with many competing interests as opposed to the *Gazette de France*'s monarchialism. The portrayal of competing bodies posed a challenge but adding insult to injury was the parlementary constitutionalism available. In short, this theory advanced the notion that the ancient law of France guaranteed individuals and corps particular rights or privileges. The most potent of these was the argument that the parlement held the office of its magistracy by right, and efforts by monarchs to alter this were despotic. To cynical Frenchmen, merely printing these views constituted their advocacy, but the *Gazette de Leyde* often went further. Through placement or weighting or even occasional editorializing, the *Gazette de Leyde* moved toward an endorsement. Interestingly, upheavals by the *peuple* received little or negative attention, with the assassination attempt on Louis XV serving as a good example.[81]

Evidently at other periods such aggressiveness scarcely entered the Leiden newspaper. Indeed, from 1771 to 1774, and again from 1776 to 1784, the *Gazette de Leyde* made the king virtually the sole significant focus of political activity. A few exceptions occurred, but basically this paper came to closely resemble the *Gazette de France* in the central place it granted to the monarchy.[82] This was precisely where the Bourbons hoped to be.

The context provided by the *Gazette de Leyde* helps explain the domestic reporting of the *Courrier d'Avignon*. While the latter paper certainly was no equivalent to more aggressive foreign papers, it shared their attitude in a muted fashion. When others expressed support for various degrees of resistance, the *Courrier* at least managed to describe France as a country with competing interests. As such, this newspaper collaborated in undermining absolutist claims. Not surprisingly when her relatives remained quiet, she followed suit. Despite this limit, clearly the *Courrier d'Avignon* possessed the courage to challenge directly the monarch.

If the *Gazette de Leyde* with these attacks hovered near one pole and the *Courrier* constituted the other end, what can be concluded generally about the treatment of France in the foreign political press? As the century wore on, this reporting provided an indirect rebuke to Versailles by reinforcing and expanding the *Gazette*'s own tendency in covering foreign countries to treat a range of political actors beyond monarchs. As such, the gazettes were indicating, not so much a specific alternative, but the possibility of difference from prescribed absolutism. The bigger the difference, the more the imagined alternatives might grow. An audience, restless under absolutism, would have been likely to pay attention to the critique, though its members too would have been mindful that not all reports gave unalloyed praise.[83] Second, the gazettes could cover France's difficulties in foreign policy in a sustained manner. While the current state of knowledge about the overall treatment of foreign affairs remains limited, clearly earlier periods contrasted with the overtly, if somewhat qualified, positive treatment during the American Revolution. And criticism of the king's domestic administration flourished except from 1772 to 1774 and 1776 to 1784.

As the above summary suggests, chronology demarcated important changes in the gazettes. One might use 1772 as a crude marker dividing the entire period. On the early side were reports that contained some degree of domestic critiques of the monarchy and mainly guarded coverage or worse of foreign policy. Missing, however, was significant criticism from observing foreign alternative regimes. Later, all these tendencies were reversed, doubtless to the general approval of French authorities. While not relishing indirect critiques from reporting the new political structures in other countries, the government found them easier to withstand than direct blasts on domestic and foreign efforts.

If in the second period contemporaries witnessed a significant decline in criticism of the Bourbon government, a more in depth examination of the final decades of the Old Regime reveals another interesting detail. The confluence of all these trends meant that during the American Revolution the gazettes – largely taciturn but still supportive on domestic matters while clearly if not completely endorsing foreign policy – overall covered the monarchy positively. On the other hand, in the immediate crisis preceding the French Revolution, the *Gazette de Leyde* seized the opportunity to participate in the upheaval. And the glow of the American Revolution also faded. The era of positive feelings really ended in 1784.

The new organs that began to emerge during the more quiescent period provide the subject of the remainder of this chapter. Panckoucke's widely circulated periodicals remain generally unstudied, but some research suggests that in their assessment of France they differed from the foreign gazettes. Two major periods bear observation. In 1778 after the *Journal de Bruxelles* (merged for its political reporting with the *Journal de Genève*) became the political part of the *Mercure de France*, its reporting on the revolutionary wars fell under the sway of Vergennes, who wanted to use the press to bolster support for French policy. This influence manifested itself by largely favorable reporting of the Americans and British opposition to George III's policies.[84] In general, this reporting yielded praise for French foreign policy. The consistency of reporting was great enough that its readers might imagine, like those of the *Gazette de France*, that matters proceeded exceptionally well with setbacks pushed to the side. Certainly, this slant affected mainly England and America, but these topics were important enough to alter the entire perspective. As such the periodicals were favorable; but by tilting so far toward the English opposition and American revolutionaries, the paper simultaneously provided new problems by supporting political orders very unlike those of France. Not as a text book for revolution but as a suggestion of the limit of absolutism and the possibilities of major change, these reports revealed politics antithetical to absolutism. In sum, although the vicissitudes of the political coverage diluted both these messages, reporting during this period favored French foreign policy and inadvertently opened wide the window on challenging politics. Allowing a positive drum roll for American ideology threw up the specter of alternative approaches to government; associating French foreign policy with this popular colonial rebellion gave the government one of its relatively rare unqualified successes with public opinion. But contemporaries likely were more impressed by their government's success than by alternate ideals. This difference with the foreign gazettes, though difficult to calibrate, surely seems to fall in favor of the king.[85] A second variation from the gazettes occurred when the *Gazette de Leyde* and its comrades took advantage of government relaxation of controls under Turgot (1774–76) and again after 1784. Panckoucke's papers also showed more though not nearly as much spunk. Criticize domestic and foreign policies (the latter much more clearly than the former) they did, but far less often and with great circumspection.[86] Thus, insofar as the new periodicals deflected the tendencies of the foreign gazettes, they favored the monarchy.

What was published in the *Journal de Bruxelles* after 1778 characterized the entirety of the *Affaires de l'Angleterre et de l'Amérique* and most of the life of the *Courrier de l'Europe* when under French domination from 1778 to 1784. The *Courrier de l'Europe* like the *Affaires de l'Angleterre et de l'Amérique* reflected royal policy by systematically printing favorable reports about domestic critics of George III and his adversaries across the Atlantic. Simultaneously, like the *Journal de Bruxelles*, these periodicals produced many articles tacitly supporting foreign policy. These views, by glorifying the Americans and English opponents of George III, lent support – and this surely was the reason Vergennes appreciated these organs – to the ministry of foreign affairs. However, the *Affaires de l'Angleterre*, more than any other journal, produced, with few cautions, propaganda for the American cause that released the poisons of problematic political forms. The *Courrier de l'Europe* did the most to spread notions of the English system of liberal politics. These papers, though indirectly questioning France's governmental arrangements, still offered praise for foreign policy. They seemed in this way to lean toward the monarchy as did both the foreign gazettes and Panckoucke's organs. It ought to be added that the *Courrier de l'Europe* enjoyed a fling of independence before 1778, well beyond the other gazettes, but also so brief as not to affect the overall pattern described here. Some of this assertiveness continued after 1778 and this makes all assessments even more complex. Nonetheless, such variations may well be regarded as transitory and negligible. By 1784 after the end of the war, Vergennes set the *Courrier* free so that it behaved in a fairly spritely manner like other gazettes.[86]

Linguet's *Annales politiques* was unlike any other periodical and extremely idiosyncratic, with somewhat unclear targets. Indeed, Linguet in the short term advocated absolute monarchy as the best course open to the French people. Yet, he reached this conclusion through a radical attack on the social structure and every minister serving Louis XVI.[88] Despite this rather confused viewpoint, the *Annales politiques* possessed great popularity which might have allowed it to reshape the form of the political information available. Although the size of its press run remains uncertain, it eclipsed all other papers whenever it appeared.[89] Yet, for a number of reasons it did not fundamentally alter the presentation of views on France. Much of what Linguet had to say was quite abstract. He rarely commented on particular policies or developments. How his commentary actually related to France highly depended on the readers' interpretation. This rendered his critiques at least as indirect as the gazettes' treatment of English and American politics.

Even though the *Annales*'s arguments did not significantly change the course of the French press, Linguet remains very important. It would not be an exaggeration to see in Linguet a celebrity, the like of which has become more common in our century. Likewise, the public appeared more impressed by his language and his courage than his specific viewpoint. In fact, from the beginning of Linguet's journalistic career, these two elements – personality and the willingness to shock – are the clues to understanding him. The editor's earliest confrontations were with the Enlightenment establishment of the Académie française which he powerfully attacked as unworthy on a number of grounds. But in the debate over the Académie the reasons pale compared with the clash of personalities that occurred.[90] For further determining of the impact of Linguet, a later confrontation with Vergennes proves interesting. The minister complained about the journalist's strong language rather than his rationales. Indeed, the minister recommended that the "employee" (i.e., Linguet) who wrote the piece for one of Panckoucke's journals ought to be fired. In reply Linguet failed to justify his reasons or even his language but instead relied on his individual rights and declared: "The employed person is spoken here of as a lackey who may be let go when one is discontented with him." But, continued Linguet:

> The one called here a person...would never have agreed to be humiliated as a placeholder only dependent on the caprices of a publisher. The only way this can happen is if at the bar of literature all the rights of a citizen are removed without reservation and if the publishers and the lawyers are above the laws and the courts.

Significantly, Linguet closed by demanding his rights and refusing to sacrifice his honor.[91] This battle, like much of Linguet's career, can be reduced to a conflict, not over differing viewpoints, but over exaggerated language and the personal claims of Linguet. While it was the editor who raised his rights in this dispute, elsewhere he became a factor even without his involvement. The readers' construction of Linguet as a combatant implied criticism of Old Regime politics. In Linguet they saw a man standing for individual rights and vociferously defending his position. Yet this remained only another oblique attack on France to be added to the biting, but largely abstract prose of his paper. When one combines his tangential critique with the paper's irregular schedule of publication, the critical power of the *Annales politiques* appears much reduced. The *Annales politiques* had a very short run in France, permitted to enter only from 1777 to 1780, although much smuggling occurred in other periods.[92] It may have been officially restored after 1784 but denuded of much of its most radical material.[93] Even when it was allowed to circulate, Linguet's erratic work habits guaranteed a sporadic publication record.[94]

All told then, because the *Annales politiques* irregularly mounted abstract and oblique attacks, its power remained somewhat limited. Surely, the paper was far less significant than Linguet himself who took center stage far more consistently than he could issue the *Annales*. He was quite successful in using other means to portray himself as an embattled hero thwarting unfair authorities. And the reputation of the *Annales* also grew during the Revolution, because its example became all the more significant in the maelstrom after 1789. Nonetheless, in its own times, its importance should not be overrated.[95]

Such an assessment of Linguet largely contributes to the view that the new entries on the journalistic scene generally maintained the pose struck by the foreign gazettes in the 1770s and 1780s. Although they shifted the content and shape of reporting, mainly by increasing support for foreign policies and deepening the praise for alternative political structures, they did little to change the overall depiction of the French government. However, Linguet should not be completely discounted nor should Panckoucke's journals after 1784. Doubtless, the extraordinary circulation of these last papers undermined the turbulence building in the rest of the press in the mid-1780s.[96] While Panckoucke dampened problematic reporting, Linguet went in the other direction. But still his views remained indirect with many limits. In general, all these differences only add nuances to the vision of France articulated by the gazettes.

Having shown the view of France in the foreign political press, one might assess how problematic this medium proved to be. The press before 1772 certainly contained a spate of news challenging the monarchy. Domestic difficulties paraded through these papers. Reviewing foreign affairs in the *Courrier* and the *Gazette de Leyde* suggests a confusion at best. If anything, criticism stands out. But this is not the entire story for the period 1745 to 1771. Prior to the late 1750s the government severely restricted the circulation of all the foreign gazettes except the *Courrier d'Avignon*. Competing with this depleted field and one circumspect periodical was the largely statist *Gazette de France* whose circulation, and relative self confidence as well, likely overwhelmed the opposition. Only in the very late 1750s and 1760s would the full problematic nature of the press manifest itself when the *Gazette de Leyde* and several periodicals like it entered the realm. In this long decade up to the Maupeou coup, periodicals truly were difficult, at their worst spreading parlementary constitutionalism throughout the kingdom. Even though circulation remains uncertain through this period, the effort by Maupeou and his colleagues to suppress them after 1770 suggests a distribution substantial enough to undermine the earlier effectiveness of the *Gazette de France*.

Although the last years of the Old Regime witnessed a far less troublesome press, and even a supportive one during the American Revolution, two further comments are necessary. The indirect critique provided by the gazettes' publication of English and American politics and by Linguet's personal individualism were not decisive during the Old Regime. But as the concluding chapter discusses somewhat more, this approach had its role to play by contributing to long-term generalized complaints about the Old Regime. Second, in the last two years immediately proceeding the convocation of the Assembly of Notables in February 1787, the press became challenging. Still one should not overstate the revival, because the popular powerful journals of Panckoucke diluted this tendency. Nonetheless, this change attests to the revolutionary stirrings immediately on the eve of the Revolution.

Whatever turbulence the press possessed in the waning decades of the Old Regime, this analysis indicates that the ideas presented were insufficiently sturdy to allow us to envision a press which undertook sustained criticism of the government. Matters were, however, somewhat different on questions of style. With the *Gazette de France* and, indeed, other periodicals, the government might be satisfied with the substance of reporting. But the dictates of absolutism required a timelessness and a monopolization of information. Even the earlier papers, by keeping a schedule and distributing information, disrupted the situation. To be certain, their approach had its limits as news came fitfully and uncertainly. But as the century wore on, the press became more and more troubling as it better mastered time and information. And Linguet, at least for his use of time, presaged the revolutionary situation. His was a temporary, high water mark of change, for the comparison with the *Révolutions de Paris* indicates that in neither clarity nor time did the Old Regime achieve revolutionary standards.

Even if the methods of reporting were surpassed by those of the Revolution, they did make the medium more troubling throughout the century. Did their strengthening however, at the end of the Old Regime, revise judgments about the relative quiescence of these periodicals? The new periodicals that delivered sharper and more timely images were on the whole those that possessed less problematic information. Without important challenging information to communicate, the changes in time and space provided another perhaps heightened, but still indirect critique. In considering, for example, American revolutionary events – however well – these papers could not demonstrate that strong a value of a new sense of time or clarity. The exception may have been Linguet whose language was so extraordinary, but his residence on the political land-scape proved too brief to alter it. In addition, he expended much energy on "indirect" subjects, undermining the new sense of time he was imparting. Stylistic changes, thus, provided abstract critiques. As with other such criticisms, they contributed to general discontent, but not to creating particular, and more important crises. The most positive aspect of reporting on this period for the king was the American Revolution. However qualified, this very good news – it seems to me – had more value than Linguet's extraordinary prose coupled to other periodicals' indirect admiration for more democratic regimes.

In sum, contemporaries found the political press was a dynamic medium that over time reported fewer troubling events even as it still treated other more distant problems. Interestingly, the government in part engineered this trade-off because, as will be further discussed in later chapters, it both suppressed the reporting of domestic events and sponsored periodicals that would better further its purposes. At least during the waning years of the Old Regime these governmental efforts were successful. Without denigrating this achievement of setting and realizing objectives (all too rare even today), one must also note that fixing such deliberately repressive goals may also reveal short-sightedness or weakness – systemic or immediate – in which officials could only choose among poor alternatives.

2

THE AFFICHES

Appearing in the middle of the eighteenth century and rapidly pro-
liferating at the end of the Old Regime, the affiches were largely forgotten
during the Revolution. With attention riveted on the political news from
the capital, papers produced in Paris dominated local productions cen-
tered on commerce and provincial information. When the local press
expanded, it mimicked the national press, not the affiches. In this
environment, many affiches ceased to exist altogether. Late to arrive,
early to expire, the affiches have been forgotten even by historians.
Scholarship on the press, mainly undertaken by historians interested in
politics or literature, has often ignored these periodicals with their
reputation as advertising.

But the affiches, in volume alone, constituted a significant segment of
the press and indeed were more than a locus for advertisements. Produced by leading printers and in most cases related to the intellectual
elite of the particular province,[1] this genre of publication also published
commercial information such as exchange rates and ship arrivals, as well
as commentaries on moral questions, information on the local academies, political news, anecdotes, and more. This extraordinary variety of
materials originated with any number of authors. Advertisers probably
submitted their own notices,[2] although editors clearly imposed some
order upon them. While the staff of the paper wrote some pieces, local
residents submitted many; and items were also borrowed from other
papers. Despite the selection and editing of such pieces, such submissions conformed significantly to the author's goals.

In order to ascertain the contents of these papers filled with so many
types of information, this chapter focuses on the general perspective
adopted by the press, endeavoring to estimate for each type of coverage
how problematic it proved. After quickly examining the minor interest in
politics and religion, the chapter turns to the affiches' main subject: the
vision of society that emerged through a variety of coverage. To assess
this viewpoint, one might simply note that, whatever the variety of actual
practices, contemporaries equated the Old Regime with the primacy of

the nobility. In other words, traditional society depended for its solidity on the dominance of the Second Estate. Advocating other positions meant some sort of critique. To be certain, with the primary purpose of the affiches commercial, one might expect some sort of elevation of non-traditional ideals. Yet, the affiches also had connections to Old Regime elites, so their stance – especially outside of advertisements – was no foregone conclusion.

Assessing the message of the affiches in so many texts requires sampling. Appendix II provides the full rationale for the selection, but a brief synopsis is in order. This chapter is based on the entire run of the *Petites Affiches* based in Paris from its inception in 1751 through 1786 and complements it with representative periodicals from the provinces. Although a similar paper began in Lyons at the same time, only one of the early years survives. This chapter utilizes that year, but the interpretation of the early period must essentially depend on the Paris paper. For later decades, however, many more papers were available for sampling. Selected for the period 1755–1764 were affiches from Lyons and Bordeaux as well as the *Annonces, affiches et avis divers de province* which, though published in Paris, focused on an audience outside the metropolis. Consulted for the decade, 1765–1774, were journals published in Rouen, Orléans, and once again the paper in Lyons. And for the period extending to the Revolution, I returned to the Orléans affiches as well as others in Lille and Poitou. Yet constructing a general picture from these many sources could lead, if everything printed was analyzed, to an overall view that had little resonance in any one paper. Because readers consumed these papers individually, rarely seeing another, one paper might emphasize notions which remained totally unavailable in another. The goal here remains to ascertain what was generally available in these sheets.

Published weekly, or at most bi-weekly, sold for an annual price as little as six and no more than nine livres, and most often consisting of four pages (8 x 11 inches), these papers devoted some space to almost every subject, even formal politics.[3] Political views occasionally emerged unexpectedly, when, for example, the affiches published edicts or announced social events and funerals, or printed certain kinds of poems. For the most part, whatever the occasion, these papers supported monarchical power without question and the ecclesiastical authority related to it. In this last area, these provincial periodicals also criticized the Church's opponents, the philosophes, even though as we shall see, much of what the affiches printed about society seems to have followed the Enlightenment program in their own informal way. Later sections in this chapter consider such indirect support but here lies an opportunity to consider how the affiches specifically dealt with king, Church, and philosophe.

Given the nature of the reporting, the affiches did not provide well articulated interpretations of formal politics, but their articles encouraged the view of an all-powerful and benevolent Bourbon monarchy. Even though eighteenth-century French kings faced political opposition, this press all but ignored this opposition by publishing only royal edicts,[4] omitting the pronouncements of intermediate bodies like the parlements and local magistrates. These periodicals supplemented such indirect statements of royal omnipotence with panegyrics, most commonly focused on currently reigning kings.

A couple of examples of the rather sentimental approach to French kings must suffice here, although modern readers would doubtless enjoy scoffing at attitudes and a mode of expression now reserved more for rock stars than political leaders. The March 6, 1783 issue of the *Affiches du Poitou*, celebrating the peace with England, claimed that shepherds were singing the following verses:

Our prince, this tender father
Fills the object of our wishes
He gives us peace and ends war
And gives us subjects much happiness.
Peace which our king has given us will embellish our days
In thankfulness our hearts leap with joy
In celebrating this beautiful day
Of Louis we sing all your glory
And henceforth our echoes
Singing along with us, celebrate your victory
Your virtues and your goodness.

But such gushing sentiments were hardly the first time the affiches had used this kind of language about Louis XVI. At his coronation the *Annonces, affiches et avis de l'Orléanais* (January 6, 1775) had produced the same kind of verse and in the process had extended the praise back to Henri IV.

His tender goodness reminds us
This first Bourbon so cherished
This immortal, this Henri the Great
For kings the most perfect model.

In such circumstances it remains unsurprising that the affiches' general approach to royal difficulties was a discreet silence. And when they commented, they invariably gave monarchical justifications. While political pages like the *Gazette de Leyde* complained loudly about the suppression of the parlement by Maupeou,[5] the Orléans paper was busily publishing the royal explanation, emphasizing the new and now free system of justice.[6] This affiches repeated the monarch's claim that his reform stemmed from an effort to rectify financial abuses. Predictably, when the press generally supported the monarch as it did when Necker in 1781 sought to stifle criticism by publishing his *Compte rendu*,[7] those affiches that mentioned such matters joined in the chorus of praise. Of course, these few efforts, which tended to deal with royal responses without detailing the initial problem, indicate that the affiches could have been more supportive if they had been more active. Nonetheless, their silence remained helpful to the kings.

And the affiches showered praise on French kings by glorifying family members and allies. The death of the Duke of Burgundy, a popular heir to the throne, elicited a number of poems. The *Petites Affiches* (May 4, 1761) commented about such works ". . .there are some pleasant verses, touching details, and praise much more beautiful than any flattery. How many hopes have we held for this young prince. He dies!" For some of the French such emotion for the Duke indicated displeasure with the crowned king, but one must recall that the affiches coupled such attention with very positive reporting on all the Bourbons.[8] Queens, including even Marie-Antoinette, received very flattering notices.[9] And other kings, linked by marriage or alliance to the French, attracted favorable attention. Regarding the visiting King of Denmark, one paper exclaimed that he, like Solomon, would be the lawgiver to the North. Protector of wisdom, he would be a good father for his subjects. And concluded the article:

O Prince, under your laws the golden age will be reborn
If I were not French, I would wish you for my master![10]

These final lines not only focused praise directly on the Dane but indirectly on the Bourbons as well.

Underpinning the claims of the French royal house to power was religion and the Catholic Church. The affiches showed favor to ecclesiastical authority as toward the king. Curiously, despite the provincial location of most affiches, they seldom cited local bishops or other local churchmen. Even among these scattered reports, the regular clergy were featured more often than the parish priests.[11] The affiches seldom emphasized that part of the Church which could be somewhat rebellious toward hierarchy. Rather, they tended to focus on abstract beliefs and the hierarchy – areas providing little or no problem to the king.[12] Commenting on a book on Christian morality, the *Petites Affiches* of April 20, 1761, proclaimed it an excellent work whose eloquence could produce noble sentiments and lead to piety.

Despite the general inclination of the affiches to praise the Church, the *Affiches de Lyon* (January 13, 1768) reviewed a book on the clergy, noting that "the merit of this precious collection is attested by the esteem it enjoys. All the controversies raised in the kingdom regarding dogma, all the rights of the ecclesiastical judicial system, so much desirable as contested, all the temporal privileges of the French clergy are laid out here in the most interesting way for all the orders of citizens." The criticism embedded in this remark, which mildly chastises the Church by speaking of the many problems facing the clergy, appears an aberration.

It is worth noting that the philosophes, as individual intellectuals or as a movement, scarcely received notice.[13] Enlightenment ideas certainly did surface, but without recognition of their authors. And the affiches covered the provincial academies but almost always without calling attention, even in a covert way, to their important links to the philosophes.[14] Impregnated with Enlightenment notions, these reports generally left the connections implicit. When mentioned, the philosophes were more often attacked than praised. The *Affiches du Poitou* in the June 28, 1782 edition published the following poem to the philosophes:

What is this arrogant troop
Of presumptuous reasoners
Who with an imposing haughtiness
Preach their ostentatious dogma.
Devised in their vain systems
Where little in agreement with one another
They prepare their poison for us
And in their prideful drunkenness
Seem to offer wisdom
In order to insult reason.

Along with this verse, which surely went beyond ordinary disdain, the philosophes would have found other criticisms, directed at them in general[15] or at their heroes including Voltaire[16] and Rousseau.[17]

Although criticism prevailed, the affiches could at times recognize the Enlightenment positively. Since the publishers of the affiches were printers and booksellers, they often used their periodicals to advertise their own materials.[18] Inevitably Enlightenment works populated these offerings. And Rousseau[19] and Voltaire[20] earned positive mention, and the movement likewise received praise. The *Annonces, affiches et avis de Normandie* (April 22, 1768) printed an article on an academy of *belles-lettres* in Caen. This piece argued that the scientific method invigorated a philosophy which now benefitted monarchs and subjects alike. The reference to science makes clear that the philosophy praised was that of the Enlightenment.

Despite such traces of support for the philosophes, the affiches generally held these thinkers at arm's length and instead enthused about Church and monarch. In a few of these papers, however, a minor strain suggested some limits to royal power. This sprinkling of articles proves worthy of mention, more because of their arguments than their number.

A few articles, suggesting restraints on monarchical prerogative, advocated moderation, the laws of Christianity, and concern for the happiness of one's subjects.[21] With the exception of the last, such proposed restraints constituted very traditional discussions of constitutional limits on French kings.[22] The failure of challenging thinking to penetrate into this political writing, suggests the way that the monarchical point of view on political matters really held sway in this medium.

But discussions of power were far from the main subject of the affiches. Instead these pages were mainly dedicated, either in ads or articles, to social and economic comportment. Here lay the focus of the affiches and, as will become apparent, their message in this area proved complex. But on one topic, they were clear. For the most part, these journals excluded, by failing to mention them, the poor and laboring people, or as contemporaries labeled them, the *peuple*. The affiches omitted them from the obituaries they printed. The English press of the same period often included the poor, largely as perpetrators of crime. The columnists there used their reports to criticize the lower order. But no comparable stories ran in the affiches.[23] The clear meaning of ignoring the poor and destitute was their isolation from their social superiors. Even as criminals they could not be noticed.

The affiches' treatment of the working poor would seem totally compatible either with the Old Regime or its detractors. Whatever the more inclusive role outlined for the poor in the more distant Christian past, elites had by the eighteenth century largely come to believe in ignoring the impoverished. They were no longer necessary to central functions of elite society; their best role would be avoiding crime and staying out of sight. In the end, for those who could not manage on their own, institutions would serve the "deserving" and punishment would dispense with the rest. Such a consensus meant that the affiches' indifference to the poor posed no challenge.[24]

Still, occasional breaks occurred in the press's silence and deserve attention because, while they did not fundamentally undermine the general approach, they do provide interesting observations about the poor in the eighteenth century. Of particular concern were employment ads.

To clarify matters, one needs first, however, to examine the occasional comments about the laboring classes. These items picture the *peuple*, defined in the eighteenth century as those depending on manual labor, as flawed in character. The April 29, 1761 issue of the *Affiches de Lyon* published an article supporting lotteries. This piece claimed that such games would benefit the *peuple*: "The domestic and artisan will spend their surplus that they would have formerly lost at the cabaret. The hope of winning has not only corrected the debauchery of this class of people, but it has gotten the artisans to work seven days a week." Suggested in this article is that gambling among the people was at least a lesser vice than their shiftlessness and licentiousness. Other scattered pieces in the press also referred to the poor – whether employed or not – as ignorant and easily corruptible. A churchman explained his intervention in the lives of the peasants as necessary because their poverty left them open to many prejudiced attitudes that could be exploited. The moral of a tale about an erstwhile holy man of peasant stock proved the point that the poorly educated may be easily misled.[25]

Having indicated such shortcomings among the *peuple*, these mur-murings in the affiches also suggested work as that group's one appropriate activity. Clearly the author of the article on lotteries thought it desirable for artisans to go to the workbench every day, applauding that workers were no longer taking off one or two days each week. A poem entitled "Idle Laborers," also published in the Lyons paper (April 15, 1761), expressed the view that hard labor was the people's proper function. A few snippets give the flavor of this piece:

> Deprived of all the wealth that their work gives
> The sad laborers live in indigence
> Destined from birth to the rudest work
> They feel neither pleasure nor rest.
> In vain poetry makes of their lives
> The fortunate story of tranquil richness. . .
> These enchanting portraits, made to impress us
> Do not offer real benefits for those who could enjoy them.
> Alas! What can they do? Scarcely the light
> Streaming from the sun beginning its brilliant course
> Work calls them; by a thousand efforts it's necessary
> To force the ungrateful earth to yield its treasures. . .
> Night alone ends their fatigue.

After emphasizing the hard, cruel work of the cultivators, "Idle Laborers" seeks to justify this toil. Here the author develops two different strategies. First, the *peuple* will escape the vices inflicted on their betters. Although this tack includes the extremely exceptional view of the *peuple* as morally superior to the educated, it also reinforces the role of work for the laborers. The second justification for all this travail is its utility to the state. The poem continues:

> Useful to the State in peace and in war
> You serve in all times the masters of the earth
> Louis, will he be forced into war?
> You are free to avenge him by bearing soldiers.

Thus, work and parenting become the moral outlet for the people.

The occasional articles in the affiches which focused on workers not only relegated them mainly to the world of work, but also emphasized the barrier between this portion of society and the rest. "Idle Laborers" takes up this subject directly by questioning whether, subjected to so much toil, workers might grow restive. Here the poem answered:

But no, do not listen to the voice of vengeance
Mortals, you are aware, that wise Providence
Wishes that diverse ranks distinguish human society here
Even in your troubles adore his design.

Other articles encouraged the notion that the *peuple* must remain in their place. The Normandy paper (March 30, 1770) carried a story of two men condemned to pay a fine of 150 livres for mistreating a servant, but whose penalty had been overturned. The affiches happily concluded that "This sentence reestablishes two known citizens, gives honor to the judges who have retracted the first judgment, and shelters masters from the insults of domestics." Such an article clearly implied that servants should not accuse their superiors. Yet another article in the same paper (November 9, 1770) indicated the inevitability of social distance. The affiches recounted an anecdote about a Scottish gentleman at the court of Charles I. This Scot always dressed like a farmer, and one day a domestic ignorantly barred him from the court. Charles offered to hang the servant, but in the end all was settled amicably. The implication here is that the servant behaved criminally by not recognizing the essential distinction of the gentleman. In this story social superiors, even those in disguise, should remain fundamentally recognizable to all as possessing high rank. This account of class cross-dressing reinforced the message of social rigidity.

But the affiches did allow one interaction across the great divide separating the haves and the have nots: charity. Naturally, in stories on this subject, the rich appeared as the active participants while the poor remained passive recipients. The *Annonces, affiches, et avis de Normandie* published several pieces which encouraged the wealthy to give to the people. Such was the acceptable form for class relations.[26]

By using charity, the affiches could combine the wealthy giver and the passive *peuple* with appreciation of royalty and, more relevant for our purposes here, with a view of the proper morality for the object of these gifts. The affiches from Orléans[27] reported that the Princess Marie-Antoinette and the Dauphin, while walking in their gardens, observed a child who was carrying soup that they learned was for his family. Upon inquiry they found that the boy's father was employed as a gardener on the salary of a little over a livre per day. Marie-Antoinette gave the lad four pieces of gold but discreetly followed him home. When the father received the gold, he immediately worried about the money and whether it was stolen. The princess, listening through the window, opportunely announced that she had given the money. She turned to her husband, the future Louis XVI, described the scene as tender, and declared that they and others of wealth should give such gifts all the time. Marie-Antoinette's comment provides the proper moral for this story by prescribing the desired role for those of higher rank in regard to the laboring classes. And the gardener, honest and hard-working, indicated the prescribed behavior for the recipients of charity.

A fascinating piece in the *Affiches de Lyon* (June 23, 1761) on the public hospital reinforced this notion that the recipients of charity must work. This report noted that some had continued to give money to beggars out of a false sense of duty. The article frowned upon such practices as encouraging begging and gave an account of Lyonnais who were discontinuing this practice:

> . . . the vagabonds who have escaped our investigation, fearing that they will be deprived of a liberty that they abuse, have fled far from our walls and have carried elsewhere their laziness and indecent clamor . . . the Lord who has blessed our enterprise and the zeal of our of our comrades will not leave our neighbors defenseless and the professional beggar, seeing himself banished from city to city will be forced to look for work . . .

In advocating a resolute unwillingness to give charity to beggars, this article underlined other discussions about the necessary qualifications for charity and the deserving poor.

These scattered commentaries, taken together, reinforced the general disapprobation with which the affiches portrayed the lower classes. The papers focused on their weak character, their destiny in work, their isolation from the upper echelons, and their need for a straight and narrow course to be set before them. Such occasional stories did little to alleviate the exclusion implied in this overall treatment. And, in fact, such negative remarks provided justification for affiches otherwise omitting the *peuple*.

Even if these comments which sprinkled through the affiches only deepened the rejection of the inferior orders, the advertisements which appeared primarily in the affiches of Lyons and Normandy and the *Petites Affiches* during its last decade presented a somewhat more positive image of the *peuple*. The advertisements concerning this layer of society were basically announcements by workers looking for positions or employers hoping to fill particular places. There was a reasonable balance in what posts were advertised. Most notices were for domestics but many related to artisans or clerks. Notices were commonly brief. Workers described the position they wanted and the kinds of skills they possessed. While employers used the same two categories, they could often be even more terse, failing to mention any particular requirements. And workers could, on occasion, be quite voluble in this regard. Whatever the difference in what they included, both sides usually omitted discussions of salary. And in the rare instance when the ads raised the question of recompense, they still never discussed monetary remuneration, but the availability of housing and other amenities. This omission is significant in the light of recent research which has emphasized the important role of money in the eighteenth-century workplace.[28] Failing to mention salary at all may add nuances to those assertions about the importance money had achieved in the workplace.

The many advertisements from both potential employers and employees appeared similar, but substantively emphasized different criteria. The appeals from workers promised many different abilities that might be crudely grouped into four separate categories: special skills, appearance, character, and intellectual abilities. The attributes promised varied a great deal according to the post sought. Wet nurses inevitably promised good milk. The *Affiches de Lyon* ran the following lines: "One Bernarde, wife of Joseph Chanci, with milk of four months; she is 28 years old; they live in their own house which has considerable space."[29] This ad, of course, extended beyond skills, to emphasize the comfort available in their large residence. And the reference to the husband was undoubtedly a claim to respectability, a value that will be more fully discussed below. Other workers touted skills appropriate to their proposed employment. Domestics promised a wide range of abilities including cooking,[30] shaving,[31] cleaning,[32] driving carriages,[33] strength,[34] making liqueurs,[35] sewing,[36] and doing the laundry.[37] Of course, servants could list several of their attributes together as one did in the September 18, 1765 issue of the *Affiches de Lyon*. That female servant, who claimed to know especially well what women needed, numbered among her skills the ability to store jellies, brew liqueurs, and wash and iron fine linen.

Various workers also emphasized their appearance. One woman applying for work in a "bourgeois" cabaret described herself as clean.[38] A man, wishing to work in a store selling silk, noted that he possessed a pleasant face.[39] Another, very important facet of these ads was their emphasis on the applicants' exemplary behavior. Workers sometimes claimed loyalty,[40] sweetness,[41] and agreeableness,[42] but they tended to stress their good families[43] and good references.[44] For example, the *Affiches de Lyon* carried a notice from a young man, who sought a job in a business involving either gold or silk, and who promised that his family could vouch for him.[45]

But in depicting themselves, laborers went beyond reliability, physical attributes, and skills to note their mental abilities. The high frequency of this sort of claim even suggests an insistence on the significance of these traits. Among these appeals was a knowledge of the city and the vagaries of the customs;[46] while another promised a special understanding of older people.[47] Along with these particular claims were others that resonated throughout these ads. Some promised shrewdness, including one "young man of 20" who announced great savvy as a clerk.[48] Perhaps, the most common promise was the ability to read and write. In addition, computational skills – usually, but not exclusively, counting – were listed.[49] The *Affiches de Lyon* (November 12, 1766) published an interesting ad incorporating and expanding many of these claims:

> A young man with the ability to read, write, and count, and who has studied much and knows well how to be a servant, would like to become a domestic; he has the ability to govern the business of a household.

This hopeful noted his intellectual abilities and his educational background, and expressed a wish for a supervisory position. He was not the only one who desired such authority as an earlier notice in the *Affiches de Lyon* indicates:

> For chambermaid a girl of good family presents herself. She knows needlework and related areas. She knows how to repair gloves and sew; she also understands all that is necessary for efficiently running a house.[50]

Though more subtle than the other ad, this young woman still put forward her wish to supply direction.

These advertisements supplied by workers in the columns of the affiches thus developed and enhanced the laboring classes' image in the affiches. Although these notices constituted an effort to escape the silence imposed on them, much of their copy did not actually challenge their inferior position. Self-descriptions emphasizing skills, reliability, and appearance did not equate them with the elite – probably the major readers of the affiches. Nonetheless, when workers claimed mental abilities, including the ability to manage, they were intruding on the turf of the upper classes.

But such claims to possess intellectual skills and thus to enter into some kind of partnership with the social elite did not remain uncontested even in the employment ads. Although sharing the form of the workers' ads, announcements by employers emphasized different traits. When employers looked to fill positions, they sometimes stressed exactly the same attributes as workers claimed. One advertisement emphasized reliability as it indicated the employer was "looking for a young man as a domestic, 15 to 18 years old, who is already known. . ." by a respectable resident of the city.[51] Another ad emphasized skills by calling for someone particularly able in sewing and hair dressing.[52] Even though some ads from potential employers and employees could strike similar chords, the workers far more emphatically stressed their mental ability. Only impressionistic evidence yet exists in regard to this argument, but one issue of the Lyons affiches which contained numerous help and employment wanted ads lends considerable support for the notion advanced here.[53] In this issue, workers claimed that they could style hair, sew, launder, clean, serve a table, give a shave, and drive a coach. Furthermore, several promised excellent recommendations. In addition to these assertions of special skills and faithful service, the workers also stated that they could read, write, and in two cases, speak foreign languages. Yet the ads seeking employees said nothing about the need for such intellectual abilities. They emphasized skills – cooking, gardening, driving a carriage – morality, and strong letters of reference. Such desires ran counter to the claims advanced by would-be employees.

These implicit rebukes to workers' pretensions seem then to leave the peuple largely outside the affiches. Such employment ads appeared only in a small minority of these papers anyway. In the end, these advertisements, linked to the commentary regarding the peuple, remain marginal in amount and their message did little to overcome the exclusion implied by the general silence regarding the lower classes.

Although the overall message thus conformed to the press's indifference toward the poor and did not particularly challenge elite views on this matter, something did exist here. The description of the charity of Marie-Antoinette sounded a personal note, long since discarded elsewhere in the top echelons of society. Far more significant were the voices of the workers seeking jobs who clearly reveal, once again, that the bottom of society often will not acquiesce in the negligible roles assigned it. Slipping into the press was a discourse, however crowded out by others, that, while not altering the general tone of the affiches, shows a lodestone of popular attitudes and resistance. And the self-image of the peuple is compelling. By claiming intellectual ability for themselves, working men and women also claimed a new status for themselves. Such aspirations also suggest that ultimately they desired the goals of their social superiors, rather than desiring a fundamentally separate lifestyle. Such evidence would seem to further the view of the poor that Daniel Roche has developed for Paris.[54]

But in the affiches' main subject matter – social and economic questions – it was the educated elite that provided the special object of attention. To understand how these papers covered this subject, first I will examine the articles, comments, and occasional items that appeared throughout. Treated separately will be the message generated by advertisements, because, as will become apparent, these columns provided a different, though complementary, point of view.

What emerged most prominently in the pages of the affiches was an attack on a degenerate lifestyle based on luxury. The contributors to the affiches found nothing positive and a long litany of ills attributable to this vice. In an article on the provincial academy of science, the *Affiches de Lyon* (December 13, 1769) reported such a discussion about luxury. Arguing that this vice would be difficult, if not impossible, to eradicate, the article focused on containment. Nonetheless, the piece began with extremely negative assumptions about luxury and its deleterious side-effects: "Considered as the acquisition of property, luxury stimulates cupidity, excites pride, and foments debility. Consequently, it depraves morality, confuses the ranks of society, and undermines the sinews of subordination."

On other occasions, the affiches identified luxury with yet other failings. Indeed, this part of the press often attributed problems in agriculture to this characteristic. According to the *Affiches du Poitou* (October 2, 1783), for every 100 jobs created in the luxury trades, 100,000 were lost in the countryside. In addition, able workers became impertinent, lazy lackeys when employed in the luxury trade. This report uncannily echoed and made more specific an article that had appeared fifteen years earlier in the *Annonces, affiches, et avis divers de l'Orléanais* (September 23, 1768) that argued: "The vice of luxury encourages a soft life among masters and domestics, which has prodigiously multiplied the number of sedentary arts. This increase, so often praised, has simultaneously ruined agriculture and health." Infected by luxury, farming and physical well-being suffered. Other affiches pursued other tacks in blasting indulgence in material goods. For example, the *Annonces, affiches, et avis divers de Normandie*[55] noted that luxury hardened hearts and inhibited contributing to charity.

Related to luxury were a number of other vices that the affiches likewise condemned. As the examples of the evils of luxury reveal, contemporaries connected this vice to a long string of indulgent behaviors. But one of the most often cited by-products was laziness. The manner in which the Poitou paper deplored laziness created by luxury reveals the former as a target and the connection between the two despicable characteristics.[56] The *Affiches de Lyon* (May 1, 1765) picked up the same cudgels, attacking passivity as one of the major failings that led to unhappiness. Also linked to luxury and routinely condemned was voluptuousness, or rule by the physical passions. Only weakness could issue from such goals, warned the affiches. Passions tyrannize and lead to unfortunate results.[57] Finally, such feelings further encouraged luxury as well as "vanity and cupidity" while destroying "relationships, friendships, gaiety."[58]

Targeting luxury in particular and focusing as well on the concomitant ills of laziness and voluptuousness would seemingly be related to other interests of the affiches. The press was concerned about how seeking financial advantage in relationships undermined the family. To the eighteenth century, depraved and fickle individuals contracted a marriage as a matter of financial advantage or "interest." Some direct evidence indicates that the affiches viewed those involved in depredations related to luxury as incapable of solid marriages. One article raised fears that those who used artifice and manners to attract a mate could not attain true love.[59] Another piece argued that such egotists would likely be utterly incapable of marriage.[60] But the affiches did not explicitly argue that decadence, which might produce no marriage or flawed marriages, most likely resulted in mercenary marriages based on interest. Nonetheless, this seems logical, especially since such marriages could satisfy the need for luxury if not passion. Perhaps, indeed, this concern about "interest" in marriages emerged from a broader disdain for luxury.

Whether directly connected or not to the anxiety about luxury, the hostility to interest as a focus for marriage took up considerable space in the affiches. This appears all the more fascinating in view of the important role actually played by interest in marriages in a wide range of the social spectrum. In a review of a play, the *Affiches de province* (September 26, 1764) made clear its hostility toward the antagonist who married for money. This individual, also characterized by a certain frivolousness, provides additional weight to the suggestion that such unfortunate marriages resulted directly from the vices derided by the affiches. Yet another play praised in an affiches criticized interest.[61] In this theatrical production, a baronet promised his daughter to a big businessman instead of a young officer whom she loved. When she and the officer decided to elope, the baronet found them out but then offered to support them financially, even at great personal risk. Seeing her duty, the daughter renounced the officer and swore obedience. At this moment, the businessman arrived and observed that his betrothed loved another and intended to marry him only for the financial advantages to the family. Witnessing this, he renounced his claim, resolved to unite the two lovers, and was successful in this quest. Without following the many implications of this story, one should note how in the happy ending the marriage for interest fails to take place, and the romantic attachment supplants it. But the *Petites Affiches* (March 29, 1759) spurned subtlety by denouncing such relationships: "The marriages of interest engender caprice, indifference, bad treatment; it's a just punishment for sacrificing the sentiment of attraction for a fortune that could never soften a heart. . . ."

Whether or not the fear of a decadent lifestyle was connected to lambasting marriages constructed on interest, such hostility to luxury helped to produce the sexism infecting these affiches. Ever since biblical times, men had connected depravity to women. To explain why women were regarded as they were in the affiches requires detailed investigation into the intellectual world of these papers. But for now it seems safe to assert that, except for a small elite, most publishers and contributors –

almost entirely male and influenced by Rousseauist conceptions – would have identified active women with luxurious, enervating lifestyles.[62]

The affiches followed and reinforced the societal strictures regarding women by linking decadence to women and warning against their participation in public life. For example, the *Affiches de province* (March 31, 1762) carried a story on Christine, the daughter of the Swedish king, Gustavus Adolphus. Heir to the throne, she voluntarily renounced it and remarked that women were unequal to the task because "The ignorance of women, the weakness of their souls, their body and their mind render them incapable of rule." Likewise, the Lille paper (April 26, 1782) published a scathing attack on female autonomy, citing a case of a woman who, trying to gain her independence, was willing to see her husband consigned to the galleys.

One last, rather tentative target of the affiches was erudition. Scattered through these journals were a few remarks which perceived difficulties arising from sophisticated instruction, though these comments failed to link this vice to others. Nonetheless, one can track these murmurings here and there through the press. One contribution found learning in Greek and Latin worthless.[63] Suspicion could also spread to extraordinary intelligence as revealed in a scathing attack on Voltaire in the February 15, 1782 issue of the *Annonces, affiches, et avis divers de Flandre*:

> . . . even if you possess the greatest genius which has ever surprised the world, you deserve only public indignation: in fact, what monstrous glory is there in overturning all the useful ideas, in inconsiderately shaking, unfortunately with success, the foundations of good society, to unhinge and even to break completely these sacred ties, the ties so sweet which attached me to my father, my king, my country!

This eruption of anti-intellectualism surpassed other remarks in the affiches but only established an outer edge. In this reasoning, the author would still seem to validate rationality by his endorsement of "useful ideas" and be mainly interested in attacking highly sophisticated ideas that threatened societal calm and important hierarchies.

In opposition to such undesirable comportment – defined as luxury, laziness, voluptuousness, mercenary marriages, female assertiveness, and intellectualism – the affiches proposed above all humility. A common compliment was to state that someone was modest. An obituary for a famous mathematician noted his modesty and concluded: "The great men of all times, Virgil, Correide, La Fontaine, Molière, Pascal, Newton, Mabillon, etc. were modest."[64] In a similar way, a contributor to the *Petites Affiches* (August 21, 1760) in considering the Greek philosopher Epicurus praised him for opposing "haughtiness, assertiveness, disdain, invective, modern sensitivities (these are his own terms), and embracing modesty, equality, simplicity of manner in words and bearing. . . ." Clerics who followed such ideals likewise received positive coverage.[65]

The emphasis on simplicity and reticence also infected the affiches' notion of proper education. The simplicity mentioned in the statements on education meant not so much humility as a lack of affectation. The affiches asserted that the human heart was good and needed only an opportunity for exploration. No journal pronounced more completely on this subject than the Bordeaux paper (January 15, 1761), which published a series of letters from a self-proclaimed "Dutchman" who commented on various aspects of French life. One epistle commenced by noting that French education performed admirably in producing adventurousness and athleticism but "the heart and reason have lost their rights." By forcing young children into public speaking and applauding all their efforts, the French failed to learn about secrecy and the advantages of a controlled society. More attention seemed to focus on dancing and the ability to make war. "At home" continued the Dutchman:

> education is simple, but tends to a more useful end. Manners consist of knowing the truth of one's heart. We concentrate on making our children honest men and women; we encourage them in love of country, indulgence for their neighbors, forgiveness to insults, necessary compassion for the unfortunate, prudent spending, a wise liberality, courage of soul in the face of danger, pure morality, controlled conduct, good faith, and sincerity. We try to form them into men and citizens. In France, one creates machines.

This final remark highlighted the affiches's goal for education. The image of the machine as the result of an undesirable education only illuminated what was expected. People fashioned machines from raw materials into a cold instrument unrelated to the original substances. The articles in the affiches advocated staying close to the simple materials.[66]

Embedded in the definition of proper education was another positive theme in the affiches: the commitment to nature and consequently to a natural law emanating from it. Evidently, a schooling designed to evoke an already extant goodness in individuals is predicated on the pre-existence of an internal natural goodness. Despite accepting this view in educational theories, the affiches made few explicit references to natural law. One exception appeared in the *Affiches de Lyon* (April 15, 1761) on pagan religion. This article discussed how these primitive people, regardless of their low state of development, accepted virtue and thus revealed the universality of a beneficent human nature. Such a statement was a commitment to natural law. Emphasizing the same point was a poem in the *Affiches de Bordeaux* (June 18, 1761):

> It's your reason that our fathers
> Leading with hesitant steps

Freed them from their misery . . .
Living under the law of nature
They maintain a sure route
Guided by your clear light
Enemies of slavery
Love alone provided the transportation
Toward a perfect equality.

Less voluble on a theory of natural law, the affiches strongly inserted hard work in their litany of desired characteristics. In reporting praise for an academician of Rouen, the *Annonces, affiches, et avis de Normandie* (January 10, 1772) noted that he owed his success in letters and arts to the constancy of his effort. In another article on the Academy of Sciences in Lyons the orator waxed lovingly over the advantages of work. His analysis not only explained his belief in toil but also focused on many of the evils opposed more generally by the affiches. As reported in this paper:

M. l'abbé Pernette finished the session by reading a speech on the necessity and advantages of work. He was convincing that two obstacles ordinarily prevented man from being happy: the tyranny of the passions and the unfortunate events of life. Work prevented the fatal effect of the passions . . . . If laziness is the mother of vices, work is the father of virtues. The injustices on the part of men, disorder in business, the destruction of a fortune, poverty, the loss of dear ones, even certain illnesses find solace in the exercise of the least work. M. l'abbé Pernette concluded that no situation exists in life where work is not a useful and agreeable resource, and he finished by observing that work contributes to the repose of the soul as sobriety procures the health of the body.[67]

Thus, the affiches endorsed the same intensity of effort – though surely not necessarily manual exertion – for the elite that it had favored for the workers and the destitute.

But the positive ideal that emerged most prominently in the articles of the affiches was the construction of a proper family ordered by love and devotion. They used these terms without definition, so their meaning demands closer scrutiny. Different affiches emphasized various aspects of the family but all coalesced around deepest affection as the generating force for marriages.[68] When this sort of journal discussed courtship, it encouraged, not physical attraction and certainly not financial advantage, but sentiment.[69] Indeed, one article clearly expected that physical love must await marriage.[70] The precise meaning of the sentiment of attraction remains elusive but a poem decrying artifice among lovers suggests by contrast that the proper emotion was that of an honest, unreserved meeting in which two personalities would reach immediate harmony.[71] Nonetheless, the specific emotions involved remain unclear except that, opposed to voluptuousness and money, this appeared to be a kind of romantic, yet rational decision.

The affiches were not particularly more loquacious on the proper relationships within a marriage. While this press made innumerable references to the role of love between the couple, it spent very little time discussing what this may actually have entailed.[72] Indeed, the explicit message about marital relationships lauded the stability of marriages, discouraged separations, and counseled longevity.[73] The *Affiches du Poitou* (November 11, 1784) reported a celebration involving a 73-year-old husband and his 76-year-old wife on their fiftieth anniversary. Recounting the activities, the Poitou paper detailed how one of their grandchildren had led them to their church where a joyous assembly met and received them with songs and dancing. Everyone was thrilled that the couple had "lived together during such a long course of years." Interesting as this was, it pictured marriage more an achievement vital for the public and revealed little about the inner workings of the relationship.

Despite glossing over marriage, the affiches gave great attention to the relationship between parents and children, and here they overtly suggested mutual love and respect. From the very beginning parents ought to care deeply about their children. The *Annonces, affiches, et avis divers de province* (May 7, 1760) endorsed a book on child care which precisely described the correct treatment of the newborn. The book depicted in detail the articles needed for the crib and addressed such areas as sleeping, nursing, cleanliness, dental care, dressing, and suitable exercise. The article closed by labeling the book an interesting one that could protect those "fragile deposits of nature." Other articles in various affiches discouraged swaddling[74] and supported mothers' breastfeeding their own children.[75] And many items testified that parental concern intensified as the child matured. Often the affiches referred to such relations as based on "natural sentiments."[76] Such sentiments received illustration when the paper based in Lille printed a letter from an English noblewoman to Vergennes, the French foreign minister, which pleaded for her son to be released from a prisoner of war camp. This woman portrayed the misery of parents bereft of their son. Her husband's illness made it impossible even to inform him of their son's imprisonment and her grief was practically killing her.[77] Such strong parental attachments to a child were reflected in another anecdote recounted in the *Petites Affiches* of July 13, 1781. A woman saw her older son drowning and flung herself in the water after him. Although she reached him, his weight and the current overwhelmed her. A baker, witnessing the "tender" spectacle, was overcome with sympathy and attempted, despite his inability to swim, to save them. Using a log, he pulled them to shore. In this story, the parental self-sacrifice was so evident that it could impress and motivate others.

Parents were thus expected to be overcome with grief and to risk their own lives to save a child. In return, children were supposed to display respect as a theater review clearly shows.[78] The account concluded, "The sentiments of tenderness for an estranged son who returns to him and the respectful attachment of a good son to a dignified father made a touching impression on the numerous assembly gathered there."

The focus of the affiches on the parent–child interaction as the central aspect of family life did not completely exclude scattered stories on affection in other relationships. The *Annonces, affiches, et avis divers de Normandie* carried a couple of stories of this ilk. The October 10, 1766 issue reported a reunion between brothers. A beautiful carriage stopped near some water carriers, and a man descended to address one of them whom after a while, he pronounced to be his brother. Years of trading in the Indies with their father had made him rich, and he had returned to assist the family. This act symbolized a commitment beyond the parent and child to siblings. The Normandy paper added to this theme with another account a year later (September 25, 1767) of a family in which four generations comprising 60 people lived together in peace, friendship and *concorde*. Similarity in thinking as much as blood had made this unity possible. But these examples pale beside the much greater interest in the exchange between parents and offspring.

Having defined the family mainly as nuclear and sentimental, the affiches unhesitatingly consigned women to a special place within it. A detailed account of one article goes far to explain how the affiches understood this question. This particular piece was published three times in the sample considered for this chapter. It first appeared in the January 20, 1762 issue of the *Petites Affiches* and was reported a week later in the *Affiches de Bordeaux*. Seven years later, the June 30, 1769 edition of *Annonces, affiches, et avis divers de l'Orléanais* carried the same account. Repeating this story so often, especially over a seven-year interval, would in itself show great interest but, given the sampling technique employed here, this repetition proves practically an obsession. Although the system of reading the affiches should produce an outline of the message of each paper, this approach makes no effort to compare the fate of specific stories. For the same article to appear three times in the sample is unparalleled and suggests that a thorough search for this piece would yield many more instances.

The story that so drew the journalists' attention was entitled, "Apology for the Babbling of Women." This account began with a woman's assertion that women talk too much, destroying social life with their constant babbling. A man, labeled an optimist, justified women's loquaciousness on the ground that it helps children develop. As he remarked, "It's good that nature has desired the conversations of women always to go over the same objects, those that are the simplest and most ordinary." If they discussed complicated subjects, their speech would not be clear to children who need to understand so that they can learn to talk. Moreover, this babbling generated good, clear singing voices for women. Yet even these advantages have limits, as the spokesman for women agreed: "It becomes necessary for men to forget in the future the stories of our infancy and entirely change our method of thinking." Happily, time would cure this ill.

The implications of the story would have been quite clear to the eighteenth-century reader. Women were weak; in the end, stupid. By using the word "babbling" to describe their talk, this piece equated women with babies. And their function was clearly the home, in particular child raising.

Even when articles in the affiches did not inject the condescension of the "Babbling of Women," they agreed with its notion of the proper position for women as in the home. The *Affiches du Poitou* (June 7, 1781) published a long account about the education of women that advocated serious formal training. The author of this piece was careful to note that such education should not disrupt women's housework and should not encourage them to seek careers as intellectuals in the public sphere. Asserting that the home remained the proper place for women, the author insisted that they still would benefit from education because:

it is convenient. . . to give them some of our knowledge, as useful as agreeable, which adorns the mind, forms the judgment, and assists in the conduct of business. This knowledge can add still more to their natural charms either to entertain them from time to time, considering the pain and difficulties that they carry; or to spread greater grace in society which they soften and embellish; or to defend them from boredom and laziness which in turn can lead to disorders, or finally so that they become able to satisfy their duty and their own tenderness very early in assisting their own children with this knowledge, when they become mothers with a family, and especially those of their sex when they serve as teachers. . .

Most interesting here, in this complex advice on education for women, is the line about female "disorders" which finds laziness to be the main culprit. This assertion shows the way in which anxieties about women could easily be linked to other concerns, in this case the affiches' obsession with a lack of application. Also worth noting is the more positive portrayal of women as charming and tender. Nonetheless, the adjectives did not denote strength and power but instead a need for protection. This gallant condescension, indeed, contributed to the general point of this article, which was that education, despite its utility for business and teaching, ultimately should perfect women for their special role but should do nothing to alter their status. The kinder tone of this piece in regard to women did not change at all the subordinate place reserved for them.

With women relegated to the home, the affiches had constructed its image of the desired world which would avert undesirable behaviors. What clearly emerges in these papers is a decided preference for humility, simplicity, hard work, the family as nest, with the women safely tucked within. These positive goals stood as the rejection of an uncontrolled love of luxury, lust and the disordered family, and assertive females, all of which the affiches found objectionable. Having elaborated starkly different visions of good and evil, this part of the press located each style in very different parts of society.

Insofar as one class personified and harbored the evils envisioned in the affiches, the press identified it as the nobility. Not only did this press portray the Second Estate as haughty, it more generally castigated them and their behavior.[79] One paper, in an item on seigneurial rights, focused on one new, pleasant practice but contrasted it with the numerous other disagreeable rights found everywhere.[80] Such attacks on seigneurialism surely were aimed at the nobility. But nowhere did the Second Estate appear in so problematic a position as when nobles went to Versailles. Courtiers could not be modest.[81] The Dutch visitor featured in the Bordeaux periodical (July 9, 1761) advocated politeness as an essential part of the training of the nobility. This same visitor generally encouraged "simplicity" and direct behavior as the main focus in education so his advocacy of the opposite for the higher reaches of society appears curious. His answer to this seeming contradiction was that courtiers needed the skill. Although not equivalent to great talent, merit, or profound knowledge, courtesy was required at court, and there produced excellent results. Thus nobles had the duty to learn politeness. This comment, allegedly supporting politeness, simultaneously, though circuitously, condemned the court as shallow and artificial. Yet another periodical published the following lines about the courtiers:

> Dissipated without purpose, occupied without business
> To lose our money in all nighters
> Bored with pleasures, tired of excesses
> I believe that we are possessed by the devil.[82]

This verse precisely identified the court as the center of the luxury and decadence that the affiches elsewhere condemned.

While the affiches depicted the nobility and particularly those of the court as the locus of undesirable pleasures, this press also insisted that virtue lived in the countryside. These papers argued that not only were rural areas of the country the most agreeable,[83] but they were also the place where the most useful citizens resided.[84] And that love without artifice, so touted by the affiches, remained attainable there as well. A poem in the paper from Bordeaux (November 19, 1761) commenced:

If ever I have the choice in love
I want a country beauty
Amiable without thinking about it
And who artlessly can easily charm
True pleasure follows nature
I have seen love more than once
Playing in a field of grass.

Did this commitment to the countryside really mean that the affiches intended to elevate rustics, the plowmen and farm women, that it usually ignored or even castigated? Several reasons suggest that "country" here should be identified as a metaphor for members of the elite with a base of power outside the court. First, consider that the main opposition that the affiches noted was that between court and country. This dichotomy, a standard in English political theory, had been translated as well to France.[85] In both countries the definition of country was less that of rural society than that part of the society uncorrupted by the court. Thus, contemporaries might read "country" as a broader construct than simply those working on the land.

If country provided a wider berth for social groups than would first meet the eye, one still must assess which part of society the affiches found most qualified. Of course, the nobility – even its rural members – was already tarnished. And in papers so dedicated to business, it would be no surprise that those involved in commerce were most favored. This proves to be exactly the case. It ought, however, to be added that while many of the affiches' goals could be found elsewhere, this favorable treatment of merchants was mainly the innovation of these periodicals. Wholesale merchants, who received significant specific attention, were described as simple, good and charitable.[86] Another paper allowed the *Courrier de commerce* access to its pages, and its comments glorified such merchants as very important in the current advanced state of the economy.[87] The Poitou paper spoke more generally of the benefits of commerce, admiring the achievements of nearby Flanders and hoping for the same at home.[88] An anecdote reported in the Orléans affiches (June 7, 1771) threw considerable light on the desirability of commerce and again identified the court as a source of difficulties. In Vienna, so the paper reported, the courtiers had been assigned commercial responsibilities. "It is necessary to hope that they will be content with their fate and not use all the subtleties of individual interest to disrupt the attempt of the well-intentioned authorities and to place yet more obstacles before Commerce. . . ." By linking the court to selfishness and revealing it opposed to business, these lines suggest that commerce, as opposed to the wickedness of the court, was a truly noble activity. In elevating the commercial classes, the affiches was truly putting its own cast on "country" ideology which in England found business as corrupt as the court.

Having located malevolence and benevolence in particular zones – the court and commercial classes respectively – the affiches nonetheless showed a certain ambivalence about criticizing traditional social divisions. Even if this part of the press was prepared to throw its lot in with these middling classes, it also held back somewhat. Its prospectuses always addressed the "public," intended to include the nobility as well as the elite commoners.[89] Furthermore, some articles particularly warned about breaking social barriers within the upper echelons of society. One article bluntly justified hierarchy as necessary for maintaining stability.

> Thus after the ministers of religion who constitute a class apart, which we regard as men consecrated by rank to give lessons and examples of all the virtues to society, the military rank which imposes on itself the duty of giving its last drop of blood for the country obtains and merits first place. Independent of this sacrifice, this honor provides its sole recompense. The Magistrates come next and the nation accepts this rank because it senses how necessary it is to have able and enlightened judges and courageous defenders of the law.[90]

Another story reported in the *Affiches de Lyon* made explicit this hostility to breaking down social barriers. The protagonist was a wealthy English middle-class woman who, though she lacked proper station, copied "the airs, fashion, and the tone of the ladies of the Court." Overstepping these boundaries, she became the laughing stock of the court and the object of a plot to discipline her pretensions. Several distinguished ladies, in the manner of *The Emperor's New Clothes* but with a completely different object in mind, dressed in outlandish garb and managed to convince the intruder that such attire was all the rage. She immediately rushed out to procure the appropriate costume but when she returned newly attired, the ladies had resumed their usual dress. When the interloper saw her situation among the numerous invited guests, she swooned in confusion.[91] Of course, this vignette comments on women by portraying them as mean-spirited beings, obsessed with fashion. Yet it also provides a strong lesson against social climbing.

The countervailing messages of these anecdotes and other items indicate the complexity with which the affiches linked particular comportments to certain milieus. Some of this ambiguity doubtless sprang from the mixed feelings that the middle class held – superiority about their own station coupled with a desire to climb into the nobility. Perhaps the fairest assessment of the vision of these periodicals is that they found good in commercial society and problems with the court and, to a lesser extent, the nobility in general. Nonetheless, other articles seemed to suggest that whatever the truth of these characterizations, they should not lead to a division within the elite in which the commoners might seek to compete with their social betters. These dictums reinforcing the current hierarchy might suggest to readers that the affiches called only for a symbolic or behavioral change and did not sound the tocsin for any restructuring of the elite. What this criss-crossing advice seems to advocate is that the commercial elite set a standard to which all might aim and which might reform manners in an evolutionary fashion.

Despite the affiches' limiting their nostrums for society to persuasion, readers doubtlessly would have comprehended well the message. Most evident to contemporaries would have been the attack on the court as the home of luxury, voluptuousness, and disordered families. To be sure, some ancient authors available to this classically educated readership had denigrated these same targets. Potentially, consumers of the affiches might have regarded their contents as homilies unrelated to any specific society. But writers of the eighteenth century had excoriated the court, and nobility to a lesser extent, for these and other ills, transforming general moral dictums into specific indictments. The theorists of the commonwealthman, with their emphasis on the good of the country and the evils of the court, made the most of these distinctions. And the moral stench that Louis XV's mistresses seemed to typify only added to this theoretical attack.[92] The audience would have ineluctably seen the affiches – even if the views inscribed there were not completely congruent with others – as reinforcing the charges levied elsewhere.

Like the critique of the affiches, the ideal world imagined in the affiches – of humility, simplicity, hard work, family, female subordination, and commerce – could pose problems as well for the top echelons of society. Again, the writers of antiquity had supported many of these goals, making them virtues without a particular object to reform. Yet the intellectual climate of the eighteenth century intervened to channel such doctrines into criticism against society at the very top – the aristocratic world, surely including courtiers and possibly the nobility. A number of writers had argued the incompatibility of those *positive* ideals, found in the affiches, with the upper ranges of the establishment. Most obviously, Rousseau asserted that eighteenth-century high society lacked the very values that this press proposed. His autobiography and his novels, *Emile* and the *Nouvelle Héloïse*, reveal a man, rather a Candide, representing the same goals enunciated in the affiches.[93] Rousseau's fan mail clearly indicated wide agreement in the society both in favor of these principles and Rousseau's belief that the aristocracy opposed them.[94] Thus, the affiches, in proposing those ideals, evidently critiqued the highest echelons of society. Enough similarity existed between their notions and those of others for the latter to subsume the former. The advertisements likely did not always reinforce Rousseauism, as scanning its pages reveals many notices and reviews of the theater to which he was implacably opposed. Still the affiches and Jean-Jacques seemed most often to agree.

To be certain, some of society's attitudes, so important to transforming the language of the affiches into a broader social critique, emerged only relatively late in the century. Nonetheless, because the affiches came along at about the same time it seems fair to connect, without reference to chronological distinctions, these perspectives. They were, more or less, present along with the emerging provincial advertisers.

Guided by eighteenth-century debates, the educated audience saw the affiches as participating in the outpouring of criticism against Old Regime manners and mores. Of course, the court and nobility were not as guilty as its indictments suggested and, to be certain, accepted most ideals expressed in the affiches. Targeted individuals surely reconciled their beliefs and their maintenance of their position in any number of ways, possibilities probed to a degree in the conclusion of this work. Of course, this in no way spared the aristocracy as a group. Because the court had been condemned and the *monde*, probably also including the nobility, was seen as hostile to simple, family values, the commentaries in the affiches would be envisioned as criticism of that milieu.

The final question of this chapter concerns how the advertisements may have added to or influenced the image of proper elite behavior projected by the articles. Although great variations existed among journals as well as over the course of a life of a single journal, advertisements generally comprised about one-half of the copy of the affiches. Many, many items including goods and services were advertised. With the pages of the affiches open and free to many comers, an incredible range became possible. Books, royal offices, mortgages, real estate, educational opportunities, luxury items comprised a significant part of the items offered. The variety of the ads defies simple categorization, but a few examples may give some of their flavor. Although some notices could stretch to as long as 200–300 words, brevity was much more common. Usually the longest appeals came from individuals with unusual services or products whose appeal was not immediately apparent.

In the affiches, the reduction of all these items to one common denominator – the price – produced a message that, among its most important aspects, seemed to attack the status of nobility. Advertising high royal offices and seigneuries, which conferred nobility, and luxury items alongside such banalities as medicinal cures probably appeared disconcerting. In the system appearing in the affiches, money proved the only barrier to the top of the social strata and its culture. Yet as nobles laid claim both to distinct racial characteristics and a lifestyle markedly different from others, this intermingling led to potential challenge.

Although this situation accurately reflected eighteenth-century reality, writing it down and publishing it weekly in the pages of the affiches certainly posed a blatant alternative to the pose of the nobility.

That contemporaries recognized the theoretical challenge to status becomes apparent in an article published first in the *Petites Affiches* and reprinted in the *Annonces, affiches, et avis divers de l'Orléanais* (January 3, 1772).[95] This piece, entitled "The Philosophy of the Affiches," is worth examining closely, partly because its repetition suggests a significant resonance, at least among the journalists. Its anonymous author first exclaimed about the rootlessness of the present world typified by all the belongings shifting from family to family. Within less than a generation articles change hands and are reshaped. From all this one could conclude that no "real possessions" existed; everyone was a mere renter. Three important examples particularly troubled the writer. First, he noted, "The great seigneuries and important offices, which constitute the titles of the distinguished families by the names of *houses* . . . are not sheltered from these revolutions, marriages, alliances, deaths, exchanges, and shifts in fortune." Worried about the changes for important families, the author broadened his concern to include human pleasures which, because of the constant sale of luxury items, seemed so fleeting. Finally, the solidity of commercial activity appeared threatened by the column on exchange rates.

The emphases in the "Philosophy of the Affiches" reveal that not only did the structure of the ads challenge a latticework of privilege which defended a distinctive nobility but also attacked the solidity of the society in general. This piece went beyond noble prerogatives and lifestyle to reveal anxiety over even commercial wealth. Evidently, the ads proclaimed the situation that already had transpired but this also flew in the face of the stability that was supposed to be a benefit of the Old Regime.[96] This contradiction doubtless underlay the concerns of the writer.

Evidently then the general structure of advertising provided problematic material to the status quo, but some genres of notices provided special messages. At this writing, three special subtopics have been examined, all of which add to the general impression created by the advertisements. Colin Jones' highly focused study of medical advertising posits that the commercial notices about medicine undermine the privileged medical world. These materials tended to challenge privileges even below those exercised by the nobility. The affiches assuaged the fear that confidence in doctors would wane by assuring a happy community of producers and consumers, benefiting from the advance of medicine.[97]

Notices for the sale of royal offices further challenged the status quo. Such ads constantly undermined the image of office-holders by stressing the cost-benefit advantages of these offices. The conferral of nobility and special privileges were important selling points as the effort to market the office of Conseiller du Roi promised:[98] "Office of Conseiller du Roi, Chevalier of honor at the Bureau des Finances of Caen. It grants nobility and all the prerogatives attached to the Treasurer of France." The Orléans affiches (November 21, 1777) did not even bother to give the specific name of an office with attendant rights that it advertised: "Considerable Office, with some very honorable and very lucrative functions and responsibility for only three months. This office is one of the best in the government; it gives nobility and great prerogatives. . . ." This announcement also clearly indicates that other aspects than just the conferral of nobility and privileges could be used to encourage buyers.

Such appeals – status, profit, and little work required – were employed elsewhere. An advertisement in the *Petites Affiches* (June 15, 1778) promised the potential purchaser that the office would not be onerous by noting the comfort of the job. Another ad went even further by noting that only two hours of work per week would fulfill that office's functions. Yet another different approach guaranteed a substantial income, promising a return of at least five per cent.[99] By the standards of the day, this represented an excellent investment. Yet other notices elaborated on this theme of financial return: "Office of Conseiller du Roi in the Election of Estampes, with 300 livres of wages and annually yielding in collections more than 75 livres; also one is exempt from [the taxes of] the *taille*, the *Droits de gros*, and the *Entrée des vins*."[100] Other notices highlighted social distinctions as did this squib for the sale of a judgeship in the Duchy of Elbeuf: "These sorts of offices were created to command the guards of the forests who because of distance lack supervision; those who hold these posts in the provinces hold a very honorable rank."[101] In addition, ads might even emphasize the quality of life where an office would be held.[102]

Despite all these different appeals, service to the state or the public never received mention. Such ads inevitably undermined the prestige, if not the desirability, of these posts by conveying an impression of self-seeking that was insulting to the honor that the state required of its representatives. In a way, these notices posed a problem for the governmental elite as a political entity for they seemed to be denigrating or demythologizing a class of public servants.[103] Here then was another form of attack upon a different area of privilege.

No category of advertisements can rival that for real estate which constituted from a quarter to over three-quarters of any individual journal's advertising. Studying these notices, which also related a message difficult for the Old Regime society to accommodate, is no easy matter. The mere volume of material creates problems. In addition, the differences in real estate: for rent or sale, as well as the type – land, apartments, buildings – all lead to difficulties in categorization. Sorting through these complexities reveals yet another concept sent through the affiches.

The ads for real estate communicated a message by their selection of attributes emphasized. By virtue of selling an item in a particular fashion, each ad validated the appeals selected. And what was most striking is the way that sellers relied upon and mixed together two kinds of claims. Jostling for attention in these advertisements were appeals that treated properties with reference to current use and those that focused upon potential. Two examples, one following the other in the Orléans affiches (February 22, 1771), may help clarify this distinction.

House, on rue du Cheval rouge, where hangs the sign *La tête noire*, occupied by the sieur Baudeduit, who pays 300 livres annually, *to sell*. See M. Gaillard, Notaire, rue du Poitier.

House on the rue des Juifs, consisting of two lower and two upper rooms, with a granary above, wine cellar, court, garden with hut and wall, pits and other facilities, *to sell*. There are warranties for the buyers, who will be allowed to seek legal redress. See M. Garnier, Notaire, rue du Bourdon blanc.

Evidently, the first ad focused upon the present situation of the building, by noting only its occupant and his rent. That information alone suggested that this property would attract a buyer mainly through its current disposition. To the contrary, the second concentrated on its size and facilities, creating its appeal quite differently. The owners sought to sell it by explaining its general attributes, regardless of its present or immediate past circumstances. This advertisement attracted by showing how a property could be more than it currently was.

The real estate portion of the affiches contained a wide variety of appeals both to specified and open-ended uses. Ads exemplifying the former technique often named the social class of the occupant or the luxuries presently installed. Alternatively constructed notices might mention price or the ability to increase income. And, a substantial portion of the advertisements mingled the two genres of appeals.

To go beyond this co-existence of differing claims requires a systematic approach to determine the mixture and change over time. Using the three major categories of real estate in the affiches, this investigation focuses first on sales of land, then sales of buildings, and finally the rental of apartments.

The land offered in the affiches included everything from seigneuries to scraps of arable fields, but mostly entire farms involving buildings as well as land. Assessing the nature of the advertising made it necessary to take a sample of ads from each affiches. For each journal three groups of five issues were selected, spaced out as widely as possible over each decade. For those journals considered here for more than one ten-year span, samples were drawn for each decade. Within these 15 issues, each ad was separately examined to determine the kind of claims included. Appeals were placed into appropriate categories. To accomplish this, various subcategories that related to the larger issues – use and potential – were identified. The general category of current use included a series of subcategories: the rights the landholder could invoke, the past income of the property, the luxuries located there, and the current use. All these tended more to explain the value of a property as a continuation of what it had been. Alternative ads concentrated on the price of a property, its condition, the area, its facilities, and the ability to increase income. Price was included in this latter category because the content of the notices made clear that this indicator was used to assess future profitability and thus related to calculations about open-ended investment. This and other such claims seemed more suitable to envision a variety of possibilities. Of course, none of these categories was entirely irrelevant to each type of purchase, but the way categories clustered in individual ads suggested the divisions here.

Each of these subcategories was duly counted, with a minuscule number of appeals that did not conform to any pigeonhole left aside.[104] Once all these ads were analyzed, the raw numbers (how many in each subcategory) were totalled for each periodical and then converted into percentages of the total. For example, if the advertisements of a journal contained 400 separate appeals with 40 concerning rights, then 10 per cent was listed for this category. These figures were averaged with others to create composite scores for the entire four decades surveyed and for each decade. By combining percentages instead of recomputing the raw numbers, each periodical received equal treatment. This seemed more representative than permitting one paper, heavily laden with ads, to overdetermine the outcome.

Table 2-1 indicates that the ads contained a mixture of both sorts of claims, but that the greatest emphasis lay on the open-ended approach. In fact, these notices were 50 per cent more likely to discuss potential than present use. On the other hand, they did not rely on the most optimistic form of claims about the potential as they rarely envisioned the return from the property increasing. Nonetheless, the message delivered here by the affiches emphasized thinking in economic terms which focused on the possibilities, not the present limits.

Table 2-1 Types of claims used for land sales
by percentage[a,b]

Rights	10
Income	17
Luxuries	4
Use	8
Use total	39
Price	6
Condition	5
Space	25
Facilities	25
Income could increase	8
Open-ended total	62

[a]Weighted for equality among papers
[b]Does not add up to 100 because of rounding

Table 2-2 Types of claims used for land sales
by percentage over time[a,b]

	1755–64	1765–74	1775–86
Rights	13	7	9
Income	20	16	13
Luxuries	5	5	4
Use	8	8	7
Use total	46	36	33
Price	9	5	4
Condition	7	5	1
Space	16	29	31
Facilities	23	26	29
Income could increase	2	1	1
Open-ended total	53	65	71

[a]Weighted for equality among papers
[b]Columns may not add up to 100 because of rounding

Furthermore, the tilt toward open ended announcements further intensified over the course of the century. Table 2-2 shows this comparison (with the decade 1745–54 omitted because only the *Petites Affiches* survives in substantial numbers from that period). These data reveal that by the end of the Old Regime, open-ended advertising was more than twice as prevalent as the alternative.

The validation of potential over the present may also be found in the claims employed to advertise buildings for sale. Using the same categories and the same analytical technique, this research also produced equivalent results as reported in Table 2-3.

Table 2-3 Types of claims used for building sales by percentage[a,b]

Rights	1
Income	1
Luxuries	23
Use	9
Use total	34
Price	3
Condition	5
Space	32
Facilities	26
Income could increase	0
Open-ended total	66

[a]Weighted for equality among papers
[b]*Affiches de provinces*, 1755–64 omitted. The sample of this paper included no ads for buildings.

Approximately twice as many claims emphasizing prospects were listed over more close-ended appeals. Few buildings would hold any rights as is evident from the results, but the minority style of advertising could and did focus on the luxuries presently in these buildings. One difference between the notices for buildings and those for land was that the former changed little over time, and the same percentages were maintained.

The notices for rented apartments (Table 2-4) also sent a message through the conflict between claims focused on the present situation and those on the future. However, the subcategories that contribute to each concept were different than for landed property and buildings. The appeals that focused on the present included the luxuries currently installed and the social status of the tenant currently occupying the place. On the other side of the equation were the price, the condition, the space, and the facilities. Although such categories had to be shifted slightly from those used for analyzing the other ads, the procedures – and for the most part the results – remained the same.

Table 2-4 Types of claims used for apartment rentals
by percentage[a,b,c]

Luxuries	24
Tenant status	9
Use total	33
Price	3
Condition	5
Space	32
Facilities	26
Open-ended total	66

[a]Weighted for equality among papers
[b]Column does not add up to 100 because of rounding
[c]*Affiches de provinces*, 1755–64 omitted. The sample of this
paper included no ads for apartment rentals.

The same proportion, two to one, prevailed here as elsewhere, as in the notices the possibilities exceeded the present. Although these percentages fluctuated over the course of the last decades of the Old Regime, the overall situation little altered.

Thus, the ads for different kinds of real estate communicated the same message. In their lists of appeals, advertisers revealed a strong tendency to sell the product by relying on the open-ended characteristics. As such, they validated a kind of economic calculation which, though including both sorts of claims, favored one over the other.

The most interesting aspect of this preference for the possibilities over the status quo was the extent to which this stance was out of harmony with the Old Regime. Contemporary economists had linked the reigning establishment to an economic system favoring security and certainty over exploiting the possibilities. Even though the charge was partially unfair, the Old Regime symbolized caution.[105] When the ads of the affiches touted real estate for its potential, educated readers would see these actions as encouraging an economic approach antithetical to that of the established regime. In short, by implication, the structure of appeals in these papers assailed the Old Regime's economic system.

The three excursions into specific genres of advertisements provided critiques of the controlled economy and privileges, targets beyond the aristocracy. In fact, these particular observations raise the possibility that the more general framework of commentaries and advertisements presented an alternative to more than the top of the elite. The most compelling argument, noted by the affiches themselves, is that depicting a country where everything is for sale undermined the entire mechanism running the social structure, not just its apex. Still a price for everything is not necessarily incompatible with privileges (at least those regarded as mainly economic) in a controlled economy – important characteristics of the Old Regime. As a critique then, the affiches provided a message whose extent remains unclear.

What could have made these disparate critiques more thoroughly challenging is the way that they validated what Jürgen Habermas labeled the public sphere. Habermas envisioned a growing part of society, fundamentally commercial in nature, that strongly emphasized home, family, and self-control. It would seem that the contents of the affiches mainly supported one or another part of this vision. They could provide, in Habermas's schema, the backbone for an alternate civil society, based on a series of values, often crudely labeled *bourgeois*. Advocating such a public sphere, these periodicals were in effect contradicting its social alternative: the world of aristocracy, privilege, and a managed economy. Of course, members of the Old Regime elite were about as likely as others to believe in the ideals of this public sphere. However, whatever the views of these individuals, this set of ideas attacked Old Regime society and economy as it supported the intellectual underpinnings of an alternate. Here then, as elsewhere, these criticisms produced an effect, not because they were accurate characterizations, but because contemporaries believed them.[106] Finally, one may speculate that the various social critiques spilled into a political challenge to the monarchy. Habermas has certainly seen it that way. He argues that private values (like those in the affiches) constituted the staging area for an assault on power.[107]

But without a Habermasian frame which fitted messages in a way to elevate their significance, support for a bourgeois lifestyle becomes limited. Encouraging this are the complications in the articles' critique of the aristocracy and the important minority viewpoint in real estate ads. When the affiches directly addressed class, some ambivalences emerged. This less speculative and perhaps more convincing approach still provides a politically problematic discourse. Problematic because even though the monarchy was by the eighteenth century disassociating itself from this "torpid" society, it still embraced elements of tradition. Absolutist monarchs had been unable to break completely free from the grip of tradition.[108] So while the affiches launched no direct attacks on the king, this reduced representation of what was desirable eroded a foundation that even the king connected to royal domination. And some critics believed the monarch was totally dependent on this social system;[109] he could not avoid being injured by ricochets.

3

THE LITERARY–PHILOSOPHICAL PRESS

While both the gazettes and the affiches had a fairly narrow focus, the rest of the press took up a wide variety of subjects from science to poetry. Yet it is worth considering these periodicals together because, whatever the specific interest of a magazine, it was involved in examining part of the great seamless web of knowledge for the general elite. During the eighteenth century, the educated understood such categories as history, science, philosophy, geography, but ranged widely among them. One area possessed implications for another. Because of contemporaries' broad interests, magazines that ranged widely over various fields may all be grouped together. Another rather different factor that encourages considering these journals together was the manner in which they, unlike the local affiches, appealed to, and were perceived as belonging to a national market. Moreover, they conversed with one another and assumed that readers could follow the various ends of these dialogues without explanation.[1] For the sake of convenience, we may call these literary–philosophical journals, or, because they had a much greater tendency than either gazettes or affiches to publish long pieces, discussion journals.

While sharing general subject matter, the approaches of these papers varied. Some used book reviews, others extracts or philosophical ramblings by a journalist or contributor, or a combination of these and other techniques. And some of the periodicals tended to polemical bombast, others a calm and reticent style.

Given the large size of the discussion press, it would not be particularly surprising to find that virtually every contemporary idea found some resonance in these magazines. Of course, some concepts appeared more frequently and occupied greater space than others. Pornography never reared its head. But the great historian of the press, Eugène Hatin, claimed that there was scarcely a writer whose ideas had not received some attention,[2] and an overview of the press reveals, above all else, a cacophony of voices.

To try to narrow this subject and ask a question that links this chapter to others, it seems reasonable to inquire how comfortable was the berth provided to concepts that challenged traditional notions of Church and state, the pillars of the Old Regime. A final concluding note to this chapter considers how much the notions in the journals challenged, not only such abstract underpinnings, but the Church and state as they presented themselves in the second half of the eighteenth century.

As a first attempt to sample ideas that were at least problematical in theory, one might examine how the most radical views emerged. One extreme of the ideas this press could carry can be consulted in Nina Rattner Gelbart's important study of the later renditions of the *Journal des dames*.[3] Begun in 1759 strictly as an entertainment magazine, the *Journal des dames* sometimes embraced notions that accepted but far exceeded the High Enlightenment. When conservative Maupeou-led ministers entered government in 1769, they suppressed the paper. But when those ministers fell, the *Journal des dames* once again became a viable property.

Purchased by Madame de Montanclos, the *Journal des dames* returned to exploring new, treacherous turf. When this noblewoman sold the magazine to Louis-Sébastien Mercier on April 19, 1775, he took it even further into troubled territory. During the year and one-half that he ran the *Journal des dames* before new, conservative authorities arrived in power and quashed the enterprise, he plunged into controversies.[4] Attacking the injustices of the Old Regime, Mercier berated the privileged theaters, the academies, the government periodicals, and even the royal ministers.

Gelbart's study reveals how Mercier combined his basic interest in plays with broader concerns.[5] In a favorable review of *Observations sur l'art du comédien et sur d'autres objets concernant cette profession* by d'Hennetaire, the former director of the Brussels royal theater, Mercier praised its revelations: "the true vanity of actors is laid bare . . . by one who knows . . . from inside . . . the abuses to which the public falls victim." Mercier further castigated actors in no uncertain terms as philistines. But in this issue of June 1775, Mercier also cited a speech by the naturalist Buffon who, despite his normal alliances, attacked the privileged theater.

In the journal Mercier endeavored to influence the new king Louis XVI to create a government designed to protect law and embrace work and austerity. This journalist believed the parlements, not the central royal administration, seemed to provide the best political hope. In other articles, Mercier supported the freedom of the press and the abolition of slavery.

The configuration of ideas found in the *Journal des dames* labeled by Gelbart as *frondeur*, conformed to a loose definition: support for those most radical thinkers of the eighteenth century who accepted the High Enlightenment but went beyond it. The Enlightenment might in theory oppose privileges but accept the role of the academies;[6] Mercier would have none of this. In his appreciation of the parlements, he was also embracing the extraordinary decentralization proposed by those bodies from the mid-century onward. Such a collection of notions, emphasizing equality, were nonetheless shared by other periodicals, all of whom endured little better than the *Journal des dames*. Evidently these beliefs made a short-lived arrival in the press.

Also included, but barely, was materialism, the notion that, denying free will and spirituality, contemporaries undoubtedly regarded as the most extreme ideology of the time. The periodicals in fact largely ignored this phenomenon and its leaders D'Holbach and Helvétius, with the few mentions almost exclusively negative. The *Journal encyclopédique* favorably examined this intellectual strain,[7] but far more typical of the notice it received were shrill denunciations in the *Journal de Trévoux*. As will become apparent, this paper could exhibit considerable ambivalence toward the High Enlightenment philosophes, but support given to their various positions scrupulously avoided mentioning any contributions by materialists. Yet attacks on the former could spill over. As will be explored more fully below, the *Journal de Trévoux* deprecated the lack of religious faith exhibited by proponents of the High Enlightenment. This, of course, could be applied to the materialists as well.[8]

But beyond these relatively mild critiques, the *Journal de Trévoux* specifically criticized the materialists in extremely severe terms. One can measure this periodical's view by examining the three-part essay published in late 1758 on Helvétius' *De l'Esprit*. The debate continued into the next year, but the core of the editor Guillaume François Berthier's response to this work was concentrated in some 70 pages scattered through the September, October, and November issues. This critique ranged rather incoherently, with frequent shifts in tone and approach. The journalist often attacked his target, withdrew to find a new angle, and then charged again. To some extent Berthier's review resembled a running commentary on *De l'Esprit*.

Berthier argued that Helvétius's book was worse than any other advanced texts. The journal noted that Helvétius went far beyond "any *Incrédule* [Berthier's synonym for the philosophes] who has written lately."[9] In this way, Berthier excused related intellectuals from contributing to such views while at the same time damning Helvétius. The journalist reiterated this point by discussing the sources Helvétius had drawn upon:

> In a word, there are primordial notions of justice and injustice: notions that the Creator has imprinted upon our soul, to illuminate natural law. These are the foundations of all morality: only individuals such as Hobbes, Spinoza, Mandeville, Collins, &c. have dared to assert otherwise.

Despite the open-ended possibilities of the "et cetera," this list of the guilty clearly pulls the High Enlightenment out of consideration. The review elsewhere criticizes Montesquieu in another context, but such indictment of the philosophes remained the exception.[10] And in concluding his overall critique, Berthier reiterated that in attacking the materialists, he differentiated them from the standard bearers of the High Enlightenment. While stating that he knew he had not pleased the author of *De l'Esprit*, the journalist also asserted that his commentary would not anger "the true Philosophes."[11] The general context indicated the *Journal de Trévoux* meant with the invocation of philosophes to point toward the figures of the High Enlightenment.

Not only did the *Journal de Trévoux* seek to portray the materialists as different from and worse than the High Enlightenment, it launched a withering attack. Atypically for that periodical, the journalist made his point by personal assaults. A substantial portion of the critique highlighted in a particularly insulting way the mistakes the author had made. The review used the argument of the materialists that nothing would better prove this philosophy than the thinking of its partisans. With this challenge laid down, every error went to prove mental feebleness of these scorned intellectuals. To drive home the point, the review was packed with specific citations of mistaken sources, misunderstood quotes, and other problems. And the review also launched direct attacks on *De l'Esprit's* reasoning: "Here is raised a well-founded doubt: one wants to know if the author of *l'Espirit* [sic] has a clear idea, clear and precise of the passions. . . ."[12] Elsewhere, Berthier argues that students with six months of philosophy could refute Helvétius's essential claims. In addition, one article noted obscurities, poor definitions, and frivolous principles.[13] Such *ad hominem* remarks no doubt stung.

The review also countered the claims of the materialists, on philosophical grounds, going over them point by point. Sometimes Berthier partly refuted these views by arguing logically against them. But his main approach, other than personal aspersions, was forecasting their evil results. First and foremost, the journalist warned of the regrettable effects of the attack on religion, but he went even farther. Quoting the author that "men are not evil, but dominated by their interest," Berthier surmised that this meant that no real liberty of choice between vice and virtue existed. What would the results be: "the encouragement of crime and libertinage, in fact an increase in the most abominable practices. In these circumstances no laws could stand against a Catalina."[14] In the next month's issue, the journalist responded to Helvétius's argument that the rights of men consisted only in compacts among individuals. Under such circumstances, there would be "no mutual and natural guarantee of the possession of the territory occupied by diverse nations: from which it follows that the strongest people will be able to strip the weakest, and the most adroit will be able to take advantage of the least able."[15] That charity would likewise disappear, was one of the variety of dire predictions that filled the remainder of the review.

Certainly, some of the assaults on the materialists mirrored those on the High Enlightenment. But, by labeling the materialists as different and more problematic than the encyclopedists, and by resorting once again to personal animadversions, the *Journal de Trévoux* made clear that it considered materialism as being beyond the pale.

The *Journal des dames* and the *Journal de Trévoux* indicate how little the discussion press dealt with the boldest ideas. But what was included? As a start in the proper direction the single most important topic might be a systematic investigation, beyond the asides regarding the *Journal de Trévoux*, of how the periodicals treated the High Enlightenment. The question possesses validity because this intellectual movement provided more material for the discussion press than any other intellectual strain. This question is not new; indeed it has been framed previously. Scholars want to know about this treatment in order to reconstruct the daily cultural and intellectual context of Old Regime France. Relevant historiographically, this approach is not an anachronistic way of comprehending the literary–philosophical press. The struggle over such ideas raged within certain social groups who would have evaluated these periodicals in much the same way.[16]

Focusing on the press's appreciation of the High Enlightenment requires some definition of these ideas. This is no place for a history of such beliefs, but it is difficult simply to borrow one of the extant schemes. Some discussion of the press's reception of radical notions has already occurred, but greater specificity still is needed. The Enlightenment provided the main body of the problematic ideas in the eighteenth century. General agreement ascribes certain minimal characteristics like secularism and individualism. But scholars have defined many subparts, most significantly, the High Enlightenment.[17] Its adherents – henceforth in this work the term "philosophes" will be exclusively reserved for them – believed in the worth of the individual and improving the individual's life. A person's talent, not his or her legal privileges of rank, ought to determine the future. In addition, the philosophes were epistemologically committed to empiricism. Suffusing all was a general belief in deism and, by extension, natural law. They remained blind to the way that empiricism could conflict with these latter ideas. In fact, they believed that deism, with its benevolent God, guaranteed that human investigations would confirm a belief in natural law. A beneficent deity promised the veracity of the mind and the positive didacticism of nature. All these concepts were looped together amicably. The *Encyclopédie* was the greatest single collective work of the philosophes. Embodying the above principles, it added, through its overwhelming size, a quest for knowledge to the philosophes' agenda. Viewing the Enlightenment in this way is, for some, unorthodox, as customarily historians treat this movement as a unitary whole. But closer scrutiny has revealed many strains. Adopting the concept of the High Enlightenment makes it possible to chart a more coherent set of ideas that lay at the heart of the entire philosophic enterprise of the eighteenth century.

With the import and definition of the intellectual movement in place, one might yet inquire about the method of the following analysis. To be certain, these ideas never existed in isolation and were jousting not only with contrary but related notions that could lay claim to the term "philosophic." Consequently, when one asks how this movement fared in the press, one is only inquiring into how someone conscious of these particular categories would have assessed the journal's reception of the High Enlightenment.

It should be added that even though these concepts attacked either the royal government, Old Regime society, or both, the social and political establishment did not necessarily reject these challenging ideas. Indeed, as Simon Schama has clearly shown, the most hospitable place for these notions was among the elites.[18] Even detractors accepted parts of these programs.[19] One of the real problems of those nay-sayers was that they lost the ability to label the ideas they accepted and had to agree that they were borrowing rather than claiming as their own what they approved. Or put another way, these elites, though they had changed or believed they had, never were able, or thought it necessary, to show that the Enlightenment critique had lost its force. Such were the paradoxes of the Old Regime that must have played into its demise.

With this background, one can again pose the question: How did the High Enlightenment fare in the discussion press? Inevitably, given the number of journals, weighing the relative importance and staying power of each periodical requires great judgment. Again focusing on opposite ends of a spectrum to illuminate the whole, this chapter selects examples along a spectrum defined by its receptivity to the High Enlightenment. As Nina Gelbart has eloquently argued, a *frondeur* press, carrier of anti-elitist ideals, emerged in the 1770s. With its roots in the *Journal des dames*, this collection of papers so threatened authorities that they had to extinguish it. According to Gelbart, contemporaries clearly comprehended these periodicals' agenda of promoting a set of radical notions.[20] Curiously, while the *frondeurs* – often called the radical Enlightenment – at least shone for a brief moment in the press, the more staid, more acceptable High Enlightenment barely earned open recognition and advocacy through journals clearly founded to defend it. It was only in 1755 with the *Journal encyclopédique* that a journal actually was established in the name of the philosophes.[21] Perhaps, their extraordinary antipathy to the criticism levied by the press discouraged them.[22] No other journal ever committed itself so visibly to the Encyclopedists' cause. Also attached, though more quietly, to the philosophes' cause was the *Journal étranger* and the *Gazette universelle de littérature, aux Deux-Ponts*.[23] The *Journal économique* and a few others committed to physiocracy obliquely contributed. Although the philosophes generally rejected physiocracy, the physiocrats commonly supported the High Enlightenment, so some indirect support did emerge.[24] Another source of encouragement to the philosophes' cause came from periodicals called spectators, imitators of the famous English paper of the same name. While these journals did not espouse the views of the High Enlightenment, their emphasis on the human decency and common sense morality of the common man shared much with the High Enlightenment's emphasis on the individual's goodness.[25] But by the second half of the eighteenth century, the spectators were dying, losing their force as a genre and lessening its usefulness as an ally for the Enlightenment.[26]

Evidently then, such periodicals granted a safe, but not very wide, berth for the High Enlightenment. Of course, any of these periodicals could loom large to certain individuals. But if one asks, as this chapter does, how did this nexus of ideas *generally* fare, none of these journals achieved great visibility. Without a substantial, aggressive group of magazines, a relatively less committed approach ends up representing the leftward end of the spectrum.

And there existed a solid block of journals that my serious but, given the sample size, inevitably cursory review found largely hospitable to the High Enlightenment. Among the most positive, and therefore useful to sample, were the *Mercure de France* under the editorship of the philosophe Jean-François Marmontel (August 1758 through January 1760) and the *Journal des dames*, from 1763 to 1766, a moment of confrontation yet one milder than the later period. Another important reason for selecting these two are the availability of excellent studies on them by Jacques Wagner and Gelbart.[27] Other considerations played a part. Showing how the government-sponsored *Mercure* and the perennially financially exhausted *Journal des dames* could share the same approach provides illuminating variety.[28] Selecting the very different *Journal des dames* and *Mercure* gives further evidence of the wide reliance on a restrained approach to the Enlightenment. The editors of both papers were committed adherents to the High Enlightenment; yet their publications showed only muted support.

To provide a textured example of how the Enlightenment penetrated the *Mercure*'s reporting, it seems desirable simply to describe carefully a single issue (August 1759). With that question in mind an appreciation of how this paper understood the High Enlightenment may proceed. But to comprehend this reception, the general style of the publication must be considered. A tone of reticence marked the 29 entries and more than 200 pages of the monthly edition of the *Mercure*. The staff had only composed five pieces; the rest were extracts, letters, or short tracts. None of these items displayed a polemical tone. The *Mercure*, in a long obituary of the economist Jacques-Claude-Marie Vincent de Gornai, chose to praise the deceased for a moderation that it shared:

> His simple eloquence, animated by an interesting warmth, shows that the discourses of this virtuous man sustained the cause of the public weal, yet never lessened the solidity of the discussion. . . . As incapable of taking a dominant tone as of speaking against his belief, his manner of presenting his viewpoint was not imperious except by the force of his proofs.

The obituary concluded with praise for de Gornai's patience, candor, politeness: the very qualities that the journal's own style embodied.

In fact the strongest assertion the *Mercure* contained came not from the journalists but from a letter in a debate over vaccinations against smallpox. The exchange is worth following. The author of the letter, M. Gaullard, first restated a question put to him by another physician, M. de la Condamine. "What," queried the latter "is the goal of M. Gaullard. . . . Is it to deprive those ill with smallpox of all help? Is this where this new doctrine tends?" To which, Gaullard responded: "I admit that I had not foreseen that objection; the reason I argued as I did is that the sentiments of humanity are stronger than the fear of contagion." Although Gaullard's initial question seemed somewhat aggressive, the fact that it was purely rhetorical lessened the air of confrontation. De la Condamine had not directly attacked Gaullard in this interchange. In addition, the latter turned the other cheek in his response, dissipating any controversy on the spot. And this interaction was the most highly charged in this issue.

As will become relevant in the overall assessment of the *Mercure* and the Enlightenment, much of the content of the paper in August 1758 was for all practical purposes unrelated to any new ideas at all. Sixty-five per cent of the pieces (but only 31 per cent of the pages) fell into this category. It seems worth focusing on a few representative articles to give a full flavor of these works. Included were a number of poems addressing general problems of the human condition: love, death, friendship, self-doubt, loneliness, success, and more. Three snippets provide examples of these efforts:

On the Death of a Friend
Of virtues, of glory, he taught me the way
The Arts gave him their light
For him even the greatest obscurities posed no problem
Assemble his writings, still dear and lasting
With a delicate, sure touch, memorable monuments;
Keep a record of what survives him:

From the cares of his friendship this care is a payment.
Keep his memory from the night of the grave.

To a Young Woman Whose Brother Had Obtained a Regiment
Beautiful Iris, your brother is surely worthy
Of obtaining from his king the most desirable posts;
And if ever one ought to be granted a favor
You will for him have his Regiment.

To a Maréchal of France, on Embracing a Pretty Child Who
Resembled Him
Before all loves I tremble
As much as the Enemy must tremble before you
But by an impulse both sudden and sweet
I embrace this one because he resembles you.

These verses address their subjects with a sentimentality and banality different from the more practical and serious High Enlightenment, not to mention any other more strident ideology.

Poems did not completely dominate this category of materials seemingly utterly indifferent to the new ideas. Included also was a ten-page essay on dignity whose rather common sense remarks seemed at best oblique to the various fresh notions invading the century. And the *Mercure* also published a critical review of a play that panned the major protagonist as disagreeable and the acting and script as weak. None of this appeared relevant to the High Enlightenment; similarly bland was the synopsis of a very complicated play about Greek gods. Finally, of the same ilk were notices of four puzzles and two books: one on how to price and sell wood, the other on exceptional cases tried by the Châtelet that had led to revisions in case law.

In addition to all these items, the *Mercure* also published a great deal that, though not so labeled by the editors, might be linked directly to different parts of the High Enlightenment. Twenty-seven per cent of the pieces, but 47 per cent of the copy, comprise this category. Included were articles that clearly could have been composed earlier without reference to the Enlightenment, but which contemporaries would have linked to it. Consider a review of a play in which true love conquered mercenary motives in the courtship of a beautiful young woman. Although this theme had been discussed since time immemorial, in the context of the eighteenth century it contributed to the Enlightenment's emphasis on the passions and individual liberty. Connected to this article was a long discussion (13 pages) of man and morality. This piece intended to refute directly a low opinion of man. Instead the essay argued: "Two principles lead men, passions and reason. From there, its definition: *reasonable animal.*" With these two elements so central to the thought of the philosophes, it is difficult to imagine that readers would not have linked this argument to the High Enlightenment. It could have been written earlier, but to the eighteenth century it was associated with the philosophes.

But examine also the debate on smallpox vaccinations. Because that exchange bore on practical, applied science rather than theoretical, it in structure shared the philosophes' own approach to this subject. The philosophes were heavily responsible for the particular application of empiricism. Consequently, this category of the press included pieces, with ideas born before the Enlightenment, and others whose existence depended in part or in whole on the philosophes' intervention. What they all shared was that, though not identified as such, contemporary readers would have instantly connected them to the High Enlightenment.

Finally, the *Mercure* published two articles (8 per cent of the articles, 18 per cent of the lines) which openly praised the High Enlightenment, and they are worth careful consideration. The first summarized Jean le Rond D'Alembert's "Essai sur les eléments de philosophie ou sur les principes des connaissances humaines." Marmontel's discussion of this work repeatedly praised the great names and slogans of the High Enlightenment. Witness the beginning of the analysis:

> This essay in which may be found the seeds of the article, *Eléments*, in the *Encyclopédie* is a more considerable treatment than found in the new edition of *Mélanges*. The importance of the subject and the noble, wise, and forthright manner of treatment, merits one's focus upon it; the tone of the philosophes and the spirited character of M. D'Alembert does not show itself more evidently than in this piece.

Mentioning the philosophes and their classic *Encyclopédie* in such positive terms in itself openly supported the High Enlightenment. And the article also advanced a key proposition of the Enlightenment by positing that knowledge was empirical, rather than the result of grasping the great chain of being. Finally Marmontel's discussion also included yet another significant claim: ". . . Bacon and Descartes appear [in D'Alembert's essay] as restorers of experimental physics. M. D'Alemenbert [sic] who knows so well the obligations of the philosophes to these men, reproaches them also for having been more doctors of speculation than of practice." Yes, continued the journalist, the "lazy pleasure of meditation and conjecture" created genius but without action it led to nothing. The *Mercure* stressed that the High Enlightenment was committed to knowledge's application.

In a second article directly endorsing the High Enlightenment, the *Mercure* reviewed a travel account of China. Its conclusion clearly supported the philosophes, and was, according to Wagner, the most definitely positive of Marmontel's editorship.[29] The journalist appealed:

Permit me to close this extract by reflecting on the spirit of the philosophes that some say brings honor to our century while others ill-humoredly dispute this. The true physical and astronomical system of the heavens is certainly known; the shape of the Earth is determined, never has anyone penetrated so deep under its surfaces; the theory of useful arts engages the best minds in Europe; the history of men, places, and times develops from day to day; the bank of information that barbarity had broken is reconstituted from all places; peace, abundance, the population are recognized and proclaimed as the only objects of politics, moderation, justice, humanity . . . pernicious prejudice, old errors and false system accept and submit to the ascendance of reasoning and frivolities finally concern only the frivolous. Such is the point of view from which I envision the present century, and I do not believe that there has been another in the annals of the world worthy of the name of the Philosophic Century.

This expression of confidence, both in its beginning and its closing, directly linked these achievements to the philosophes and showed a strong and inclusive allegiance to these intellectuals and their movement.

Connected with the *Mercure*'s endorsement of the High Enlightenment was its silence about revealed religion. This issue, however, in an article on China did contain one barb. Spoke the *Mercure*:

The Court of Rome . . . surely has argued less against the age of the world than against the spinning of the Earth; and I would dare to predict that in the end however it will be constrained to allow us to turn.

Except for this, the Church and revealed religion figured only in the announcement of a book appearing in French and Italian on sacred and profane history. By and large, these sparse notices among two hundred pages indicate the *Mercure*'s indifference, whether feigned or not, to the subject. Yet the *Mercure* by virtually ignoring the Church, was actually limiting support of the Enlightenment. To be sure, omitting the Church promoted a secular view of the world. But, more important, the failure to evaluate works on the Church from a critical perspective defanged the High Enlightenment. More than any other subject, the Church provided the alternate to the philosophes' notions, so not publishing an enlightened critique of religion missed an opportunity to underscore the secular view so essential to the High Enlightenment. Much the same argument might be made about the complete absence of specifically political works. Of course, the government would never have allowed Marmontel to turn the *Mercure* towards politics and religion, but whatever the source of this lacuna the shape of the coverage was seriously affected from what it might have been.

Jacques Wagner's work on the eighteenth-century *Mercure*, with special reference to Marmontel's editorship, extends the above case study. While Wagner's interests and focus differed from mine, he also found similar characteristics, including placing this issue of August, 1759 among the most favorable to the High Enlightenment. One quantitative piece of evidence is particularly illuminating. Wagner shows just how little attention the *Mercure* usually paid religion. Only 2.19 per cent of the titles (2.17 per cent of the total lines) dealt with theology. The editor never treated ecclesiastical history, although contributors wrote a few pieces. Altogether, the *Mercure* largely abandoned direct comments about the Church and theology, and it did not print criticisms from other angles.[30]

Thus, the *Mercure* illustrates the tentative approach to the Enlightenment. First, the cautious language posed a problem. Calm in this way, the editorial endorsements of the philosophes as well as the writings based on Enlightenment themes lacked punch and were indeed somewhat obscured by so much unconnected froth and technical material. Reinforcing this was the relatively small effort at opinion making which represented the philosophes but did not urge them on. By not covering the philosophes as individuals and by leaving implicit their battles, the *Mercure* denuded their cause of an important part of its meaning: its role as a movement. Furthermore, without the context of the struggle, the ideas appeared less significant. All these stylistic devices and selection of material made it very difficult to appreciate the High Enlightenment. Finally, even after this lukewarm endorsement, the journals did not make available the most powerful notions on religion and politics. Although reticence was a common approach among periodicals, the combative world of eighteenth century intellectual life did not really encourage compensating for this quiet.

One could argue that readers could have compensated for much of this. Furthermore, because readers knew the government censored references to Church and state, arguably they might have been likely to add back the critical edge otherwise lost. However, with so much other febrility, both in style and open engagement that experience taught had no relation to the authorities, the audience would have had a difficult time envisioning tendentiousness regarding religion and politics for the *Mercure*. Even the philosophes, who knew first hand about government censorship, apparently believed that Marmontel was expressing far less than the government would permit. Consequently, with so many factors suggesting this journal willingly held back, reporting in the *Mercure* seemed difficult to push beyond a cautious embrace of moderate Enlightenment ideas with implications, but not forcefulness, for stronger ideas. This was positive, but its limits are readily apparent.

The *Journal des dames* illustrates further how cautiously treated were the philosophes. The journal went through a number of incarnations, sometimes an adventurous magazine and on other occasions less so. In March 1763 its publisher was Catherine Michelle de Maisonneuve, a wealthy widow, who turned for assistance to male collaborators, in particular Mathon de la Cour. These men supported the High Enlightenment. Eventually in 1766 she withdrew, remaining nominally in charge but actually leaving the paper in bolder hands. But during her period of dominance (1763–66), the *Journal des dames* fit easily into the model of hesitant advocacy of the Enlightenment.[31]

The same reticent style that had marked the *Mercure* mainly dominated the *Journal des dames*. Indeed, it practiced an oily obsequiousness toward authorities. In praising the Queen, the head censor, and others in power, the *Journal des dames* paraded its tameness. Still, though cowed, the editors were not completely without spark toward authors, if not officials, and occasionally derisive language crept into their pages. An article published in January 1765 containing extracts of a book entitled *Le Porte-Feuille d'un homme de goût*, concluded with a witticism: "I can assure the author that if a compilation can disgust the public, then it is certainly his. . . ." Nonetheless, such remarks remained rare indeed.

The *Journal des dames* had originally been designed to furnish a steady diet of pabulum, or as the original editor put it, *"riens délicieux."*[32] In the founder's mind such material was all that women wanted. Even though the history of the *Journal des dames* showed nothing could be further from the truth, the *riens délicieux* continued there, as in many other periodicals. Scanning the *Journal* produces an entire range of these pieces. Opening the issue of May 1765 was a poem, "Sunrise," whose theme was that no matter how impressive the sunrise seemed, to God it remained but a cinder. The September issue reviewed a symphony celebrating love. Earlier in January, the *Journal des dames* published a little piece, "The Tears of Ismael," about a woman who planned to leave a man who loved her. In parting, she burst into tears, enrapturing him, and he exclaimed, "Such immortal ties enchain my soul to yours." Under the rubric, *Pièces fugitives*, this periodical served up substantial helpings of similar sentimental fluff.

In equal measure, the *Journal des dames* dealt with moral and social questions in which the point underlined the views of the High Enlightenment but where the periodical avoided overt mention of the connection. Many of the pieces took up the ancient theme of the triumph of true love over arranged or mercenary marriages, which, though banal, certainly harmonized with the tunes of the philosophes. Exemplifying this tendency to publish materials supporting the Enlightenment, even depending on it, without mentioning the movement was the story of "Sidney and Silly, or Munificence and Recognition."[33] This long account, some 45 pages of a novel by Baculard d'Arnaud, provides the text of the travels of Sidney and Silly. Sent to India, Sidney discovers Silly, a displaced Frenchman fighting on the Indian side, who recounts his story. Raised in Paris, he was bookish, sensitive, and honest. When his father lost all his money, he quickly found himself an outcast. The courtiers, who thought he was amusing, trifled with him, while the men of letters, consumed with vanity, envy, and ambition, acted no more graciously. Indeed, Silly criticized all levels of wealth and all social groups. When he contemplated approaching the rich, "his rage spilled over at this idea. They are prostituted by their vices, to all crimes. Only their insolence equals their inhumanity." The "bourgeoisie" were no better. They were "occupied only with their fortune, because they attach all consideration, all pleasure, their entire being to this, they calculate the extent of their happiness and reputation according to these revenues." Even the *peuple* cared only for money. Silly finally was forced to leave France without his beloved because love could not triumph over wealth. Hearing this, Sidney took up Silly's problems, aided him financially, and arranged his return to Paris to marry his love. Silly then turned to commerce: "Although a French gentleman, he had the courage not to blush to have made this choice which is far better than being . . . in the antechambers of grandeur and fortune." According to the narrator, he had matured from being a misanthrope to becoming a man. This story, filled with themes from the High Enlightenment, especially that of hard work triumphing over sloth, went beyond mere compatibility with the philosophes. The condemnation of Parisian society clearly echoed the critiques in Montesquieu's *Persian Letters* and Voltaire's *Candide*. Yet though it rehearsed questions raised by the Enlightenment, "Sidney and Silly" remained silent about this connection.

While the *Journal des dames* scarcely mentioned the Church or the state, it directly associated itself with the High Enlightenment, though less frequently than its indirect bows in that direction. The paper contained positive references to the philosophes, especially Voltaire, while Marmontel contributed frequently. In 1764 and 1765 the magazine praised the favors bestowed by Catherine the Great on the lions of the High Enlightenment. And in a subject which exceptionally implicated both Church and state, the periodical participated in the campaign surrounding the Calas affair. The *Journal des dames* published Voltaire's plea and then when the King exonerated Calas, the periodical feted his generosity.[34] Nonetheless, these open pledges of fealty paled compared to the philosophic pieces that the periodical never labeled as such.

Thus, characteristic of the issues of the *Journal des dames* from 1763–66, like those of the *Mercure*, were a calm tone and three main approaches – (1) indifference to the High Enlightenment, in this case more traditional and sentimental than technical (2) the presentation of implicitly philosophical writings, and (3) open advocacy of the High Enlightenment. And as in the *Mercure*, the last category trailed the other two. Furthermore, the almost complete omission of Church and state permitted but also toned down whatever support other articles lent to the High Enlightenment. But the ladies magazine, unlike the governmental paper, also carried a few items that fit none of the larger categories. Other new ideas that went beyond the High Enlightenment received some attention. Criticism of the philosophes' hyper-rationalism appeared in a series of articles advocating an educational system based on patriotism, exercise, music, and other skills that the philosophes would have embraced but only after placing rationality at their head. [35] These other ideas remained relatively marginal, however, so that the overall impression the *Journal des dames* gave of the High Enlightenment was cautious acceptance, in largely the same pattern as had the *Mercure*. But these additional topics in the *Journal des dames* do remind us that, even though many journals backed the High Enlightenment, they rarely conformed to any specific general pattern. Taking into account additional case studies would develop these variations, including those papers with a stronger polemical style.

At the other extreme from papers like Marmontel's and Maisonneuve's stood two groups of periodicals that took a far more negative view of the philosophes. One was a small contingent focused on the defense of religion. The leaders of this pack were the Jesuit *Journal de Trévoux* and the powerful and mercurial, as well as clandestine and illegal, *Nouvelles ecclésiastiques*. Founded to defend the Jansenists, this latter periodical evolved along with their political positions. Although the significance of the *Nouvelles ecclésiastique* likely looms large in present historiography because of its emphasis on a significant role for Jansenist jurists, only a few ephemeral journals seem to have shared its cause. Typical of these were the *Journal chrétien* published in 1754 and the *Journal ecclésiastique*.[36]

Related but still different from the religious magazines was a group mainly defined by a rabid hostility to the philosophes. This hatred formed the core of these journals' existence. While the religious journals shared the antagonism, other agenda mattered as much to them. Included in the relatively secular, anti-philosophic group were three papers edited by the abbé Desfontaines, three by Elie-Catherine Fréron, and two by Simon-Nicolas Linguet.[37] Interestingly and coincidentally, the papers shared not only perspective but also tone. In a periodical world often characterized by reticence and oblique references, these journalists presented their views straightforwardly, similar to less inhibited media of the era.

Even though these religious and anti-philosophic magazines remained few, the significant role that several of them assumed in eighteenth-century literary controversies meant that they composed a considerable node at the negative end of the spectrum showing the reception of the "new ideas." In-depth case studies of the *Journal de Trévoux* and the *Année littéraire* allow examination of one of the most important periodicals from both the religious and secular clusters.

It is important to underscore how these periodicals differed from the *Mercure de France* and the *Journal des dames* in terms of expressiveness. Because all the more anti-philosophic magazines were outspoken, contemporaries would have understood their views mainly in their open remarks, rather than finding them filtered through patterns of reporting. Even when indirect commentary played a role in the *Journal de Trévoux* and the *Année littéraire*, the direct views expressed within each proved the most important.

One of the most important journalists of the eighteenth century was Elie-Catherine Fréron. Born in Quimper (Brittany) in 1718 to a master goldsmith, he migrated to Paris in 1734 to continue his studies at the famous Jesuit school, Louis-le-Grand. Although becoming a novice, he quit the Jesuits in 1739. Jean Balcou, in his magisterial biography of Fréron, accepts speculations that Fréron left orders after being discovered at a theatrical event. The Jesuits' loss was, however, journalism's gain for he soon found work with the abbé Desfontaines. There he learned much about the periodical business and also pursued his own literary career. About the time that his mentor died in 1745, Fréron launched his first periodical, *Lettres de Mme la Comtesse de XXX*, whose point of view and style mimicked those of Desfontaines. Aggressive language and vigorous anti-philosophic opinions earned Fréron enmity and the closure of this paper after only one month. But he refused to leave literary life and, aided by the protection of the Polish king, who was Louis XV's father-in-law, in April 1749 he launched another publication, *Lettres sur quelques écrits de ce temps*. The authorities, again for largely the same reasons, interrupted this publication. The shifting tides of influence again relented, allowing the journalist in 1754 to found the *Année littéraire*. Although this paper encountered serious interruptions, it published monthly (300–400 pages per issue). Possibly Fréron released his monthly issue in sections, a batch every ten days. The periodical lasted through Fréron's death in 1776, with a series of successor journals enduring until 1790. During that period, this massive undertaking reviewed about 12,000 books.[38] Under Fréron's stewardship, this paper seems to have earned more attention than any, except Linguet's *Annales politiques*, and it continues to interest today.

Although this discussion would seem to indicate the rejection of new ideas in *Année littéraire*, Fréron actually had a very complex relationship, at least with the High Enlightenment. Balcou has treated him as an anti-Voltairean Voltairean.[39] Fréron was obsessed with the philosophes, and he attacked them enough to give offense though he hardly repulsed all of their ideas. As this account unfolds, it will be apparent that these contradictory attitudes were able to coexist partly because Fréron's anger essentially fixed on the philosophes as individuals. Of course, the attacks on them implicated their beliefs by depriving their views of their moral context. But as the ideas also possessed an existence apart from their authors, or from even the movement as a whole, the way that Fréron focused challenges on the philosophes, while tarnishing the Enlightenment, left some opportunity for supporting this system of beliefs.

Yet the *Année littéraire* certainly did attack the philosophes on purely ideological concerns. As a nationalist, Fréron blasted the cosmopolitanism of the advocates of the High Enlightenment. One incident beautifully illustrated the journalist's position. At mid-century, the French "public" divided over following the musical approach of their countrymen or adhering to that of the Italian opera. The first elevated the librettist and stressed simplicity of composition while the reformers preferred to advance the autonomy of the composer. The philosophes strongly sided with Italian innovators. In February of 1752, Grimm opened the attack, claiming supremacy for the outsiders, and Jean-Jacques Rousseau soon allied with him.[40] In both the closing issues of the *Lettres sur quelques écrits de ce temps* and his newly inaugurated *Année littéraire*, Fréron lambasted the philosophes and defended French music. Fréron asserted the superiority of his country's music which he found noble and sweet. Indeed he assumed the mantle of interpreter of the national sentiment. He stamped his patriotic indignation on an entire issue of the *Lettres* and exalted "our symphonies that are performed in Prussia, our motets the strongest in Europe," and finally our music which "can be felt by all nations." In Fréron's view, everyone was jealous of France's superiority. But more important for the purposes here was the equal animus Fréron expressed toward the philosophes. He believed that the Genevan Rousseau symbolized the problem because as an outsider, his allegiances lay elsewhere. But Rousseau was only a part of the philosophic movement that showed insufficient appreciation for things French.[41]

The *Année littéraire* also took umbrage at the philosophes' assault on Christianity. For example, in a dispute over religion, Fréron added the warning: "the *Encyclopédistes* should treat such delicate matters with more prudence and judgment. . . ."[42] The mildness of this rebuke revealed that his concern with religious transgressions remained rather muted. Nonetheless, Fréron, though no dévot, argued in the pages of his paper that a general commitment to Christianity, particularly Catholicism, provided the fabric holding together civilization. And he charged the philosophes were guilty of shredding this necessary protection.[43]

Neither such aesthetic nor religious interests, whatever their import, proved the center of the *Année littéraire*'s attack upon the High Enlightenment. Fréron found its personnel, not its program, most objectionable. He devoted far greater space and emotions to the philosophes themselves

103

than their ideas. Balcou's study of Fréron, a relatively overlooked work which is enormously informative about the French intellectual scene, has identified the years 1770–74 as the apotheosis of Fréron's antipathy to the philosophes. For this period, Balcou has provided a careful analysis of how the journal dissected its prey.[44]

Desfontaines had made Voltaire his primary target, and Fréron continued this approach. In all his publications, the editor of the *Année littéraire* pursued Voltaire, and the 1770s witnessed the aging of both antagonist and protagonist but no reduction in animosity. Fréron believed Voltaire a liar whose writings were largely indifferent toward the truth. The *Année littéraire* reported an anecdote transmitted from a friend of Bolingbroke. The paper noted that Voltaire stated about a biography of the English Queen Anne, "I need to know only the principal facts and their dates; in a word, I only require a canvas; I designate myself to fill it."[45] Not only was Voltaire untruthful, according to Fréron, he by his disrespect dirtied everything. Voltaire had ridiculed the great Condé by pointing out the latter's mental instability, and Voltaire's hostility for the Church lacked solemnity; in all this Voltaire exceeded bounds of decency and sullied everything.[46]

In addition to such charges, the *Année littéraire* further declared that whatever Voltaire's skills had been, age had stolen his intellectual acumen. Though once possessing the gift of producing memorable barbs, he had become far less subtle and interesting.[47] Finally, the magazine harped relentlessly on Voltaire's exile to Ferney. The periodical taunted Voltaire that he would never have an opportunity to return to Paris. In the preamble to the 1772 issue, Fréron continued these charges:

> I have never left France to allow myself the despicable mania of impudently writing these absurd horrors against religion, public honesty, the country which gave me birth, and my compatriots. I have not sought out an asylum at the extremities of the kingdom in order to be able to flee deep into foreign territory far from the just punishment due to a vile slanderer, to an obscene writer, to a shameless satirist. It is in the heart of my country, in the capital among comrades, under the eyes of the guardians of the laws of literature, that I have taken, and that I hold, and that I will resign the pen when my trembling hand will no longer be able to hold it.

This attack on Voltaire's sanctuary gave yet more muscle to the charges leveled at the lion of the High Enlightenment.

Although Fréron spent the most time disparaging his arch enemy, he also attacked others in the circle of philosophes, including La Harpe, D'Alembert, Marmontel, Diderot, Deslisle de Sales, Saint-Lambert, and Condorcet among others. They, like Voltaire, were all charlatans, who might use any occasion to falsify evidence.[48] They misunderstood

Fénélon, the nobility of the Crusades, the lessons of the Church.[49] Perhaps even more than their alleged misrepresentations, the *Année littéraire* loathed the pretensions of the philosophes, and depicted these men as hopelessly self-important. In its review of a work by Deslisle de Sales, the magazine ridiculed the effort as an attempt to inflate that philosophe's self-importance.

> Kings, descend from your throne and make room for the phi-losophe; criminals will disappear; the golden age, peace, inno-cence, and morality will descend from heaven. People, fall at the feet of the benefactor of humanity; bend your head, prostrate yourself before the *eternal being*, the *sublime being*, the *being par excellence*, the *most responsible being on earth*, the *only being who has the right to your homage*, since he has only been placed on this sad globe *in order to cure you of all evils stemming from life*; the heavens are silent; the divinity no longer speaks to us; it is sufficient to have around us the *Interpreter* of the holy laws of *Nature*. Let the philosophes be henceforth our only guides, our only masters, our only legislators; it is from them that we will learn to become wise, honest, good, humane, compassionate, sociable, happy. O my comrades! O my brothers! O my friends! Admire, cheer, admire the philosophes.[50]

Deceivers and egotists in these biting phrases, the philosophes also appeared in the eyes of the *Année littéraire* venal and conspiratorial. Contradicting a point in the *Journal des dames*, Fréron assailed Diderot for greed after selling his library to Catherine the Great.[51] And generally, the magazine portrayed the men of the High Enlightenment as searching for a handout from the rich.[52] Needful of money, the philosophes caballed to capture the sinecures and salons. Fréron saw himself as a truth squad to flay the philosophes and those they seduced. He singled out the women of the salons for special criticism.[53]

Reinforcing all of these attacks on the new ideas and their carriers was a sarcasm that historians have linked, in particular, to Desfontaines, Linguet, and Fréron. What made this kind of expression especially remarkable was its relative absence in the rest of the press. Whatever the balance elsewhere between politeness and polemics, no one could touch the virulence of Fréron and his compatriots. Both the extent of Fréron's assaults, coupled with their tone of ridicule, exacerbated the attacks on the philosophes because readers were so unaccustomed to this language in the periodicals. It might, in fact, be argued that the unconventional style, at least within the press, of the *Année littéraire* attracted readers far more than its ideas. Desfontaines, whose works fathered Fréron's, saw his popularity rise when he adopted this demeanor;[54] Fréron's success may have depended on the same style.

An interesting example of how the language of the *Année littéraire* made this magazine such a devastating weapon can be found in the sarcasm and wit visited upon the rather hapless La Harpe after the publication of two of his translations of Suetonius. Fréron's review of the translation of Suetonius's *Twelve Caesars* in the January 11, 1771 issue, declared that it lacked justice, elegance, harmony, agreement, and warmth. The bulk of the article systematically dismantled the quality of La Harpe's rendition, claiming to have found 104 errors. Fréron underlined these errors by repeatedly insisting that this number emerged without any systematic effort to locate them. However harsh was the substance of this criticism, its bite was made measurably sharper by several extremely sarcastic remarks scattered through this 36-page rendering. Toward the end of the analysis, the journalist offered two gratuitous insults. The first read:

> Before translating a Latin author, it is necessary to understand the original text; it is necessary to know the language into which one translates it, it is necessary to have some style. All that is missing from M. de la Harpe.

The *Année littéraire* did not merely assault this publication on its internal weaknesses; its author had to be directly, unambiguously implicated. Fréron's language here conjured up a vision of a bewildered La Harpe, intensifying the actual criticism. An even sharper rapier wit was deployed in the devastating conclusion. The last few lines of the review recounted an anecdote about a famous professor who promised an *écu* to anyone finding a mistake in his works of geometry. However, "if M. de la Harpe had the treasure of Croesus, and promised such a recompense to those who would locate his mistakes and solecisms, I would soon become one of the richest individuals in the kingdom."

On January 20, in the very next number of the *Année littéraire*, Fréron returned to the attack, this time focusing on the preface of the translations of the *Twelve Caesars*. Space prevents detailing the long, blistering attack mounted there but the introductory remarks gave a sense of the flair used to bring down opponents. These sentences, comprised largely of expressions in series, generated in the original French a kind of a prose poem whose ups and downs served in themselves to ridicule La Harpe. The magazine treated the defects as follows:

> In the magisterial and decisive tone that he [La Harpe] assumes in his *Discours préliminaire*, one appears to hear a Despot of Literature who promulgates decrees, appreciates the genius and richness of languages, reforms the laws of history, traces new plans to treat with even more grandeur and with more philosophy, and who, in the examination of works of this sort produced by the Ancients and by the Moderns, fixes the degree of esteem that each of them must

occupy in posterity. This strange discourse, where good sense, taste, and truth are mortally wounded on each page, where the most incurable mediocrities announce themselves with a revolting haughtiness, and besides are nothing more than a reheating of used observations, than a desultory compilation of scraps, rags, and common-places taken from everywhere without a principle of selection, without connections, without amounting to a whole, without connection to the version by Suetonius. I'll not go through all the indecent satires, all the false judgments, of this preliminary piece.

Amused by the rhythm, readers would have also found much cleverness in the imagery of phrases such as the one where a prostrate truth in the throes of death bloodied the rest of the text. And these few sentences provide just the beginning of a sustained effort to dismantle La Harpe's essay.

Finally, the attacks in the *Année littéraire* were extremely persistent. Never letting up, Fréron continued to attack, needle, and harass opponents. In the issue released on January 30, 1771, the magazine published yet a third devastating critique. Fréron used this article about a competing translation of the *Twelve Caesars* by de la Pause, as a pretext to criticize La Harpe again through invidious comparisons. As the *Année littéraire* sniped, "The version of M. de la Pause, although it does not have the merits of being completely exact and faithful to the text, at least is French."

Thus, vibrant vituperative language gave weight to the blasts against the philosophes. Personal charges, in their intensity as well as in the large amount of space devoted to them, overshadowed the complaints about the hostility of the High Enlightenment toward Christianity and nationalism. Two observations about the tilt of this anti-philosophic onslaught seem in order. First, its emphasis on personalities closely resembles the resentment of the Grub Streeters identified by Robert Darnton toward the figures of the High Enlightenment. One wonders if the Grub Streeters may have been building not only on their own career frustrations but also on a discourse of complaint, created by Desfontaines and perfected by Fréron. How paradoxical that these radicals might owe debts to such conservative men. Second, a reminder of an earlier argument, the emphasis on the personal in Fréron's attacks, evidently helps to explain the pro-philosophical attitudes that he also exhibited. By focusing on individuals and not programs, Fréron could advocate various specific elements of the High Enlightenment without so directly contradicting this evident strong animus toward these thinkers.

Whether or not directly disagreeing with the attack on the philosophes, substantial parts of the copy of the *Année littéraire* advocated significant elements of the High Enlightenment. In the main, this support came in the paper's praise of books and other works which would have been understood as propounding the ideals and methods of the philosophes. Fréron seldom admitted any sympathy for the movement but his subterranean allegiance would have been inescapable to readers.[55] Taken together, such endorsements mounted up to a substantial undercurrent of support for the High Enlightenment.

But before turning to his positive views of the philosophes, it is worth a brief detour to see how Fréron's most important subject – literary criticism – fits into this entire pattern. About fictional works, whether plays, poetry, novels, or stories, Fréron could be, and often was, brutally frank. Usually his excoriations did not reach the heights he reserved for the contemptible philosophes, but critical he was. Sometimes he linked his negative evaluations to the High Enlightenment, which in his view debased literature. A defender of classical ideals, he believed the philosophes threatened them.[56] Nonetheless, he seldom made this connection. This silence, in the midst of a paper that rarely kept silent, evidently undermined such a bridge. Furthermore he sometimes even supported the efforts of philosophes, including their interest in the bourgeois *drame* and foreign literature.[57] In this combination of silence and confusion, it would have been difficult for readers to link the general approval toward classicism to an attack on the philosophes, since for the eighteenth-century audience the High Enlightenment was far more an ideological statement than the endorsement of particular literary forms. Thinking this way, most readers would not have been inclined to tie the discussion of a specific form to any position on the Enlightenment. And, even those inclined to make these connections would have found it difficult. The adherents of the Enlightenment generally opposed classicism, but not uniformly. Exemplifying this was the most visible of all philosophes, Voltaire, who advocated classicism.[58] Furthermore, critics of the Enlightenment might still support their opposition's literary efforts. With the philosophes divided, with Fréron somewhat ambivalent and quiet on this, the audience of *Année littéraire* might have found it hard to relate the philosophes to the paper's diatribes regarding literature. This failure to blame the philosophes would seem to dilute the anti-philosophic message delivered elsewhere. Apparently Fréron did not find the philosophes as thoroughly evil as one might expect.

The *Année littéraire* also went so far as to support a number of causes clearly understood to be philosophic. Indeed, in the same pages in which Fréron was lambasting La Harpe, he was also siding with the philosophes on particular issues. The *Année littéraire* printed a letter discussing the forms of ceremonial address and listing the difficulties caused by so much overlap and confusion. But then, the epistle concluded:

Were there only these inconveniences, which are very real and very odious, the actual formulations of our addresses ought to be forever proscribed. I then invite all men of good will and intelligence to join me in helping to destroy this vicious custom and substituting there the language of reason and truth.[59]

Thus the *Année littéraire*, attacking the established system by the buzz-word "reason," sounded exactly like a philosophe. That same month the magazine printed several other articles putting forth Enlightenment notions, including a book review of Buffon's work on birds. As the architect of the theory of natural science accepted in and promulgated by the *Encyclopédie*, Buffon was inextricably connected to the High Enlightenment.[60] This relationship did not dissuade Fréron from seconding the naturalist's point of view and even launching a paean of praise to him:

The author here treats with as much eloquence as philosophy the instincts, customs, habits, and faculties which distinguish them [birds] from all other species of animals. You will find there, sir, as in all the same author's discourses preceding each section of the natural history, these grand views, this observant and attentive genius, this sagacity in deciphering what is natural from what is critical and foreign, this penetrating gaze which seizes and embraces the connections or general differences which constitute genuses and species.

In this review, so enamored was the *Année littéraire* of Buffon's science that it could even praise Buffon despite his connections to the philosophes. And other articles, particularly a review of an ethnography of Iceland, gave support by accepting or encouraging beliefs and approaches linked to the High Enlightenment.[61]

While Fréron's publication focused upon a panoply of the themes trumpeted by the philosophes, he had special favorites. One recurrent message emphasized practical happiness on this earth. To be certain, Fréron included the aesthetic pleasures associated with literature. With his love of beautiful books, rare editions, receptions, and intellectual interaction, he found the universal quest for knowledge exhilarating. But he did not overlook the mundane satisfactions of life, including the gadgets that could smooth daily existence.[62] By advocating such concerns, the marriage of knowledge to daily comfort, Fréron accepted a major part of the Enlightenment.

Also parallel to the concepts of the philosophes were physiocratic notions, especially the advocacy of free trade in grain, that this periodical embraced. When the king issued a decree liberating the grain trade, Fréron greeted this edict which "lifted the hopes of the yeomen. . . . It's a flattering spectacle for a sensitive soul to see today all Europe consider itself one and the same family which reciprocally feeds each other." He also supported efforts to stimulate trade, particularly by building canals. An article generally favoring improved transportation revealed much about Fréron's commitment to physiocracy. The *Année littéraire* noted:

The roads are as necessary as the rivers and streams. . . . By the communication that they established among men, they awaken cupidity, this fecund source of work, they multiply the treasures of nature and industry in facilitating exchanges; little by little they equally enrich diverse regions; they soften morals and polish spirit.

These remarks, by accepting the Economists' logic in which free trade spurred productivity, indicated how captivated by, and propagandistic of, physiocracy the *Année littéraire* had become. As this program became increasingly unpopular in France, the magazine retreated somewhat but continued in this general vein.[63] Evidently, focusing on physiocracy was not necessarily an embrace of the High Enlightenment whose chieftains remained divided on this theory. Nonetheless, they were related, and Fréron's commitment should be noted as part of his acceptance of the Enlightenment. And these two examples scarcely exhaust this list of topics which could include how empiricism and the science of the philosophes cropped up in these pages.[64]

Adding these favorable treatments of philosophic ideas would reinforce the claim that in many, many specific cases – indeed in most ways – the *Année littéraire* tacitly accepted the High Enlightenment while rejecting it very visibly and vociferously on three very important points: religion, cosmopolitanism, and the personal character of the philosophes. In this assault, both major ideas and the movement itself became implicated. This was an uneven balance: Fréron's extraordinary hatred for the Enlightenment figures was more evident than his silent advocacy of a series of Enlightenment values.

The ambivalence toward the Enlightenment in the *Année littéraire* appeared as well in the *Journal de Trévoux*, although in different guise. A thumbnail history can assist this examination of what that periodical accepted and rejected of the philosophes' thought. In 1701 Louis Auguste de Bourbon, the Duke of Maine, who ruled the independent principality of Dombes, decided to issue a periodical, charged with rigidly defending religion and covering the rambunctious world of letters. For these two goals, difficult at best to reconcile, he selected the Jesuits to edit the magazine. By 1702 the *Journal de Trévoux* appeared monthly, a schedule to which it generally adhered for another 81 years. Through this period a number of editors took control with numerous collaborators.[65] Because of the emphasis of this book, the post-1745 period of the *Journal de Trévoux* receives the most attention here. From 1737 to 1745, P. de Charlevoix, an obscure former missionary to Canada, edited the magazine. He ceded the periodical to Guillaume François Berthier, a professor and one of the authors of the multi-volume *Histoire de l'église gallicane*. As editor until 1762, Berthier raised the visibility of the *Journal de Trévoux* and himself became a formidable intellectual figure. When the Jesuits were banished from France, Berthier, who saw no reason to continue, resigned, but the paper lived on without him. Though deprived of its base, the *Journal de Trévoux* staggered on through several editors, watching its circulation precipitously drop until in 1777 it reportedly had only 200 subscribers.[66] During the last 40 or so years of the publishing of the *Journal de Trévoux*, its highlight was the stewardship of Berthier. Both to provide focus to this analysis and to take advantage of a cluster of valuable historical works, this case study concentrates on the Berthier era.

From 1745 to 1762, the *Journal de Trévoux* published significant information bearing on the High Enlightenment. To turn first to the reception of the philosophes in the *Journal de Trévoux* requires placing the viewpoint of that journal in context. Unlike Fréron, Berthier rarely employed extreme invective or personalities in his discussions. This was particularly true in the early reviews of the *Encyclopédie* in which a gentle mocking tone accompanied Berthier's initial hostile reaction.[67] But on occasion the journalist and his collaborators raised the specter of plagiarism, a charge which related less to the merit of the insights than to the character of their authors. Commonly eschewing both extremes in language as well as charges against individuals, Berthier most often used a restrained language while forthrightly and calmly stating his positions. Thus, not as reserved as the *Mercure* but nothing like the *Année littéraire*, the *Journal de Trévoux* mainly employed a tone of solidity but included substantial critiques. Such an approach would seem to permit the paper's enthusiastic or negative remarks to come through, without further exacerbating matters. Furthermore, the *Journal de Trévoux* covered scientific and technical subjects that related little if at all to the new ideas of any sort.[68] Such copy would seem to work as a buffer, providing some tranquilizing effect. Because eager readers could imagine no governmental pressure for such pieces, they would credit them to the magazine and a certain lack of interest regarding the Enlightenment.

Despite some dilution of the message, patterns of both criticism and support for the High Enlightenment emerged – but more the former than the latter. The characteristic of the philosophes that drew the hostile attention of the *Journal de Trévoux* was their opposition to revealed religion. In particular, the paper attacked the new ideas for their critique of Christianity – which the editors usually implicitly equated to Catholicism. This defense, not surprisingly, emerged as one of the main goals of the magazine.[69] The periodical once explained its opposition to the *Encyclopédie*: "When religion is attacked, the function of the journalist effortlessly changes into that of adversary and combatant."[70] And later in the same issue, Berthier asserted that his role included delivering "the greatest blows of criticism to beliefs contrary to religion and good morality."[71]

In order to attack those notions of the High Enlightenment that the Jesuit periodical found offensive to religion, the *Journal de Trévoux* essentially used two tactics. One approach was showing the evils that emerged from the beliefs of the philosophes, or as the paper often termed them, the "incrédules" or the "esprits-forts."[72] Included among the ills attributable to the philosophes was the damage which a lack of faith inflicted on human welfare. One book review exclaimed:

> In order not to waiver between the effects of religion and in-credulity, it happens that religion makes us happier, that it furnishes stronger and more interesting motives for virtue, it inspires more greatness of spirit and true courage. The advantage is entirely on the side of religion; and the *Incrédule*, out of respect for society of which he is a member, must never divulge his principles. Now these principles, which oblige silence because they only contribute to the destruction of society and difficulties for individuals, can only be regarded as errors when one sees God and Providence.[73]

Not only had the philosophes' notions created societal and personal havoc, but they even led to laxity and degradation. When reviewing Voltaire's *Poèmes de la pucelle d'Orléans*, Berthier foresaw vile effects from such irreligious publications and continued, "Religion, uprightness, modesty, propriety, decency, what have you become in a century in which such attacks against the innocence of public morality dare to show themselves."[74]

The *Journal de Trévoux* did not content itself with showing the malign results of unbelief, but also set about repulsing particular views of the High Enlightenment that threatened religion. The magazine confronted the philosophes when they attacked the Church's supposed failings. The *Encyclopédie* had assailed a Bishop for repressing dissent; and the *Journal de Trévoux* countered that no high Church official was responsible, but the punishment administered had been justified.[75] In addition, the periodical castigated certain beliefs of the philosophes that were contrary to the Catholicism the Jesuits understood. Although the High Enlightenment did not embrace materialism, its emphases on nature and human passions held materialistic implications. The *Journal de Trévoux* remained vigilant about detecting materialism in any form and critiquing it. For example, Berthier found Montesquieu's insistence on climate and geography as the basis for morality to be wrong. For the journalist, this view made matter not God responsible and was consequently erroneous.[76] Also disputed was the High Enlightenment's emphasis on toleration, which implied that one religion was the same as another. But the magazine rejected this position, noting that accepting tolerance on matters of doctrine "would be to arm oneself against God, against truth, in favor of error."[77]

In addition to battling directly the philosophes' lack of faith and particular views on religion, the *Journal de Trévoux* supported Christianity against the High Enlightenment by treating belief with great respect. To be sure, the magazine published little on strictly theological subjects, as less than ten per cent of its articles were on such questions.[78] Nonetheless, this periodical evidenced a deep respect for religious writings. On doctrinal matters, the *Journal de Trévoux* accepted orthodox Catholicism as a premise. And in the same issue which so negatively compared unbelief with religion, the journal noted, "Who can doubt that we do not have an extreme need of Revelation, in order to be enlightened about the future destiny of the soul." In a similar vein, in a book review, the journalist praised the work, stating:

> We have long wanted a book which provides to the reader the sentiments of the Fathers as the principal objects of Christian morality. These great men have been yet still greater by their love for God, by their dignity, their talents, their success, by the homage rendered to them by society. It's the result of what they have thought and said about the love of God and about the infinite dependence that they have and will have on Christian life experienced today . . . the book presents a tableau of the Holy Fathers and their virtues, that is to say, their modesty, charity, zeal for the glory of God, their sublime faith, their own effort to conceal their good works, etc.[79]

Such evident admiration for the founders of the Church only reinforced numerous articles that supported religion.

Although the *Journal de Trévoux* explicitly and implicitly rejected the philosophes' ideas about religion, it supported their beliefs in many other areas. And, unlike Fréron, Berthier was more often willing to admit that he did share a belief in identifiable philosophic notions.[80] Some of these beliefs – cosmopolitanism, freedom for the arts, anti-aristocracy – the Jesuit paper advocated without bothering to explain any contradictions. And such would not have seemed necessary to contemporaries for these beliefs did not contradict the all-important religious opinions held by the journal. However, in addition to these concepts, the *Journal de Trévoux* supported unlimited empiricism, even natural religion within certain limits. To reconcile this and the immutable teaching of revealed religion required explanation and, as discussed below, such justifications were frequently given.

First, one might turn to the *Journal de Trévoux*'s less controversial endorsements of the High Enlightenment. Contemporaries would not have found it particularly surprising that the Jesuit magazine would agree with the international inclinations of the philosophes. One traditional criticism of this order had focused on its loyalty to the Pope that precluded the same loyalty to a nation-state. Whether such a critique was true or not, this paper accepted a cosmopolitanism far different from Fréron's cultural nationalism. One important and revealing example was the battle over the merits of French and Italian music. Against the *Année littéraire*, the Jesuit journal endorsed the superiority of the Italians.[81] And in other areas the *Journal de Trévoux* also sided with the philosophes. In the continuing battle between the Ancients and the Moderns the Jesuit paper likewise demanded artistic creation or freedom instead of copying.[82] In addition, Berthier, like the rambunctious intellectuals of his day, was contemptuous of the privileges of birth. His magazine reviewed an English work entitled *The Connoisseur*. But with the review barely begun, the author changed voice and described a conversation with his censor about how to improve English society. The abrupt and unneeded appearance of this response signaled the journalist's desire to spread such views and seemingly about France, not England. Among a number of suggestions, the censor decried the violence of the society and blamed country gentlemen, "most of whom are born only to destroy game and bother their neighbors . . . these beings belong to the species of vegetables. . . ." Although such biting remarks remained rare and had to be delivered obliquely as attacks on England, nonetheless they reflected a more general anti-noble sentiment, perhaps stronger even than any enlightened animus toward the Second Estate.[83]

But the most remarkable High Enlightenment position held by the *Journal de Trévoux* was its acceptance of empiricism. As John Pappas, in his excellent *Berthier's "Journal de Trévoux" and the Philosophes*, points out, this periodical did not simply support science but propounded the Enlightenment view of it. Newton came to be accepted.[84] When Buffon argued that one should learn through observation, not from preordained precepts, the *Journal de Trévoux* commented that this was "an excellent theory that deserves to be transported from natural history to all other sections of the arts and sciences."[85] Observation was so important to this paper that it even supported studies which attempted to define natural religion. Clearly, however, this belief in empiricism, not to mention its offspring natural religion, posed theoretical problems for revealed religion. Berthier dealt with the problem in many different ways including the following: If all phenomena had to respond to laws empirically determined, how could one guarantee the mysteries of the faith? Because, responded Berthier, the Bible consisted of a set of empirical statements about events that had occurred. God who made the rules might also make exceptions.[86] Berthier remained, once one accepts the

114

verity of the Bible as divinely inspired, consistent with his commitment to empiricism.

Thus, the *Journal de Trévoux* was able to advocate a number of High Enlightenment notions while rejecting this movement's views on religion. Roughly comparable with Fréron, Berthier edited a paper of great ambivalence toward the philosophes – a highly visible rejection of important parts of their beliefs coupled with agreement on numerous smaller points. The substance and the extent of their ambivalence differed, but in the end both seemed to have differed overtly and sensationally with the High Enlightenment while they accepted many specific aspects.

Conclusions deduced from the *Journal de Trévoux* when combined with those from the *Année littéraire* as well as Marmontel's *Mercure* and Maisonneuve's *Journal des dames* – competitors from the opposite end of the ideological spectrum – spark further consideration. What in particular did these discussion papers argue about the philosophes' movement? One would also like to consider why the periodicals wrote or remained silent on issues, but that discussion must be left to the general conclusion of this book.

This sample of papers indicates the acceptance of the High Enlightenment with cautious adherents at the pro-philosophic end, and across from them periodicals that accepted fewer but still many High Enlightenment notions. An even closer look at these papers suggests interesting nuances. Under this lens, support for the Enlightenment's representatives and by implication the movement in general appears very thin. The pro-philosophic press did not privilege accounts of the philosophes and their combats. This encouragement remained a relatively muted theme. At the other end of the spectrum lay Fréron's outright hostility. Because Berthier focused more on ideas than individuals, his support for the former seemingly did not translate into support for the latter. Indeed, the only time when he appeared to become really exercised about the philosophes and their specific battles was when he was criticizing them. Thus, across the spectrum the philosophes received limited support and much criticism. If the intellectuals gained relatively little direct encouragement, their ideas, though somewhat undermined by the less than overwhelming support for their authors, were nonetheless widely accepted. The more conservative writers retained affection for a wide array of the Enlightenment views, even though they had many hostile gibes about some philosophic notions. The more liberal journalists at least granted the ideas of the philosophes a great deal of space. More research would be required to see exactly which ideas received emphasis. Quite evidently excluded though was the High Enlightenment's vision of the Church and politics, omitted by more moderate papers and decried by Fréron and Berthier. Still, an important vein of various philosophic ideas existed throughout the press. And because this stratum might be found in radically opposed papers, it possessed even greater impact. By *a* Fréron and *a* Marmontel – two totally disparate characters – both promoting sets of related notions, these ideas do in fact appear a part of the educated elite's common understanding. A generalized commitment to a constricted High Enlightenment seemed to be reinforced in the discussion press.

Can the conclusions based on this sample be extended to other journals in the philosophical–literary press? More inquiry is surely required for a definitive answer. And this expanded research should include pro-philosophic papers of a more polemical bent than those considered here. Periodicals from the 1780s should be considered separately to see if the government's apotheosis of the philosophes shook the general approach of the press. In addition, a more systematic analysis might compare the earlier periodicals with later ones that published after the ideals of High Enlightenment had become largely accepted and far less controversial. Also, such study must address the Jansenists' *Nouvelles ecclésiastiques*, which, even if especially atypical, appears far more hostile to the High Enlightenment than either Fréron's or Berthier's paper.[87] Nonetheless, wide reading in many other papers suggests that the philosophes garnered much attention but that overall their ideas fared better than their personas and their daily struggles.[88]

Further research into the place of problematic notions in the periodicals will want to go beyond the High Enlightenment, whose notions had, in fact, insinuated themselves into all parts of society. There were some thinkers, for a variety of reasons, who accepted the achievements of the Enlightenment and wanted to go further. This kind of thinking – often labeled the "later Enlightenment" – was far more heterogeneous than its parent. Many radical offshoots appeared, but these new ideas often had little in common. Perhaps the most important accretion other than the ideas of the already discussed materialists and *frondeurs*, was sentimentalist literature à la Rousseau and Diderot.[89]

But the Enlightenment was not the only source of reformism in the prerevolutionary decades. From the parlements, the French royal courts, emerged a critique of absolutism and both the suggestion and practice of a local government designed to providing for the individual. Perhaps the most amazing aspect of this "libertarian" point of view was its source, the parlements, which were after all officially wedded to the monarchy. Such a dependency would have, it seems, kept the judges quiet. But a tiny minority within, the Jansenists, with a long-term hostility to repression, developed a thorough-going critique of hierarchy. Another political theory – the commonwealthman – also rattled about the kingdom, as evidenced by the references in the affiches. This notion may be crudely summarized as the belief that both the court and big business were inevitably corrupt and that virtue rested in the independent provincial. No particular institutional base emerged for this concept, even though it might have been most easily appropriated by the parlementarians. Of course, other notions existed, and individuals could use, in various combinations, all of them.[90]

How these other significant beliefs fared in the press requires further research. Yet one may state with relative confidence that both commonwealthman ideas and Jansenism made only a relatively modest appearance in the discussion periodical. Perhaps, the political nature of the latter ideology, as well as its dangerous implications, encouraged the literary, philosophical, and scientific press to omit such notions. Furthermore, despite the seeming omnipresence of commonwealth or "republican" ideas, they apparently were not that integral to bookish culture that formed the heart of the periodicals. As such, they rarely surfaced in the press and the vigilance of the government should not be discounted for both of these streams of belief. Without the benefit of any scholarly attempt to evaluate the press generally for Rousseauian sentimentalism,[91] speculation based on scattered materials becomes necessary. Discussion journals seem to have held an ambivalence similar to that toward the High Enlightenment. The ideas, which spoke directly to an inner goodness in man and a lack of primal depravity, seem to have fared better than the intellectuals involved. In one way, however, these two versions of the Enlightenment appear to differ. The later strain always had to coexist with the implicit and explicit critique by the High Enlightenment. Yet because the "Rousseauists" proved more favorable toward religion and evinced greater indifference to politics, their notions converged on the limited view of the High Enlightenment in the press. Overall, then, the periodical press apparently endorsed in roughly parallel ways the ideas of the High Enlightenment and Rousseauian sentimentality, even if not their authors.

Because these two currents of thought constituted extremely important parts of the literature of the century, spreading their notions made the periodicals a participant in the dissemination of the "new ideas." Evidently such participation was limited. But whatever the hesitations, the ubiquitous and sizeable treatment very likely gave a substantial lift to these movements. Confirming as well as enriching these findings will require not only new investigations but expanding the inquiry into the discussion press beyond its treatment of the "new ideas" and reconsidering the categories used here to define these problematic notions. Still these conclusions provide a launching pad, if not a resting place for such inquiry.

Evidently such positive reportage on the "new ideas," even though moderated in many ways, targeted the abstract theoretical underpinning

of Church and monarchy. Although both bodies had reformed themselves, they had never quite given up traditional justifications for their
legitimacy. The "new ideas" allowed in the press did not directly attack
these structures, but obliquely and subterraneously these non-Christian
ideologies undermined them. And the omnipresence of such notions
perhaps gave these views an added jolt.

On immediate rather than theoretical grounds, one must admit that
the king had very little to fear from the press as he had already accommodated himself to most of its ideas. His greatest problem was, it seems
to me, the ready acceptance of these notions which were ultimately
antithetical to much of his *raison d'être*. Royal adherence to such views
could have only assisted a monarch in the long term if he could locate
notions within compatible to his rule. This effort would prove fruitless
but in the short term seemed to insulate him from the view that he was
outdated and outmoded. This differed for the Church. Even though it had
also made many changes, as evidenced by Berthier's *Journal de Trévoux*,
this periodical remained more progressive than most of the Church. The
discussion press, though avoiding direct discussion of religion, clearly
introduced notions problematic to the general worldview of the Church
then in operation.

Such an evaluation of the discussion press adds to the mix created by
the affiches and the political press. The three presses managed some sort
of indirect critique of the monarch, although they ranged from tepid to
fairly challenging, especially in the case of the newspaper. But as the
century wore on, periodicals posed little present danger and even
granted active support. Regarding society and the Church, however,
difficulties in press coverage continued, though still without clear immediate confrontations.

Such a message, fairly tepid overall, still disputes two commonly made
claims about the Old Regime. Most scholars implicitly treat the press as
holding no troublesome ideas at all. Clearly this statement fails. But
somewhat contradictorily, these same historians also hold that the world
of print was increasingly challenging to the Old Regime.[92] This claim,
impossible to square with the common view of the impotent press,
simply ignores the latter or renders it irrelevant. But the newspaper, with
its political reporting at the end of the century, could dampen the
adventurousness of published material. And much of the rest of the press
shows a stream of criticism with variable currents. Suggesting a revision
to the view of the Old Regime as the site of a rising crescendo of criticism,
these findings also modify the historiography of the French Revolution –
a subject to be pursued in the conclusion.

Part II
MILIEU

4

EIGHTEENTH-CENTURY JOURNALISM AND ITS PERSONNEL

Gazetier – one who writes a gazette: a good gazetier must be a quick learner, truthful, impartial, stylistically simple and accurate: this indicates that the good gazetiers are very rare.[1]

This opinion of newspapermen, published in the *Encyclopédie* summarized the eighteenth-century view of contemporary journalists.[2] An article on journalism by Diderot in this same compendium was equally negative. After explaining how demanding the publication of a periodical would be, he noted that no journal organized itself well enough to achieve the goal. But Voltaire, who far more than Diderot believed himself to have suffered at the hands of journalists, assailed them even more vigorously in the *Encyclopédie*. Although he disdained newspapermen as subservient, he aimed his sharpest barbs at the authors of literary magazines who, he claimed, wrote solely for money. Able to earn little through praise, these devils resorted to personal assaults and malignities to enhance sales. Still, lamented Voltaire, reason and good taste dictated that such reprobates would reap only scorn and oblivion. The great philosophe added that if these journalists wished to accomplish something, they might desist from their meddling and fill their periodicals with useful announcements.[3]

Negative, then, was the *Encyclopédie*'s assessment of all those who produced periodicals, a group collectively referred to in this chapter as "journalists." Naturally, allies of the philosophes put forward similar ideas regarding the press, and Deslisle de Sales, a lesser light influenced by this coterie, wrote his book about journalists with a pen dipped in vitriol.[4] More tellingly, François-Denis Camusat, who was, if anything, hostile to the philosophes, expressed virtually their opinion of journalists.[5] Perhaps the treatment accorded journalism by the *Encyclopédie méthodique* shows how widely these sentiments were shared. Although the editors hired to produce this massive revision of the first *Encyclopédie* were heirs to the Enlightenment, the publisher and editor-in-chief were closely tied to journalism. Charles-Joseph Panckoucke, organizer of the *Encyclopédie méthodique*, had made much of his fortune by acquiring in the 1780s many of the most prominent French periodicals, and J.-B.-A. Suard, the editor-in-chief, initially achieved a reputation among the men of letters by directing the *Gazette de France*. Yet, while the second encyclopedia revised and expanded much of the first, the articles by Diderot and Voltaire and the anonymous definition of gazetier – practically all the early volumes had to say on this subject – also constituted virtually everything the new version offered.[6]

Although modern scholars have increasingly studied the periodical press, the eighteenth-century assessment of journalists remains the latest general characterization we have. This is regrettable because a comprehensive view of this group could assist scholarship.[7] Historians and specialists in literature have written biographies of many individual practitioners, including a few book-length studies. An analysis pinpointing common features of the people producing the press would help specialists identify the distinctive qualities of their individual subjects. In addition, a knowledge of the journalists will help to explain, in the conclusion of this work, the periodicals' content. Most important, an examination of journalists permits significant insights into the society of letters in general. As will become apparent, the men and women of the press commonly belonged neither to the already intensively examined circle of literary giants nor the Grub Street crowd. Rather they were foot soldiers in literary life; thus they may add to our understanding of this important stratum whose members undoubtedly outnumbered the intellectual leaders and in their day possessed greater significance than their more tawdry competitors.

A new evaluation of journalists will, of course, take a different shape than that the philosophes and others offered two centuries ago. The grave has swallowed up the injured egos of the past, so no longer must one focus upon the faults and strengths of journalists. More interesting to modern investigators of any occupational group are questions that may be answered somewhat more dispassionately about social background, educational levels, career choice and development, journalistic endeavors, motivations for commencing and ending journalistic jobs, overall publication record, and financial success. This study explores these general topics.

Nonetheless, the number of individuals practicing journalism makes it impossible to answer such questions for the entire group. The *Dictionnaire des journalistes* contains over 400 biographies of eighteenth-century figures.[8] Furthermore, additional research turns up dozens more that any comprehensive survey would have to consider. Consequently, for this chapter I developed a representative selection of papers between 1745 and 1786 and analyzed the individuals who made editorial policy for these periodicals.[9]

Understanding the organization of journalistic enterprises helps to explain why the focus here falls on the framers of editorial decisions. Clear separations between publisher, editor, and journalist generally did not exist in the eighteenth century. Indeed, individuals often performed all these functions. Thus, a study of the editors includes a substantial portion of the entire journalistic personnel. However, solid reasons exist for eliminating those who served only as either publisher or journalist. Most of the former group saw the paper as an investment, stayed away from daily operations, and cannot be termed journalists in any meaningful sense of the word. They deserve a separate study. On the other hand, those who merely wrote for periodicals – either as correspondents or as regular employees – certainly qualify as journalists. However, at most papers they labored anonymously so we know only those who became famous under other circumstances. Such skewed evidence would make this group appear more celebrated than was likely and thus dictates its omission. These writers will be best understood when some scholar uncovers extensive records for a periodical that identify a cross-section of these reporters. In sum then, this study concentrates only on those who made editorial decisions regardless of whether they did so with or without subordinates and superiors.

I constructed a sample of papers from 1745 through 1786 that reflects at least some of the diversity of this medium. (For a more complete explanation, see Appendix II.) I elected to follow one governmentally approved journal – the *Gazette de France* – throughout the entire period, and I did the same for one paper published in Paris, one in the provinces, and one outside France. I then divided the forty years under consideration into ten-year segments and placed all periodicals that endured over three years into the appropriate periods where they belonged. Organizing these decadal groups into three geographic categories – Paris, provinces, and foreign – I selected two papers from each grouping by random sample. In total then, with the exception of 1745 to 1755 when only one provincial journal existed, I examined ten papers per decade and, subtracting the four periodicals that covered the entire period, twenty-six papers in all.

This selection process of papers made a huge, potentially unmanageable block of information manageable, but the choices created certain biases, more systematically discussed in the appendix. But without a doubt, the requirement that the periodical appear for three or more years eliminated ephemeral journals and those who worked on them, and this study can only claim to investigate the personnel of relatively stable publications. Also, the complexity already created by this methodology prevented selecting according to other important variables – especially the kind of news covered (e.g. politics, literary developments, etc.), so that the accurate representation of all sorts of journals cannot be guaranteed. Geography was emphasized in this part of the analysis over genre (the focus earlier) because one could reasonably hypothesize that representing different areas was more necessary to obtain the full range of editors than would be different types of publications. Nonetheless, on a practical level, the deliberate and random choices combined fortuitously to cover all the general categories of periodicals. Finally, the decision not to employ a strictly random sample determined that any statistical measures ought to be considered as very crude. But these caveats, taken together, indicate only that this first effort to write a prosopography of journalists must remain a somewhat impressionistic survey of the personnel who operated the stable core of papers.

This procedure generated a total of sixty-two men and four women, whom, despite the variety of their duties, one might simply term editors. Even with the definition articulated above, ambiguities remain that would allow scholars to classify individuals differently. Furthermore, considerable disagreement exists in the literature on the actual dates served. The evidence presented should be considered in this light.[10] Analyses of groups of this size are best directed toward exploring broad composite characteristics even though the sample intended to test geographical and chronological differences. Nonetheless, despite the small size of the sample (hard to expand because of the time consuming nature of the work), I looked at a wide variety of subgroups. And, indeed with one exception, attempts to find distinct entities based on geography, time, or genre of periodical among this group of editors have all failed. However, the one exception – nine male editors of the provincial press – is so dramatic that it deserves separate treatment following the broader analysis of the other editors. For the fifty-seven individuals comprising this larger group, scanty source material requires deleting ten – including two women – from consideration. (See Table 4-1 for the results of this survey.) [11]

Table 4-1 Periodicals sampled and their editors[a]

Periodicals sampled for the entire period[b]

Gazette de France 1745–86
 Arnaud, François (1762–71)[c]
 Aubert, Jean Louis (1774–75)
 Boissy, Louis de (1750–51)
 Bret, Antoine (1775–83)
 Collet de Messine, Jean Baptiste (1771–74)[d]
 Cournand, Antoine de (1784–?)
 Dubois-Fontenelle, Jean-Gaspard (1783–90)
 Marin, François-Louis-Claude (1771–74)
 Meusnier de Querlon, Anne-Gabriel (1752–53)
 Mouhy, Charles de Fieux de (1749–50)
 Saint-Mars, (1750–51)[d]

Sainte-Albine, Pierre Remond de (1733–49, 1751–62)
Suard, Jean-Baptiste-Antoine (1762–71)
Petites Affiches 1751–86
Aubert, Jean-Louis (1751–90)
Affiches de Lyon 1750–86
De la Roche, Aimé (1750–90)[c]
Courrier d'Avignon 1745–86
Artaud, Jean-Baptiste (1775–84)
Cheisolme, Pierre Joseph (?-1772)
La Belonie, François (1749)
Morénas, François (1733–42, 1750–75)
Outhier,   (1740s)[d]
Roubaud, Joseph-Marie (1775)
Tournal, Sabin (1784–93)

Periodicals sampled for the decade 1745–1754

Nouvelles ecclésiastiques 1745–54
Fontaine de la Roche, Jacques (1729–61)
Journal économique 1751–54
Boudet, Antoine (1751–72)
Boudet, Claude (1751–72)
Nouvelle Bibliothèque germanique 1745–54
Formey, Jean-Henri-Samuel (1746–59)
Pérard, Jacques (1746–49)
Cinq Années littéraires 1748–52
Clément, Pierre (1748–52)

Periodicals sampled for the decade 1755–1764

Affiches de province 1755–64
Meusnier de Querlon, Anne-Gabriel (1752–76)
Annales typographiques 1758–63
Darcet, Jean (1760–63)
Goulin, Jean (1760–63)
Ladvocat, Jean Baptiste (1760–63)
Morin d'Hérouville, (1758–61)[d]
Robert, (?)[d]
Roux, Augustin (1758–63)
Affiches de Nantes 1757–64
no one identified
Affiches de Bordeaux 1758–64
Labottière, Jacques (1758–84)
Labottière, Antoine (1758–84)
Gazette de Bruxelles 1756–64
Gouvest, Jean Henri Maubert de (1759–61)
Gazette de Cologne 1759–64
Jacquemotte, Gaspard-Antoine (1753–64)[d]

Periodicals sampled for the decade 1765–1774

Journal des dames 1765–68, 1774
Maisonneuve, Catherine-Michelle (1764–68)
Mathon de la Cour, Charles-Joseph (1764–68)
Mercier, Louis Sébastien (1774–77)
Montanclos, Marie-Emilie de (1774–75)

Sautreau de Marsy, Claude-Sixte (1764–68)
Année littéraire 1765–74
Fréron, Elie-Catherine (1754–76)
Annonces, affiches, et avis divers de Normandie 1765–74
Machuel, Jean-Baptiste (1762–84)
Annonces, affiches et avis divers de l'Orléanais 1765–74
Couret de Villeneuve, Louis-Pierre (1771?-94)
Couret de Villeneuve, Martin (1764–70?)
Bibliothèque des sciences et des beaux arts 1765–74
Boué, Marie-Elisabeth (?)[d]
Chais, Charles (1754–65)
Dumas, Charles-Guillaume-Frédéric (1754–79)
Guiot, Jean (1754–79)
Hop, H.   (?)[d]
Joncourt, Elie de (1754–65)
La Fite, Jean Daniel (1754–79)
La Fite, [Mme] (?)[d]
L'Héritier,   (?)[d]
Gazette universelle de littérature, aux Deux-Ponts 1770–74
Dubois-Fontenelle, Jean-Gaspard (1770–76)

Periodicals sampled for the decade 1775–1786

La Nature considérée 1775–81
Buchoz, Joseph (1771–81)
Journal de lecture 1775–79
Leuchsenring, Franz-Michael (1775–79)
Affiches du Poitou 1775–86
Chevrier (1781–89)[d]
Joyneau-Desloges, René Alexis (1773–81)
Annonces, affiches, et avis divers de Flandre 1781–86
L'Epinard, Joseph Paris de (1781–91)
Gazette de Leyde 1775–86
Cerisier, Marc-Antoine (1785–87)
Luzac, Etienne (1738–83)
Luzac, Jean L. (1772–98)
Nouveau Journal helvétique 1775–80
Bertrand, Jean-Elie (1769–79)
Chaillet, Henri-David (1779–80)

---

[a]For the precise procedure for selecting journals, consult Appendix II.
[b]Dates beside the periodical titles indicate the years each publication was consulted.
[c]Dates beside the editors' names are those of tenure in their positions, even when those years exceeded the years sampled.
[d]Editors eliminated because of a lack of biographical material.

The remaining forty-seven directors of the Parisian and foreign press hailed from villages, towns, and cities throughout France and along her borders. Except for the central territory occupied by Maine, Orléanais, Limousin, Marche, and Berry, every other French province was the birthplace or very near to, at least one editor. They came from large cities including Paris, Amsterdam, and even Berlin, as well as from small towns including Doazit near Pau, Vic-sur-Cère in the Auvergne, and Kandel on the border between the Palatinate and Alsace.[12]

But if this one characteristic reveals diversity, patterns emerge as well. Nine journalists were born in a fairly tight triangular area, framed by Toulon, Avignon, and Montpellier, around the mouth of the Rhône. And some 150 miles north, along the headwaters of the Rhône in Lyons, Dijon, Geneva, and Besançon, eleven others were born and reared. The only other places with any density at all were Paris with four and the North Sea coast of Holland with another three. Nevertheless, since virtually 50 per cent of the editors' birthplaces were plastered along the southeast border of France, this pattern of settlement does not support the hypothesis that has been advanced regarding the exceptional literary vibrancy of the area north of a line drawn between Geneva and St.-Malo.[13] However, the data do sustain another bit of conventional wisdom which credits urban areas with a relatively high level of intellectual vitality. Although 80 per cent of the French population resided in villages and hamlets with less than 2,000 people, better than three-quarters of the editors spent their youths in larger places and over one-half in important seaports, provincial capitals, and metropolitan areas.

More original conclusions emerge by comparing the birth places of these directors of periodicals with the locales where they later practiced journalism. Only five of the forty-seven eventually worked in their home towns. People came to Paris from the farthest reaches of France and from beyond her borders as well. And while the other cities with publications such as The Hague, Geneva, and Neufchâtel drew from less distant places, they too had many visitors in their midst. Such movement reveals, it seems to me, how newspaper publishing allowed newcomers a legitimate chance. The success of the invaders conversely indicates how little these publishing centers influenced their own inhabitants, for the existence of such writers working in their environs produced no noticeable burst of activity among the residents. Evidently, immigrants to Paris found no thriving native born community of journalists to obstruct their progress. In part the low opinion of journalism may explain both the openness and this lack of competition.

Born mainly in provincial cities, later moving to centers of publishing, these editors started life with social advantages. Thirty-three of the forty-seven editors possessed discoverable family backgrounds, although one father's occupation – violinist – defied precise classification. In fact, any general sorting of these individuals' social origins involves some forcing of life's complexities into molds, but relative stability in the lives of these future editors somewhat reduces this problem. In fact, these eighteenth-century journalists essentially issued from the urban, though not merchant, bourgeoisie. Just over twenty (two-thirds of the total known) had middle-class backgrounds. Four lawyers and four royal officials sired future editors, and sons of four Protestant clergymen formed another group. Of the forty-two editors whose religion may be discerned, seventeen later directed foreign periodicals and eleven of these worshipped in Protestant – exclusively Huguenot – churches. Four other editors came from merchant families, but in each case the head of the family operated a bookstore. Above those with middle-class origins were three with noble heritage – the children of a seigneur, a naval officer, and a ranking royal official. Eight others possessed lifestyles inferior to the majority from the middle class, and, among this poorer group, three seem to have been reared in poverty – one as an orphan and two as sons of journeymen. The other five were offspring of master craftsmen so their existence, if not truly bourgeois, still may have been comfortable. But all told, the editors emerged neither from the powerful nor the unfortunate but, as scholars have established for other parts of lettered society, from the non-merchant middle class. As such, they reinforce the growing conviction that no rising group of capitalists sparked the "siècle des lumières."[14]

Not only did these editors enjoy a comfortable lifestyle, but they also benefitted from substantial education. Deducting the two women who very likely depended on tutors,[15] and eight whose educational experience remains unknown, I found that thirty-four of the other thirty-seven finished secondary school. Of this group, thirty attended schools and seminaries for advanced degrees. Although three earned law degrees and one a medical diploma, astonishingly the other twenty-six (seven Protestants among them) trained for the clergy. It is difficult to believe that some aspect of seminary training encouraged people to turn eventually to journalism. Rather, my suspicion is that school teachers, who were themselves most often members of the clergy, identified their brightest pupils for the first order. Consequently, many who took up this calling possessed substantial intellectual capacities and inquisitiveness, traits that prepared one splendidly for any sort of career in lettered society.[16] Indeed, several individual biographies of editors – especially that of Elie-Catherine Fréron – reinforce this view that it was the sort of person who entered the clergy, not the clerical experience, that explains why so many future directors of periodicals possessed such a background.[17]

Turning to the adult lives of the editors, this analysis must now pursue their several occupational directions. Career development greatly influenced all the rest of editors' lives, so it becomes necessary to follow each choice.

The most common step from respectable backgrounds and specialized training to running a periodical – true for thirty-two (all men) of the forty-seven in this survey – came, not through any interest in journalism, but because of a desire to participate in the world of letters. Although some hesitated before leaving their hometowns and student preparation, most cast their lot as writers or scholars by their early twenties. A few managed to make this an evolutionary transition, for example, sliding from priest to philosophy teacher. Four of the Protestant ministers, though none of the Catholic priests, even continued their pastoral duties. But for a variety of reasons, most of these people sharply diverged from their earlier course into the literary world, usually out of a quite independent inclination for a different career and lifestyle. Of course, exceptions exist such as that of the Jesuit who, finding his order disbanded in 1762, simply began to write for a living. But whatever their route to periodical publication, these thirty-two future editors had already experienced the world of letters.

Indeed, this large group performed a wide range of functions in literary society before they entered journalism. They composed all sorts of fiction – comedies, tragedies, poetry, and novels. Several focused on translating while others worked in editing. A not insignificant number published in the interrelated fields of philosophy and theology as well as those of science and medicine. Others worked in the academy as professors, teachers, librarians, and archivists, and several combined a variety of these functions.

Moreover, the editors were, on the whole, reasonably if not extraordinarily successful in these careers. Contemporaries, though not posterity, quite favorably regarded a few of these future editors. For example, the Académie française had already elected to its membership the dramatist Louis de Boissy when at age fifty-six he commenced his journalistic career.[18] At the other end of the spectrum rested an equally small cluster of future editors who had met as yet with little success. Among these was François La Belonie whose career as a dance master began after eight years as a Jesuit. Finally, he spent some time as a writer for the publisher Antoine Giroud, who eventually made him editor of the *Courrier d'Avignon*. Franz-Michel Leuchsenring cannot be said to have accomplished much more. Born in Germany, Leuchsenring numbered Johann Gottfried von Herder among his friends, but as this intellectual giant and his coterie came to know the future editor better, their amity turned to scorn. With his work disdained, Leuchsenring literally fled to Paris to take up journalism. Nonetheless, editors most commonly neither made it to the Académie française nor worked in such difficult circumstances as Leuchsenring and La Belonie. Although the twentieth century scarcely knows the name, François-Louis-Claude Marin held a high reputation in his day. Ordained a priest, he first worked as a tutor in 1742. His interest in intellectual life led him to resign from the Church and earn a law degree, but, most important, he began writing on a variety of subjects including history and music. Twenty years of reasonably conformist work earned Marin sufficient credit that the minister St. Florentin appointed him a censor in 1762, and in 1763 the police chief elevated him to a high position in the Librairie. His reliability in this job plus his skills as a writer brought him the editorship of the governmentally controlled

Gazette de France in 1771.[19] This man was surely not an unknown when he accepted this post, nor was Henri-David Chaillet when he assumed the editorship of the *Nouveau Journal helvétique*. In fact, his sermons and his theological pronouncements had already received recognition.[20] Overall the records of Chaillet and Marin exemplified the previous accomplishments of most of the editors.

Such achievements, of course, meant that most directors of periodicals had spent significant time in the world of letters before taking up journalism. Indeed, they were already well along in life when they took up editorial duties in any regular capacity. Seven began in their twenties, fifteen in their thirties, six in their forties, three in their fifties, and one at age sixty-three. Their median age was thirty-seven, the mean 35.2.

Why these mature, largely successful men of letters entered the world of journalism cannot be easily discovered. Most of what we know about these individuals comes from obituaries or from notices composed by contemporary historians. Such chroniclers, who faithfully recorded the activities of their subjects, tended to paint a rosy portrait of their motivations.

Nonetheless, the most credible scraps of evidence available all suggest that editors embraced journalism because personal disappointments or financial needs forced them to do so. Such was definitely the case with Leuchsenring who appears to have begun his *Journal de lecture* to increase his meager earnings and to show up his former friends. But even those with more successful careers seem to have joined the Fourth Estate when they found themselves with financial difficulties. Joseph Buchoz apparently began to edit periodicals, not only to increase the dissemination of his ideas, but also to acquire needed funds.[21] And even members of the Académie française turned to journalism in difficult straits. The playwright Louis de Boissy accepted the editorship of the *Gazette de France* in 1750 in order to earn extra income. The publisher forced him out after eighteen months of operating this newspaper because his knowledge of politics remained inadequate. But in 1755 while his comedies were still drawing poorly, Boissy agreed to edit another governmentally approved periodical, the *Mercure de France*. Marmontel, a key Encyclopédiste and prominent member of the Académie française, related the circumstance under which Boissy received this new position.

> Mme de Pompadour had me called and said to me: "Do you know that La Bruyere has died in Rome? He held the privilège of the *Mercure*; this privilège brought him 25,000 livres of rente; there's enough there to make more than one happy; and we have a plan that a new license of the *Mercure* will require pensions to be paid to the men of letters. You know them. Name those who could use the editorship and will be interested." I named Crébillon, d'Alembert, Boissy and yet some others. . . . When she came to Boissy she asked

me: "Is Boissy not rich? I believe he's at least comfortable. . . ." "No Madame, he is poor but he hides his poverty." "He has written so many plays," she insisted. "Yes but all these have not enjoyed the same success; and it is necessary to live. Boissy is so unfortunate that except for a friend who discovered his situation he would have died last winter from hunger. Lacking bread, too proud to ask anyone, he closed himself in his house with his wife and son and resolved to die together . . . when this helpful friend forced the door and saved them –" "Ah! God," cried Mme de Pompadour, "you make me shiver. I'm going to recommend him to the King."

According to Marmontel, this conversation led directly to Boissy's appointment to edit the *Mercure*, a position he held until his death in 1758.[22] Although this account probably overdramatizes Boissy's impoverished condition, it certainly supports the contention that the editors participated in the Fourth Estate out of necessity not choice. Moreover, Mme. de Pompadour's reasoning reveals that, not only men of letters, but also courtiers expected that literary figures entered journalism only when financial need dictated.

Despite the sort of circumstances which led these men to their new occupation, once in it they apparently threw themselves into this work. First, most did not simply prostitute themselves by taking up any kind of journalism regardless of their prior interests. Few mimicked Boissy, the playwright trying to edit the political reports of the *Gazette de France*. More typical were Augustin Roux, an eminent doctor, who worked on publicizing medicine, and Pierre Clément, forced out of the clergy because of his love of the theater, who reported on literature.[23] In addition, most stayed in the field for a long time. The thirty-two people in this group of intellectuals-turned-journalists spent over one-half of their lives in their new trade until the Revolution altered the terms of journalism. More precisely, these editors worked in journalistic jobs some twelve years of the twenty-one that remained to them before 1789, a useful benchmark for the collapse of the profession, if not for the medium. The median participation registered precisely 50 per cent. This dedication along with their specialization added up to significant commitment.

Interestingly, neither society nor the editors themselves believed that they had suffered any lasting stigma from their work on periodicals. Indeed, because editing did not commonly require full-time attention, all but two continued their earlier academic and literary activities. Furthermore, generally they seemed to recover the momentum possessed prior to the problem that led them to periodical publishing. Of course, exceptions exist. Joseph Buchoz, hoping to earn wealth in journalism and achieve fame, actually saw his circumstances continually undermined by investments in his own paper. More typically, Jean-Baptiste Ladvocat continued to publish in his chosen fields during his tenure as editor of the *Annales typographiques*.[24] One of his associates on the *Annales typographiques*, Jean Goulin, coupled an entry into journalism with a great increase in his other writings. In fact, before commencing journalism in 1760, the first ten years of Goulin's scholarship had yielded three publications. From 1760 to 1789 he spent over twelve years on the staffs of six different periodicals and at the same time authored sixty-five different titles. Nine academies throughout Europe elected him to membership.[25] Goulin's exceptional success is only the best example of how journalism permitted, and may have even abetted, these editors to return to or surpass prior levels of literary work.

If the principal passage into and through journalism included a long, successful initiation into the society of letters followed by a downturn and then a recovery period, others had a quite different experience. The fifteen other editors of Parisian and foreign papers adopted several approaches, but one attracted more than the rest. This group included very significant individuals as well. Four future directors – Jean-Louis Aubert, J.-B.-A. Suard, François Morénas, and Elie-Catherine Fréron – went almost directly from home and school into journalism. Each took only brief or aimless detours so that school provided their only significant experience before journalism. This led them to news writing at fairly young ages – 20, 21, 27, and 31 – on average ten years earlier than those who had formerly been teachers or writers.

Aubert, Suard, Morénas, and Fréron shared not only an early entrance into journalism, but also the reason for selecting this occupation. They all needed paid work. Suard, his education interrupted because he sided with a classmate who had duelled with a nobleman, migrated to Paris to live by his pen. He found, however, that he could talk far better than he could write, so he whiled away time in salons. He finally admitted his need for remuneration by accepting an invitation from his friend François Arnaud to help edit the *Journal étranger*.[26] A need for money likewise took Elie Fréron to journalism.[27] Identified by the Jesuits as a brilliant pupil, Fréron was already teaching at Louis-le-Grand by his late teens. But his love for the theater proved so powerful that he commonly shed his clerical garb to attend. When detected, he was shipped off to Alençon, and he feared he would spend the remainder of his life in dreary burgs. Fréron quit the Jesuits, repaired to Paris, and called upon an uncle who was a writer and who might assist his job hunt. His relative, in fact, knew abbé P.-F.-G. Desfontaines, perhaps the most accomplished journalistic critic of his day. Fréron received a job from Desfontaines that included an apprenticeship in criticism. Although scholars know less of the circumstances of Aubert and Morénas, the broad outline of their stories resembles those of Fréron and Suard.

These four initiates into journalism also spent much of the remainder of their lives prior to 1789 in this field. Suard worked 13 of 40 years, Fréron

29 of 37, Morénas 36 of 41, and Aubert all 38. Both Fréron and Morénas would have matched Aubert's lifetime commitment had various difficulties not deprived them from time to time of their journals.

Despite getting their start in and devoting most of their lives to journalism, these four also found that the profession did not in any way block their paths to success. Elected to the Académie française, Suard also became wealthy. Though he remained in debt, Fréron earned substantial amounts as well as fame and notoriety in the world of letters. Aubert's wealth remains unknown, but he exercised considerable authority within the government on the development of the press. Although Morénas labored in relative obscurity, he authored dozens of books and pamphlets on Avignon where he wrote for the *Courrier d'Avignon*. There he surely was a figure of consequence. When one considers the rather difficult problems confronting these men in their youth, journalism, rather than stunting their prospects, apparently enhanced their future.

The patterns of adult behavior of these four journalists match more than one might expect those of the thirty-two editors from literary and academic life. To be sure, the thirty-two entered journalism at middle age while the smaller cohort knew little else. Despite this divergence, both groups seemingly approached their new activities unexcitedly even though the larger cluster must have felt greater apprehension. As their lives progressed, their differences narrowed since both groups took journalism seriously, and it gave literary success to both groups.

Adding the final eleven editors to this analysis does little to alter this picture. The very diversity of the pre-journalistic experience of this remaining pool does, however, blur that aspect of the collective portrait. This last group entered journalism from very different points. Three were booksellers in their thirties; one was a very young private secretary to the publisher of the journal he eventually edited; three middle-aged Protestant ministers whose main interests were pastoral worked on a literary journal; another twenty-three-year-old minister, angry with the Huguenot Church, left his flock to commence a career in political reporting; two wealthy widows, one thirty-eight and the other perhaps elderly, bought and edited a paper to make a mark and propagate their beliefs; and one young man, Jean Luzac, trained in the law but belonging to a publishing family, apparently participated in the business to fulfill family wishes.[28] This variety makes generally diffuse the conclusions one can draw about how editors prepared themselves, but these lives do offer some slight and tentative modification to the model of other directors of periodicals. Among this group of nine were only two people – the two widows – who obviously set out to become journalists. Of course, the silence on others may mean that these two were not alone in their motivations, but evidence of an interest and eagerness to enter journalism exists only for them and suggest they provide more of an exception than an alternative.

Furthermore, even with this wide range of backgrounds, these thirteen had similar experiences to the other editors'. Indeed, they too devoted much of their lives to this occupation. They gave just over one-half of their remaining years before the Revolution to the business (14.6 of 27.5). This percentage was almost exactly the same as their peers'; similarly journalism did not damage their reputations. They all emerged at least at the point they had earlier achieved; Luzac did even better and rode journalism to fame and great influence.

Even though the editors of Paris and foreign papers greatly resembled one another, their peers in the provincial press offered a very different profile. Only one of the nine provincials, René Alexis Joyneau-Desloges, had a career profile that resembled that of other editors. Although scholars have as yet uncovered little about him, he evidently moved from law into journalism and directed at least two periodicals – one in La Rochelle and one in Poitiers. His published writings suggest that he saw himself as a man of letters, using his paper as an opportunity to express himself. Such details, though incomplete incline one toward the opinion that Joyneau-Desloges would not have felt uncomfortable with most of his equals in the capital and beyond the frontier.[29]

Nonetheless, the remainder of the provincials present quite a different appearance from other editors. The editor of the paper in Lille, Joseph Paris de l'Épinard, was an adventurer of a sort that rarely frequented journalism. Although the specific details of his life remain somewhat shrouded, l'Épinard showed up in Lille in 1776 with a wife and a large amount of money. Contemporaries believed that he had acquired wealth by agreeing to marry and then relocate the mistress of a rich man from Holland. He lived ostentatiously without any obvious means of support, until 1781 when he used some of his funds to purchase the privilège for a paper in Lille. He evinced an intense interest in his new property, promoted progressive ideas, and took an active role in the Revolution.[30]

Six other provincial journalists in this sample (Chevrier from Poitou remains an unknown) not only contrasted with their Parisian and foreign equivalents, but also shared a common background – that of bookdealer. Although three in the larger group of editors also held this occupation, a comparison reveals that the provincials possessed much more substantial assets. In sum then, editors from French cities other than Paris entered this business after having acquired a very different set of skills.

The preponderance of bookdealers reveals the dominance of a certain type of experience among the provincial editors, but fragmentary and scattered documentation makes it thus far impossible to construct a nuanced composite picture of these book merchant/editors. Nonetheless, a superb study by Jean Quéniart on the book trade in Rouen allows a general understanding of Etienne-Vincent Machuel, one of the five selected in this sample.[31] Furthermore, the evidence available on the other editors – Aimé de la Roche in Lyons, the Labottière brothers in Bordeaux, and the Couret de Villeneuve family in Orléans makes it reasonable to assume that their interests and concerns conformed in broad outline to those of Machuel.

Born in 1752, Etienne-Vincent Machuel was the last of a Rouen printing family whose labors had begun in the mid-seventeenth century. During this period no fewer than eight Machuels had served as masters in the guild of bookdealers and printers, and as many as five had simultaneously held this post. Indeed, five of the twenty-five Rouen masters operating both print shops and book stores in the early eighteenth century originated from this one family. This substantial number of participants did not always guarantee the Machuels' financial success, and indeed the family's wealth seems to have risen and fallen. However, a substantial level of comfort had been achieved by the time Etienne-Vincent entered the business. Through various inventories made of the Machuel residence during the Revolution, a general view of the status of this close-knit family emerges. Items listed included eight chairs covered in yellow damask, four others with embroidered upholstery, a desk inlaid with silver, a wall tapestry, and a gold-framed painting. Such glittering furnishings surely made the Machuels comfortable among Rouen's bourgeoisie. This family had not easily achieved its wealth, for the members had risked a great deal. From the beginning they had participated in the clandestine as well as the legal book trade, and several had been fined and even imprisoned. Etienne-Vincent also took part in this practice, but most likely he entered journalism through another part of his business. Already publishing an almanach for Rouen, he may have believed that he had the proper experience to produce a periodical whose content and periodicity would be somewhat related to this earlier effort. In any case, the *Affiches de Rouen* was and remained simply one product of a businessman with many other cares. Interestingly, whatever his motives for entering, he stayed with it – indeed, some twenty-three years. Yet one should not portray Machuel solely as a crass profiteer in his journalistic endeavors, utterly uninterested in intellectual topics. In fact, his long experience in books surely counted for something, and the contents of his affiches revealed at least some interest in these matters.

Etienne-Vincent Machuel typified the provincial editors, though evidence suggests that the others achieved greater balance than he between their economic and intellectual interests. More than the rest, he seemed to be involved in illegal books; he also appeared generally less committed to stimulating the intellectual interests of his community by promoting reading societies and their ilk. Aimé de la Roche perhaps best revealed the inclinations of this group by his tireless use of his periodical to publicize the local interchange of ideas.[32] Tentatively then, these book-dealers approached their new occupation from a long background as merchants and with a continued commitment both to their businesses and to the provincial intelligentsia. And like Machuel, once in, they stayed, as Table 4-1 shows, a significant time. Comprising the bulk of provincial editors, they characterized this general group.

Despite considerable differences, these two types of editors – national and provincial – possessed essential similarities. The producers of the nationally distributed press, located in Paris and across the borders, mainly were men of letters who regretfully took up the pen under straitened circumstances. Elsewhere editors were businessmen. This enormous difference, should not, however, blind us to one way that their motivations paralleled one another. With the unusual circumstances of those coming from the world of letters and the provincials' business background which allowed a relatively frank admission of monetary considerations, finances seem to have generally provided a very conscious motivation for embarking on journalism. In the world of letters, this would be rather embarrassing. Yet, even as all these editors sought a money making vocation, they did not abandon their intellectual aspirations. And they all seemed to stay in journalism for extraordinary periods of time. Their emphases may have been somewhat different but a basic concordance existed.

In fact, the shared characteristics of the careers in the press may explain how journalists conceived this occupation. As earlier chapters have indicated, periodicals resembled one another so some agreed-upon notions of what journalists were supposed to do must have been shared. Yet there is little evidence of professionalism. Professionalism, crudely defined as a set of internal norms governing an occupation or an *esprit* characteristic of a work environment, was, in general, new in the eighteenth century. Nonetheless, there were stirrings among many groups, but not for journalism. As we have already seen, some of the main targets of journalists – the authors of fiction and nonfiction – could castigate the editors without eliciting any defense. Surely a proud occupational group would have responded, but journalists remained silent. Furthermore, one finds virtually no commentary about how to edit or write a periodical. Press histories were written,[33] but discussions regarding work culture or techniques failed to surface. As for the two journalists who believed themselves trained in the field – Desfontaines and Fréron – others perceived them as renegades.

Perhaps one might explain this conception of journalism – a combination of shared practices and no *esprit* – at least in part by the career projections of editors. In the business over a long period, they could be expected because of their knowledge of the medium to benefit from and

136

be influenced by the work of others. Such habits might explain a tendency to formalize common journalistic practices. But the lack of assertiveness may have come from their view of their work as a response to the need to make money. As the Old Regime, even the mercantile sector, questioned this motive, so it might have undermined pride in this endeavor. Particularly difficult might have been some code of journalism, given the circumstances of these individuals' involvement. Thus the facets of their career can go some distance to explaining the ideal of the journalist.[34]

This examination of editors illuminates, not only the development of French journalism, but also of literary society in general. Revealing of the way the world of letters operated was the ability of foreign and Parisian editors to redeem their positions in learned society, even after stooping to work in journalism. This lack of derogation, even after slumming, shows that intellectuals had not adopted a rigid status system. Of course, journalists had presented the proper social and educational backgrounds originally to qualify. But their ability to recoup or retain their position indicates that the reality of the society of letters conformed, at least to some extent, with the governmental and widely accepted view that the intellectual milieu constituted a meritocracy.

This portrait of editors provides another insight into the literary community. Since many editors moved quite freely between journalism and intellectual circles, historians should regard the traits of these editors as at least roughly descriptive of writers and scholars. This suggests a connection between editors and the men of letters that yields a surprising conclusion. As future journalists attended seminaries in extraordinary numbers, perhaps this was true of literary figures. Considering French intellectual life with its general hostility to tradition as resulting from a group of churchmen seems shocking. But, in fact, this finding proves more helpful than problematic. These churchmen consisted of two groups – ex-Catholic clergy and practicing Protestants – both of whom found much to oppose in the Old Regime. One would not want to explain the Enlightenment simply as a protest by alienated Catholics and devious Huguenots, but their presence may have played a part. Ministers likewise dominated English, German, and even American intellectual life, but these clergymen did not hold antipathies toward the reigning political and religious beliefs.[35] The more advanced thinking in France may have stemmed from the kind of people who were putting the ideas forward. Scholars will know better whether this point can be sustained after they have studied more middle range intellectuals both individually and collectively.

5

THE FRENCH GOVERNMENT AND THE PERIODICAL

Interposed between the journalists and the over twenty million French people was the French government – in particular the central administration in Versailles. No other set of officials held nearly as much authority as the royal center. Until late in the reign of Louis XIV, other officials competed – primarily those in the parlements and the Church which after all also exercised secular authority. But by the eighteenth century, the royal administration monopolized the power of direct regulation.[1] Judicial officials, the Church, and other interested parties had to work through Versailles. One might still bring a lawsuit but that kind of control paled beside the authority held at Versailles.[2] In fact, by mid-century the greatest threat to royal power lay in the independence of royal provincial administrators, who often had great latitude.

States in which individual periodicals were published did possess some authority. Their power deserves study but would require investigation far beyond the confines of a general history like this. Nonetheless, some of these individual countries exerted relatively little control. Both the Dutch and the English regulated fewer aspects of reportage. In addition, important journalists had great ability to evade the power of individual states.[3] Both Simon-Nicolas-Henri Linguet and Pierre Rousseau specifically chose a locale that would tolerate them.[4] This ability to move their operations undermined the control that any one place could exert. Not atypical was the *Courrier d'Avignon*, whose concession to its location in a papal enclave, was to temper its reporting on the Vatican.[5] Doubtless, such lessened independence proved tolerable because the news most important to Frenchmen occurred in places other than the Papal dominions. Balancing the foreign governments' weakness was their general ability to deny Francophone papers admission to their market. Nonetheless, all this paled compared with the power that Versailles wielded, at home of course, but even abroad because of the large readership to which it might grant access.

Explaining the negotiations between the central administration and the press thus becomes critical for this book and more generally. As the closing paragraphs of this chapter explain, comprehending the pattern of governmental policy toward the press casts light on other aspects of the regulation of printed materials and, more broadly, on the Old Regime administration. Perhaps the most significant part of this chapter is the periodization employed. Very few other attempts, especially outside the area of fiscality, exist that describe, for as long a period as this, the development of policy. More such efforts would permit better understanding of the chronology of the Old Regime, which most often appears paced by the occurrence of problems or by the succession of reigns. But the evolution of approaches to the press developed here depended on the role of various ministries. As opposed to an Old Regime of growing problems and failing kings, this book explores different officials whose skills and techniques worked in a period that might be better likened to a pendulum than a downhill slide.

To comprehend officials' actions toward the press necessitates investigating both procedures and goals. Here "procedures" refers to the methods of administration required while "goals" means the reporting that the government thought the papers should ideally carry. These goals provide an important indicator of the actual influence exerted on the periodical press. Because journals and newspapers required the post for efficient distribution, the authorities had a means to compel cooperation. Also, the periodicity of the press gave officials a fixed target. A paper hoped to remain in business, thus making itself an easy mark. For these reasons, government policies easily generated pressure that the papers surely felt.

Comprehending governmental goals for the press is not a simple matter because very often they rested upon assumptions that went unstated in individual documents and were never systematically assembled. And even the procedures need to be set in context. Thus, teasing out the meaning of official actions requires first assessing the official baseline set for the press. Or, put another way: what did the administration intend as requirements for the press from 1745 to the Revolution? Regardless of variations in expectations, what were the basic guidelines?

C. G. Lamoignon de Malesherbes, reputedly among the most liberal authorities directly regulating periodicals, flatly stated that he decided whether to permit periodicals according to *raison d'état*.[6] The problem lies in knowing how the government defined this political consideration for the press. The rambunctious journalist Elie-Catherine Fréron understood that the press was free as long as "Religion, the state, and morality were respected."[7] These tough statements from surprising sources remain largely vague, and as will become apparent, somewhat misleading.

Ideally, the laws should provide some clear-cut rules that would indicate the inclinations or desires of the state. And a considerable body of royal jurisprudence on this matter existed. A *Code de la librairie*, published in 1723, gathered together such laws,[8] and confirmed two principles. First, publication required a privilege that granted a monopoly over that material. Second, attacks on religion were proscribed. Later edicts of 1744, 1756, and 1767 reinforced these positions. But these laws still indicate little about actual policy, or governmental disposition, because many of these published rules concern procedures for books, not periodicals. And more important, their strictures remain vague about what ideas will or will not be permitted.

There is no collected documentary base to explain what the administration expected the press to be, but it does seem that one might approach this subject by looking at two separate branches: the state press and the private (at least nominally) press. The approach here is first to establish the baseline for the latter press, evaluate its similarity to state competitors, and then examine governmental shifts in adjusting the overall guidelines to the private papers.

Sifting through the periodicals' content and officials' correspondence can allow one to approximate, at least for the period here studied, the government's intentions for the periodicals lacking any official imprimatur. Disagreement existed within the administration on the desired goals, but one may come to the following judgments about the most important topics on which the officials hoped to restrain the periodicals. On the state: Discussions of the French monarchy should focus on the king and contain a minimum of references to other authorities and political conflicts or difficulties. The activities of the government should be treated positively: at times negative information had to be included but greatly soft pedalled. Other issues – culture, natural disasters, and the like – that possessed political implications but stayed far away from formal politics enjoyed more freedom. Latitude existed for reporting on foreign affairs, but journalists should take care if a report might implicate French policies. Exactly what was tolerated is almost impossible to say, but clearly greater toleration was allowed than on domestic matters. Perhaps it might be best to say that the government desired an interpretation well along the positive spectrum but accepted that in some circumstances (e.g., military defeats) the view might remain somewhat problematic. The policy that opened this door the widest was the toleration of a fairly open discussion of allies and opponents' affairs that at least by implication, could dispute a roseate vision. But this alternate understanding could not stand unedited; rather officials wanted publishers to manage problematic news while playing up positive news. Such careful presentation guaranteed that even the non-French reporting would be largely supportive of the generally positive French reports. The difference was one of degree, with negative news accepted as long as it was placed into an overall positive picture. And there was another standard for news of relative unconcern to France which might be reported according to the wishes of editors. Almost always left untouched by these controls – though settling matters on behalf of France could have an effect – were the reports on various political structures in other countries. Although over this entire period the government thus consistently permitted some degree of freedom in presenting foreign internal arrangements, the policy in essence mutated after the beginning of the American revolutionary war. Continuing this policy in such circumstances obviously produced a more deleterious effect on the absolutist monarchy.

In the fields of literature and philosophy, the government would abide no direct critique of the Church, though as previous chapters indicate, support for the philosophes proved possible. As long as articles neither directly assaulted religion nor covered raging controversies which *ipso facto* would constitute an assault, the government tolerated such discussions. But beyond the High Enlightenment into its more extreme offspring – particularly the materialists – which emerged in the late 1750s,[9] officials apparently drew the line even if the discussions remained abstract. Clearly, the government allowed a wider berth on culture than politics. What the preservation of morals apparently meant in this context was a prohibition against overheated prose. Respectability was required, especially when reporting on individuals. One's actions, but not one's personal qualities, might be reported. Labeling as "personalities" the invective it forbade, the government by such action would make both virulent polemics and exposés nigh impossible.

To achieve these goals of reporting – which most importantly forbade frontal assaults on the pillars of the Old Regime while still allowing some oblique critiques – the government hoped to rely in part on particular procedures.[10] One was the government's insistence on prior – that is, prepublication – approval of the contents of the press. Furthermore, the existence of three avowedly state designated papers – the *Gazette de France*, the *Mercure de France*, and the *Journal des savants* – points to another procedural aspect of the governmental ideal. By 1745, the beginning point of this study, competitors already existed to the exclusive privileges held in theory by two of the state's periodicals – the *Gazette de France* and the *Journal des savants*. Evidently, journals published abroad entered France while those at home also seemed to endure. The government made special exceptions for some, and others pretended not to be journals, even as they achieved periodical status.[11] In addition clandestine journals, including the *Nouvelles écclesiastiques*, kept the government busy trying to control them.[12] Of course, such secret journals involved no compromises or deals by the government, but all the others meant some recognizable retreat. Still, the administration persistently claimed a monopoly on reporting for the governmental papers, and

141

regarded as irregular the existence of any other paper. The commitment to these three would seem to indicate that part of the administration's ideal was this small, state-controlled press. Evidently, such a press would be easily politically manipulated as well as keep the profits of journalism within France.

Understanding how such goals and procedures, which one might label constricting but not overwhelmingly tough, came to exist requires more evidence than is currently available. Malesherbes clearly believed that these aims had already been in place for some time. Perhaps they were a response to a burgeoning public interest in some cultural independence. Malesherbes, throughout his long tenure, may have turned these standards into a baseline. Although all policy makers on occasion made adjustments – occasionally more stringent, usually more lenient – these approaches prevailed as a benchmark throughout the period under consideration.

Before exploring how well the government pursued these goals and developed their processes of control in the privately held press, it is worth examining the extent of domination over the three papers with declared links to the administration. The approach here will be to scrutinize the governmental procedure and then evaluate its goals.

Oldest of the state papers and the second periodical published in France, the *Gazette de France* dated back to 1631. Founded by an acolyte of Richelieu, Théophraste Renaudot, the *Gazette* was a privately owned concern for most of its existence up to the Revolution. Although scholars have thus far only produced case studies of how the government directed the *Gazette* during certain periods, the paper's banal content indicates an overall tight control. In addition, the intervals for which solid evidence exists reinforce the impression of strict governmental oversight. First, during the early Renaudot years the newspaper was expected to be the willing purveyor of the government point of view. Richelieu composed much material to be directly inserted into the *Gazette*. Furthermore, the government supplied more neutral information to interest and inform readers. To ensure that the *Gazette* did not use the remainder of its space for untoward purposes, the government set up a committee, including Père Joseph, Richelieu's right hand man. With this strategy, the government could at the least try to guarantee that nothing negative would slip into the *Gazette*.[13]

The Renaudot family held on to the *Gazette* until 1719, but it afterwards passed through various hands becoming the sole property of the Minister of Foreign Affairs in 1761.[14] Perhaps, the government earlier also directly operated it, but that remains unclear. Until 1787, the eve of the Revolution, the foreign ministry owned the periodical, but it too hired various editors from outside the government.[15] A mémoire by one of these editors allows us to observe, at least during the 1760s, the intricate controls developed to guarantee the correct political stance. After the copy of the *Gazette* was prepared, it circulated through the government so that each minister and other top officials could make the corrections they considered desirable. Then two censors, Gerard and Rayneval, collected and assembled these changes and instructed the editor minutely on them.[16] Whether or not this procedure later remained precisely the same, other evidence points to continued tight control. For example, in 1784 Miromesnil, keeper of the seals, complained to Count de Vergennes, the minister of foreign affairs, about an announcement of some engravings slated to appear in an edition of Voltaire's work. The Assembly of the Clergy argued that the etchings should not be mentioned because they had been suppressed in France. Vergennes then struck the announcement from the proofs.[17] Such micromanagement apparently characterized the relationship with the *Gazette*.

While the precise mechanism of control surely varied over time, all evidence points to the government's general commitment to correcting deviations that it disliked. A role also existed for the government as provider of news. Richelieu seems to have regarded the *Gazette* as his private publishing house;[18] while ministers in the second half of the eighteenth century continued this practice, their purpose changed somewhat. Later officials apparently put more energy than their predecessors into providing fresh news to help the *Gazette* retain its readers. This concern was, as will be further discussed, part of an effort to compete better against foreign gazettes in the late eighteenth century. Choiseul, foreign minister from 1759 to 1770, encouraged the intendants to submit items.[19] He also recruited ambassadors, but only those to the Levant seem to have responded.[20] Despite these disappointments, the content of the press reveals the ministries themselves as a rich source.[21]

Such a change from mainly providing propaganda to soliciting stimulating articles seems to suggest that the *Gazette* of the eighteenth century possessed significant independence from government prerogatives. *But* this alteration did not portend such a radical transformation. Officials understood that the *Gazette de France* represented the government and that it conformed to even more strenuous rules than other periodicals. While it no longer produced as much propaganda, through omissions it depicted a world always essentially congenial to the Bourbon perspective. Using this more subtle approach, the *Gazette* carefully shaped coverage. In the main area that the general policy left open to private papers – a thorough if managed approach to foreign news – initial forays into this part of the *Gazette de France* suggest that this newspaper remained qualitatively different with much less permitted. And as it was expected to represent governmental positions, the government might intervene to guarantee this goal. All these controls gave this press far fewer options than the private papers.

The government limited somewhat its intervention into both the *Mercure* and the *Journal des savants*. Founded in 1665, private owners held the *Journal des savants* throughout its Old Regime existence. It always covered a vast array of subjects excluding formal politics.[22] Before the eighteenth century, the *Journal* sometimes proceeded fairly independently. With the new century, however, the government began to exercise substantial control through a variety of techniques. For the purposes of this study, one should begin with the final resignation of abbé Bignon, a well-known scholar and friend of Fontenelle, who sporadically had led the *Journal des savants* from 1701. When he quit in 1739, the state commenced selecting the chief editor from intellectuals employed by the state, most often censors. Apparently the head of the censorship reinforced the editor's efforts.[23] Pre-publication proofs were evidently sent to the Librairie, because traces remain of Malesherbes's orders calling for rewrites.[24] An even better sense of the authority and the weight of the official hand can be gained from the *Journal des savants*'s response to a governmental request:

> I have reread with care the extract of the *Mémoires*; I have corrected several dates and phrases. What I have marked by the checks, I have suppressed. Your reflection is very just, and I believe that these details, which would be acceptable in another extract, are out of place here. I had only placed them here with repugnance.[25]

Such close supervision of the *Journal des savants* may have encouraged its efforts to support official positions. Furthermore, the quite conservative nature of the *Journal des savants*'s content further indicates that officials adhered to a policy that was more active than the standard.[26] Nonetheless, the administration apparently had no procedure for inserting its own positive reportage. It corrected the existing copy rather than creating it. Some alterations in focus could occur as when Malesherbes encouraged the editor of the *Journal des savants* to review favorably a work by a prominent parlementarian.[27] But this example probably shows only a particular instance of the administration's influence rather than the promotion of any general goals in the periodical. Such an effort paled compared with Richelieu's systematic insertion of material into the *Gazette* and is at least partly related to the administration's relative indifference to the kind of news covered by the *Journal des savants*. Still, comprehending clearly the governmental approach to the *Journal* requires more information than presently available.

The *Mercure de France* was not a governmental journal in the same sense as either the *Gazette de France* or the *Journal des savants*. Each of these latter held a monopoly or privilege over a different kind of news. Taken together, they claimed to possess just about everything worth reporting to the public at large, and anyone who wished to publish had to deal with them. Though they neither covered local events nor included advertising, even for these matters the *Gazette* held the monopoly.[28] Nonetheless, the *Mercure* too held a privileged place. From its very beginnings in 1672, it was allowed to exist, squeezing out a position as a humorous, gracious, and witty periodical. Even though covering much the same ground as the *Journal des savants*, the *Mercure*'s style meant that contemporaries envisioned it as something altogether different from its two more ponderous elders. Not only was the *Mercure* legally allowed to publish, it also received a government *imprimatur*. By 1684, the king directly granted the editor a pension. In particular, the *Maison du Roi* controlled the *Mercure*, although the administration always rented the periodical out to private individuals who selected the editor.[29]

This more tenuous relationship to the government seems to have spilled over onto the governmental effort to channel the *Mercure*. Evidently, the administration normally subjected the magazine to very thorough controls as the situation from 1778 to the Revolution revealed. During this period, the *Mercure* added a substantial section of political analysis to bolster its traditional literary content. Earlier it contained only a condensation of the *Gazette de France*.[30] In these new circumstances the editor of the *Gazette de France* nominated two censors – one in Paris, the other at Versailles – to oversee the political section. In addition, the ministry of foreign affairs had the right to view copy, and a censor in Paris examined the literary portion. Suzanne Tucoo-Chala, author of a very important biography of Panckoucke, suggests that the king possessed the right to a pre-publication reading.[31]

Despite elaborate formalistic controls, evidence points to a somewhat relaxed attitude toward the *Mercure*. In 1754, Malesherbes learned of an indiscretion in the *Mercure* in which the opinions of the French and English appeared without indicating the former's superiority. To his dismay, Malesherbes found out that the censor was not examining the copy of this periodical because of its governmental status.[32] It is difficult to believe that such a practice does not indicate a certain governmental indifference. This incident suggests that however well developed the system of control, the administration somewhat lackadaisically enforced it.

Furthermore, such a lack of attention indicates that the government set lower goals for the reporting in the *Mercure de France* than for the other journals. And after 1778 officials, in their desire to stimulate sales, definitely tolerated in the *Mercure* a range beyond state periodicals but surely near that allowed by their general policy. In an exchange of letters with Miromesnil, Vergennes, foreign minister from 1774 to 1787, indicated his willingness to permit the *Mercure* greater latitude than the *Gazette*.[33] Occasionally the *Mercure* ventured beyond the government's desired limits, exceeding them in a report about Thomas Jefferson's views on the existence of God. Such a transgression went neither un-noticed nor unpunished.[34] Finally, as will be discussed below, after 1784 the administration reduced controls for all political periodicals except the *Gazette de France*, and the *Mercure* escaped beyond the usual yardstick employed by administrators. One of its editors, Mallet du Pan, was able to exploit the reduction in royal pressure and imitate, at least to some degree, adventurous foreign journals.[35] But these very last years of the Old Regime constituted an exception; during the rest of the period, the *Mercure* generally went beyond other state publications but remained within the policy formulated for private papers. Of course, given the nature of these guidelines – an orally communicated set of mutual understandings that remained uncodified – variations were possible. Nonetheless, officials generally followed their implicit rules for the *Mercure*.

The government tried to do more with its own organs than simply erect more conservative alternatives to the private press. Beyond using this press as an excuse to block new competitors, officials tried to make them attractive. As mentioned above, the goals of the *Gazette* and the *Mercure* were at least somewhat loosened to make them more stimulating. Eugène Hatin has speculated that the government took over the *Gazette* to make it stronger.[36] Infusions of cash not only propped up these journals in bad times but generally allowed a lower price than the competition. With this corps of periodicals the government promoted its own version of the world. And, as will become apparent, sometimes, as during Panckoucke's involvement, these mouthpieces could become a central part of the strategy for handling the rest of the periodicals.

Despite all the efforts by government, the public was, with important exceptions, more conscious of these papers' weaknesses than strengths. Grimm, in the *Correspondance littéraire*, no doubt expressed the reservations of many:

> . . . it is also necessary to note that the characteristics of reserve, circumspection, and decency necessary for all work which appears under the auspices of the government, will infallibly blacken liberty which can be the sole interest of a work of this nature. On how many important questions will the authors not be permitted to have an opinion? How many excellent works will they not dare to name, much less to delve into with the good faith comfortable to intellectuals.[37]

The intermittent success of the *Gazette de France* and the amazing rebirth of Panckoucke reveal the limits of this judgment. Nonetheless, a substantial part of the readership remained at least occasionally suspicious and angry.

Not only could the government often not convince the public about the worth of its own press, officials also had problems constraining the emerging journals inside and outside the realm. Likewise, the appearance of journals throughout this period that published unacceptable fare indicates that the government conceived variations in its guidelines.[38] The following account focuses upon a struggle between conformity to and expansion of these governmental goals and procedures. This chapter will also consider governmental interaction with the affiches, but their special circumstances require postponing that discussion. Left aside because of a dearth of information, is the regulation of provincial literary magazines.

Tracking policy in greater detail still establishes only the most general approach adopted. Among many variations, authorities might hold different expectations for individual periodicals. More important, the hard theoretical line of *raison d'état* enunciated even by Malesherbes, provided a contrast to the openings – even those that the general policy supplied. Surely such pronouncements colored everything and provided a backdrop to all other policies. How both of the factors raised here operated can be investigated in individual case studies.

Here then the focus must rest on the more salient operations of the central administration. Insufficient documentation exists to see how the government operated precisely in the 1740s, so analysis must begin after that point. The Librairie, which also directed the book trade, held responsibility for regulating the discussion press. Its most famous director, Chrétien-Guillaume Lamoignon de Malesherbes (1721–1794), arrived after 1750 and controlled operations for the next thirteen years.

What historians know most about in Malesherbes's approach to the literary and philosophical press concerns those produced in France, the clear majority of this genre. During this period officials generally hewed to the official guidelines for the press, though they permitted expansion as well as some debate over personalities. Understanding governmental efforts toward the French press requires examining the two levels of regulation: first, how the government granted the right to publish, and then how the administration regulated extant periodicals.

Procedurally, the Librairie deviated somewhat from the plan that limited periodicals. Malesherbes himself would have personally preferred that purchasers decide the fate of publications, but he had to work within the Old Regime legal structure.[39] Malesherbes allowed more new literary and philosophical journals, granting them either a privilege or a permission. Privileges permitted the recipient a long-term right – thirty years was not uncommon. In addition, such a grant guaranteed a field of opportunity upon which no one might infringe. But privileges remained relatively uncommon and after 1760 were largely abandoned in favor of permissions.[40] These rights lasted only a relatively short term, were apparently easy to revoke, and offered no monopoly.[41]

Although the authorities opened the doors procedurally beyond the tight nominal standard, they did not abandon their commitment to the state-controlled journals. All recipients of either a privilege or permission had to make a cash settlement with the *Journal des savants*. In addition, the Librairie tried to reduce the number of grants in order to limit the challenges to the establishment's journals.[42] Once a journal received some sort of approval, it had to stay within the subject area granted to it.[43] The settlement reached with the *Gazette de commerce* provides a good example of how the government tried to make these privileges and permissions at least seem temporary. In granting the periodical a privilege, the government allowed a period of 30 years. The publisher had to indemnify the *Gazette de France* to the tune of 6,000 livres. After the expiration of the privilege, the project supposedly would be integrated into the *Gazette*.[44] Such terms, by requiring payment and emphasizing a return, made the privilege seem more like a loan, not permanent property. And this was among the greatest security offered.

Hoping indeed to keep a cap on the number of new periodicals, the government was not always able to force supplicants to accept these parameters. Particularly corrupting was the role of significant personages. Not uncommonly, journalists included in their appeals for access their claims of important supporters. One Chevalier de Laucaussale wrote to Malesherbes appealing for acceptance of his project to publish a literary journal. Among his arguments, he noted: "to make a success of the object I have presented to you, I have urged the most respectable and powerful people to act on my behalf, as close to you as to the court." Although Laucaussale quickly added that most of all he wanted Malesherbes's assent, he had made his point.[45] The archives document that these were not empty threats as important people intervened frequently and often effectively. But the administration was not always powerless to resist, and officials sometimes thwarted these requests. On occasion, Malesherbes successfully blocked publication, seemingly to limit competition.[46]

The limits of influence became clear in the negotiations concerning the *Conciliateur*. In 1759 the would-be editors assertively demanded that they be granted a privilege as their protector, the Count de la Marche, had promised it to them. Furthermore, they requested that their privilege bar the introduction of any competitor.[47] To this request, Malesherbes opposed a stubborn calm, outlining the problems. Anyone who wished to publish a literary magazine had to settle with the *Journal des savants*. Also, the editors' plan to rely on others' extracts could not be tolerated as no one might take another's work. Finally, no one could promise a privilege that would deny the publication of other periodicals. Malesherbes was discussing a permission, but this was a distinction lost on the editors of the *Conciliateur*. Clearly, Malesherbes's goal was to preserve his procedure – permit publication, but limit the newcomers' options. Offering a little conciliation of his own, Malesherbes also pointed out that if the principals feared a foreign journal from Mannheim, some help could be forthcoming. "Since this periodical is produced in a foreign country, motives always exist for preventing its entrance in order to favor the commerce of the king's subjects." Also important were the concerns of the Count de la Marche.[48]

All and all, this interchange remained a rather abrupt reading of the rules to the prospective editors. Interestingly, the sharpness also reflected Malesherbes's hostility to the pressure being applied to hurry the process. In a separate memo to his father, who was both Chancellor and the immediate supervisor of the Librairie, Malesherbes bitterly complained that respectable people provided shelter to those attempting to circumvent regulations. Then he loosened his own diatribe against influence:

> . . . the world of publishing as all the other objects of commerce is a good to which everyone has the same right and which is susceptible to no favors. The government only watches over it to maintain public order; and for the concerns of the authors' particular interest, it is necessary to establish equal laws. Success alone makes a difference . . . only the public is entitled to judge.[49]

Of course the government was doing much more than simply monitoring periodicals, and the public was not to be the judge. Yet the practical upshot of this letter is the director's rejection of influence.

With Malesherbes's tough stand and his resistance to pressure, a new phase in the struggle over the *Conciliateur* began. Beginning in late 1759 another very active protector, the Duke de Bourbon, entered the scene. Accepting the requirements imposed, the Duke sought both to indicate the problems to the editors and resolve them.[50] Letters continued to fly back and forth, and in January 1760 Bourbon wrote the head of the Librairie that the men of the paper understood and agreed to all conditions. But Bourbon could not resist throwing his weight around, reminding his correspondent of the Duke's own "true interest" in the *Conciliateur*.[51]

Perhaps it was this effort at intimidation that led Malesherbes to play a double game. On the one hand, Malesherbes really was responsible for helping finally conclude, on February 29, 1760, a deal with the *Journal des savants* in which the new periodical agreed to pay its forerunner three livres for every 500 sheets published. So involved was the director of the Librairie that he actually wrote two of the drafts and pencilled corrections on two others.[52]

Yet also present was a pattern of delay so persistent and so unusual that it seems likely that Malesherbes was dragging his feet. On January 7, 1760, he apologized to Bourbon for not replying and claimed to have been in the countryside. Nonetheless, asserted Malesherbes, the editors "must not be concerned about their business for which they are honored with the protection of your most serene highness."[53] Despite Malesherbes's obsequiousness, the delay continued, for on March 23, even after the contract with the *Journal des savants* had been signed and the conditions for publication evidently met, Bourbon requested that the right to publish be delivered.[54] In a letter to another noble supporter but apparently meant for Bourbon as well, Malesherbes expressed his dismay that he had as yet received no permission for the *Conciliateur*. Exclaiming that the delay so surprised him that he believed a conspiracy must exist, the director also added that he had no wish to undermine the editors of the *Conciliateur* and believed their permission must have already been delivered. Yet Malesherbes could not bring himself to be completely subservient and once again noted that rules were rules.[55] Just as Bourbon could not resist throwing his weight around, Malesherbes had to put in his bid for equal treatment.

And the footdragging persisted. In the last epistle extant on this matter, Bourbon wrote on April 6, 1760, that the "privilege" had never shown up. The duke, despite an earlier understanding that the *Conciliateur* was to be granted a permission, persisted in requesting a privilege. And this time he couched his request imperiously and demanded that the privilege be awarded. The duke further asserted that Malesherbes could, if he wished, release the document, but that the director had become personally committed to withholding it. And then, his temper flaring, Bourbon exclaimed: "Do not be surprised, sir, that I will bitterly complain and I strongly request that you fulfill your engagements with me."[56] Probably, indeed, this permission never appeared, as the most reliable list of Old Regime periodicals makes no mention of the *Conciliateur*.[57]

This account, if uncertainties in it may temporarily be left aside, surely reveals aristocratic influence at its weakest. In the end, after much negotiation this periodical apparently failed to gain approval because Bourbon pushed it so hard. Although the basic conditions had been fulfilled, Malesherbes apparently punished the editors for relying so heavily upon pressure. That Malesherbes criticized in his March letter to Bourbon the effort to circumvent rules seems irrelevant since an agreement had already been reached, but it showed the director's continued anger and explained his willingness to be punitive. Nonetheless, the account also reveals something about the power of influence. Notwithstanding the ultimate result, Malesherbes both used great politeness and worked diligently on an agreement between the *Conciliateur* and the

Journal des savants. These efforts show that despite the final end, he had to cover his tracks by these other activities. To accomplish his ultimate goal required great care in providing an escape route in case it did not work. In total, the saga of the *Conciliateur* seems to suggest a role for influence, that did not at all resemble absolute power.

The story of the *Conciliateur* thus indicates, not so much by its result as by Malesherbes's treacherous navigation of procedures, the difficulty of limiting expansion in the domestic literary press. Yet the willing or reluctant compromises made by authorities in procedural matters did not lead to a change in the goals for acceptable reporting – specifically in the subjects placed off limits for the press. The authorities wanted to refuse access to any periodical that would threaten the standards they upheld on morality, religion, and the state. Indeed, they even endeavored to raise the intellectual standards for journals that provided insufficient serious fare. Malesherbes rejected a legal journal because it proved more anecdotal than jurisprudential.[58] One of his censors likewise recommended the rejection of a demand because the sample submitted was poorly written. This official deemed it that of a famished author who, interested in making money, possessed little talent.[59]

The applicants themselves promised when applying for a privilege or permission that they would never have the nerve to challenge directly governmental standards. Most often, potential publishers toadied to the authorities. One supplicant seeking to publish a periodical about ancient and new medicine partly justified his request by including his hope that his son's death in defense of the kingdom would incline the government toward his plea.[60] By resorting to such an appeal the applicant obviously meant to communicate his patriotism and support of the government that would provide no disruption to society. The Chevalier de Quinsanas, by promising the discretion of his proposed journal, evidently sought to affirm his adherence to the government's policy forbidding acrimonious personal attacks.[61]

Despite the journalists' avowed loyalty, sometimes the government still found pursuing its own policies to be problematic. Again, influence proved the culprit. When the abbé Arnauld applied to the Librairie for the right to publish the *Journal étranger* in 1760, Malesherbes wanted to reject this appeal because he mistrusted the editor and was concerned that standards would be jeopardized.[62] But it soon became evident that no less a personage than the Dauphin was pressing the case. The Chancellor, who always appeared less committed to staying the course than his son, appealed to Malesherbes for a response to the entreaties received.[63] Malesherbes tried to stiffen his father's resolve by providing him with memos that not only interposed procedural hurdles but also reiterated his view that Arnauld seemed disreputable.[64] Malesherbes asserted that Arnauld had not actually done much of the work he claimed, but instead had depended on others. Evidently, such character flaws made him a threat to the high goals of the Librairie. The Director hoped that the Chancellor would press the prepared documents into the hand of the Dauphin, but this did not happen. So weak was the Chancellor's presentation that an associate of the Dauphin understood a privilege to be already granted.[65] Such febrility produced most of the expected result: a permission, though not a privilege, to publish.[66]

Such successful pressure indicated influence forcing bureaucrats to lower some standards before publication. Nonetheless, this view finds little echo elsewhere in the archives, and generally the government had been able to insist on its point of view. Overall, they had accepted the compromises they did in procedures. But once periodicals had been authorized, the officials ended up making greater concessions in their goals than in procedures.

The desired procedural requirement for periodicals, once they had obtained either a privilege or permission, was governmental pre-publication approval of every line. To achieve this end the Librairie delegated this role to censors. For books and periodicals, the director had at his disposal 82 censors in 1751, 121 in 1763.[67]

An interesting case concerning the *Année littéraire* provides insight into the government's commitment to the process of censorship. In the issue to be published on January 11, 1754, the editor, Elie-Catherine Fréron, included a mild critique of D'Alembert, an archenemy. The censor, Morand, because of his friendship with d'Alembert,[68] sent the piece to Malesherbes for further consideration. When time for publication arrived, the copy had still not been returned. Since the printer–publisher Lambert did not know about the censor's action, he assumed that all was acceptable and released the issue. Hours later, having received Malesherbes's objections, Morand wrote to Lambert to strike certain remarks. Lambert immediately sent a letter to Malesherbes explaining everything and asking to be allowed to continue publication of the issue. He found the director unyielding.[69]

Neither Lambert nor Fréron gave up their attempts to circulate this issue of the *Année littéraire*. The publisher appealed to another censor, Lavirotte. Sympathetic, the latter argued that if "the censor found something to withhold in these sheets, it was, it would seem, completely natural first to warn the author or the bookseller. . . ." Instead, Morand had only contacted Malesherbes. This action appeared absolutely unnecessary to Lavirotte, and his reaction implied that it had been completely reasonable for Lambert to have proceeded with publication.[70] Fréron wrote directly to Malesherbes, largely restating the same case, but also speculating that the real reason for the problem lay not with procedure but the critique of d'Alembert and the influence of the *Encyclopédistes*. Fréron closed his letter by begging: "I implore your help,

Sir, more yet for my publisher than for me. He's an honest man, a very honest man, the like of which there are few among publishers. He has made considerable advances [of money] for my work. His entire fortune is involved."[71]

Fréron's appeal clearly noted that the rejection of this material was not merely a question of publishing without approval. This became more clearly evident in a further exchange of letters. Fréron had appealed to an important member of the Noailles family, the Countess de la Mothe. She, too, pleaded with the director, focusing not on any secret political agenda but on the strictness of the punishment. She also pointed out that January was the month when subscriptions were renewed so that a disruption in publication might have serious financial consequences.[72] Despite all this, Malesherbes changed nothing. He answered, "You would agree however that Fréron is often in need of correction . . . I believe that on this occasion for his own interest and to avoid a circumstance that would lead to a total suppression, it is good that he suffer this light punishment for some time. . . ." By alluding to Fréron's other infractions which stemmed from unacceptable content rather than any procedural problem, the Director was insinuating that this crisis sprang from more than a mere violation of the rules of procedure.[73] Within a week, however, Malesherbes relented. Although we only have Fréron's account of this final agreement, the journalist's reaction is plain enough. He promised *both* to follow rigorously the decisions of censors and to be careful in his critiques.[74]

The double concession of Fréron's letter shows that, whatever the role of ideological struggle in this matter, the government was intent to prove that periodicals could not appear without official approval. Clearly, Lambert believed this the main point of the incident. But it also ought to be added that this infraction, really little more than a misunderstanding, might have been handled more rapidly had it not been for Fréron's questionable record. Overall, the case proves both the commitment to censorship and the way enforcement could become entangled in broader issues.

Although the government normally achieved its procedural goal of prior official approval of all copy, one may question whether this achievement was as great in substance. Did the censors actually represent the administration? Fréron and Lambert's struggle with Morand casts light on this subject. The latter's appeal to Malesherbes certainly suggests that subservience characterized the relationship, and scholars have generally assumed that censors did their master's bidding. The director assigned tasks to these officials on a case by case basis, so recalcitrant censors might have received very little work with a consequent drop in income. And the information available suggests that most censors shared the

viewpoint of the government.[75] All and all, it seems reasonable to conclude that those responsible for reviewing copy tried to align their goals
with those of the government.

In sum, in substance and in form, censors fulfilled as much as was
possible the goals of the government. And officialdom generally appreciated the efforts of such individuals. Historians have been unable to locate
cases of the disciplining of censors; instead the only visible relationship
is one of support. For example, when Charles-Augustine Vandermonde,
the editor of the *Journal de médecine*, complained about problems with his
censor over the length of abstracts, Malesherbes flatly rejected the plea.[76]
Yet the government might question the work of a censor, as in the case of
a journalist, one abbé Brançois, who evidently objected to cuts made in
his article on religion. Malesherbes told Brançois that he must abide by
his censor's decisions. But, Malesherbes, apparently unknown to the
journalist, also wrote Salmon, the censor responsible for the periodical, to
be generous because of Brançois's age and credentials. Unwilling publicly to undercut a censor and, indeed, not even criticizing Salmon,
Malesherbes pleaded for a little leniency.[77] Such a response proves even
more the confidence placed in censors. Yet such satisfaction should not be
taken to indicate that things always proceeded as the government
wished. Numerous problems existed, but they related less to process than
to the difficulty of some decisions. For this, censors appear not to have
received blame.

However ably Malesherbes and others like him implemented procedures for publishing domestic papers consistent with governmental
assumptions, these same administrators actually opened up the range of
subjects that these journals could discuss. Formal politics provided but a
very small part in the works dominated by the Librairie, yet Malesherbes
allowed no periodicals to cross the line of acceptability in these matters.
The director insisted that in monarchical France it would be dangerous to
allow the king's decisions to be discussed. While some abstract concepts
about the ministers might be debated, the papers must remain silent
even about their activities.[78] Journalists also seemed little successful in
challenging the prohibitions on more open debate about philosophy and
religion.[79] The most interesting change in the administration's goals for
domestic periodicals related to the treatment of "personalities," what
contemporaries understood to be internal characteristics or character
traits. As policy throughout the last decade of the Old Regime permitted
extensive reporting and debate on the literature and philosophy, some
tendency always inevitably existed toward discussing individuals. Debating the actions of people could easily lead to evaluating their
motivations.

To comprehend best how wide the door swung open to allow the
discussion of personalities, one might turn to the struggle between

Fréron and Malesherbes, the protagonists in the earlier described conflict. The *Année littéraire* established a new outer limit for assaulting an individual's character; its situation thus demarcated the extreme edge of possibilities and the circumstances that enabled both this boldness as well as the governmental retreat.

Fréron and Malesherbes agreed in theory that personalities were completely off limits in the press. In this they were joined by others such as even Chevrier, one of the most outrageous polemicists, who thought nothing of appealing to the censorship to stop attacks on his character.[80] But an abstract commitment depends on the definition of what constituted an onslaught on an individual. What the journalist endeavored to do was to define an assault on personalities narrowly and to create other justifications for using the abusive tones he employed.

An incident involving Melchior Grimm goes far toward explaining Fréron's approach. In the quarrel over music, known as the "Querelle des Bouffons," Fréron, while championing French national music, declared that the philosophe Grimm only supported Italian opera in order to monopolize its promotion for himself. Contemporaries believed this a personal attack. In a letter to Malesherbes, Fréron laid out the following defense, first by defining such an assault:

> As I must reject assaults on personalities, I have figured out two kinds: some interior, if I must speak thus, the other exterior. The first attack goes to the heart of someone's character, wounding even the man: these are the most odious. Thus, if I said that such a person is a debaucher, a coward, a blasphemer, a knave, etc., this would be a very offensive "personality," deserving of punishment. . . . The personalities that I call exterior are those which are in some way outside of a man but nonetheless which can wound him as to reproach his birth, his appearance, his poverty, etc.: they are certainly much less offensive than others; but just the same I never permit myself to use these.

Fréron thus denied that he could employ these kinds of attacks, but then claimed that his diatribe against Grimm fell outside both categories. As the journalist noted: "I did not say at all that M. Grimm was a libertine, an atheist, a man without honor and without good faith." Fréron further explained that he had not accused the philosophe of any "vice of the spirit, the mind, or the body." Rather he had simply stated that Grimm hated French music because he wanted to be "the entrepreneur of the Italian opera." Such a remark tried to justify the critique of Grimm as a mere statement of action as opposed to questioning his character or disparaging his personal attributes. In addition, added Fréron, his comments were truthful.[81] In short, Fréron tried to define the crime of personalities as consisting of explicit insults to character while still allowing factual statements about activities that only implied insult. In this way, he might open wide the possibility for a great many critical statements as long as they remained implicit and based on fact.

Fréron developed yet another justification for his penchant for vituperation. Often the butt of the attacks from the philosophes, Fréron sought the right to respond at least humorously. He justified such a response by noting Voltaire's tirades which he claimed the *Année littéraire* repulsed with pure pleasantries. None of his responses were offensive; if they were, the paper deserved suppression. He really needed to write in this vein, Fréron continued, because "it was his [Voltaire's] territory, his field of battle; allow me to defend myself there."[82]

Malesherbes found such rationales, which could indeed allow slashing commentaries, to be problematic, and he strongly believed such vituperation was antithetical to the Old Regime.[83] The director followed the policy of permitting criticism of the age's intellectual discussions, both philosophical and literary. As he told one of his censors:

> M. Fréron says that the *Vie de Mme. de Maintenon* is badly written, that the author is poorly instructed about the facts, that he has tastelessly and disorganizedly rendered them; he [Fréron] is surely the master of this. If he wishes to say that the author has wicked intentions and that his collection is in some respects a defamatory libel, Fréron, even if correct, must not say this at all.[84]

For Malesherbes, flaws in a text could not be translated into assaults on a person's character, but only his abilities. And such attacks must relate only to the particular work considered and must eschew vitriol.[85] Such accusations, it seems, regardless of their purposes constituted a "personality." His main difference with Fréron amounted to a total unwillingness to discuss the author; comments on the text were possible. Furthermore, Malesherbes argued that special circumstances, including prior criticisms from the author under review, could not justify retribution.[86] Under these guidelines a person's reputation might still be wounded but not *nearly* to the degree that Fréron desired. While the journalist sought acceptance for at least implicit attacks on character and even more when revenge was a factor, Malesherbes denied these outlets.

Despite Malesherbes's roadblock, the *Année littéraire* recklessly tried to proceed. At first Malesherbes often resisted the journalist. Fréron spent time in jail for attacking the character of Madame de Pompadour's protegés. Malesherbes also banned Fréron's intemperate attacks on the *Encyclopédie*.[87]

But gradually, even though fitfully, Fréron freed himself with Malesherbes's acquiescence. Evidence for some agreement abounds as the director increasingly refused to enforce his own principles. Articulating the new limits specified for Fréron defies precision, but clearly the director expected him to assail only intellectuals, not the *grands* nor even other individuals. But how far could Fréron go with writers? When he wanted mean-spiritedly to deride their general abilities, Malesherbes sometimes allowed such charges. For example, the journalist attacked a professor as a sloppy, careless writer. Although this accusation would seem to violate Malesherbes's prior stricture against both venom and expanding an attack on a work to include the author, the director let it be published without requiring a later apology. Indeed, Malesherbes drily noted that such an attack "is a misfortune for the men of letters, but their celebrity is related to this, and their success cannot be so great unless they experience some reverses."[88] Another example of his willingness to abandon former principles was Malesherbes's response to a censor who sought to excise Fréron's attacks on Voltaire and d'Alembert:

> In the end what he has said of M. de Voltaire and M. d'Alembert is not at all literary, but as for M. de Voltaire it would too greatly injure the law of retaliation not to permit M. Wasp [the philosophes' nickname for Fréron] to retort with some personalities. For M. d'Alembert I know of no work in which he has personally attacked M. Fréron; thus I have struck the article on him.[89]

In this case, Malesherbes was veering from his own principle that past attacks could not excuse the utilization of "personalities."

Abandoning these earlier views, Malesherbes even appeared at times to enunciate a principle that entirely evacuated the field of intellectual struggles and allowed any and everything. When Pierre Rousseau, editor of the *Journal encyclopédique*, complained in 1759 about an attack by Fréron, Malesherbes responded: "I am not at all made to mix in these particular problems. . . . Authors' personal quarrels do not at all concern me. There are judges in Paris to receive complaints of all sorts of offenses."[90] A few days later, the director gave the same response to a problem raised by Marmontel.[91] In these cases, the director seemed to approve a literary free-for-all with Fréron's guidelines at most governing the fray.

More research and analysis should be able to define the chronology of this greater openness toward the use of personal attacks. In general, biographies of Fréron would seem to indicate that official tolerance of that editor ebbed and surged, with overall increasing acceptability of his scathing critiques. Although much research remains to be done, it would appear that many other journalists rushed in to take advantage of the trail blazed by Fréron. The frondeur journalists, particularly Linguet, especially resorted to this turf.[92] Nonetheless, such ground proved tricky as the government never completely abandoned its enmity to personal criticisms and remained able to select the groups protected from this hostile treatment.

Perhaps future research that would ascertain with greater certainty the overall royal attitude might also try to explain why Malesherbes succumbed to Fréron. One advantage that the journalist exploited was his many powerful supporters. In particular, Stanislas, the king of Poland who then resided at the French court, sought to protect Fréron.[93] Doubtless, another reason was Malesherbes's special relationship to the philosophes. Because he protected these intellectuals' freedom, much of which was expended ridiculing Fréron, the head of the Librairie found it difficult to curtail the journalist's right to defend himself. Involved in permitting one set of attacks, Malesherbes found it hard to censor another. To be sure, the philosophes mainly relied on less regulated media than did Fréron, but the contrast may have still posed problems. Malesherbes himself articulated the dilemma in yet another way, when he wondered how the philosophes themselves could call for his intervention. The defender of the Enlightenment responded to Marmontel's plea to quash Fréron with this impassioned statement: "How can a man of so great spirit and enlightenment who for so many years has not stopped talking with the public about the principles of government and legislation, how can he want to charge me with reforming this injustice [of Fréron]? Does he not see to what *despotism* (since it's the word of the moment) one such action would yield?"[94] In these reactions, Malesherbes was in fact arguing that a person associated with the philosophes and their calls for freedom could not deny this freedom to their main enemy. On grounds of ideology and fair play, the relationship between the Enlightenment figures and the director undercut the suppression of Fréron's charges. It remains curious how much better Malesherbes could see the contradiction than could the philosophes. Perhaps as authors, the Enlightenment figures – many of whom were thin skinned – had more to lose from this freedom than a bureaucrat committed to the cause.

Greater openness to "personalities" and some expansion of the press: such were the allowances beyond government policy Malesherbes made for the domestic press. As such the journalists were adding more areas of independence for the press to the list officially available, which only allowed some cultural debate. Personalities added to this through the general irreverence thus introduced into the mix. But, as Chapter 3 revealed, this vitality, in the hands of Fréron as well as Desfontaines and Linguet in other periods, seemed to undermine the enlightened thinkers. Thus, weakened controls promised more excitement and sales than the circulation of troubling ideas.

Before examining how this relative laxity played itself out with the foreign-based press, yet another role played by officials is worthy of notice. Indeed, the Librairie was expected to settle squabbles among journalists and their printer–publisher. Malesherbes, in particular, seems to have had no interest in this chore that he nevertheless performed as requested. The printer, Lambert, asked that the director appoint another editor for the *Feuille nécessaire*. Presumably Malesherbes obliged as he also intervened on Fréron's behalf with the same printer.[95] The Librairie's involvement here likely related to the governmental interest in keeping businesses afloat and jobs available.

The documents thus far discovered about the administration's treatment of the foreign press do not compare in number with those concerning domestic periodicals. Yet the information available suggests that when such journals applied to publish (or, more accurately, to be distributed in France), Malesherbes subjected them to largely similar though somewhat harsher procedures than their French-based counterparts.[96] One exception was the reading by the censor, a process which Malesherbes could not, because of the sovereign rights of other countries, impose on imported papers.[97] The major formal tool available to authorities then consisted of a denial of access to the postal service. Such an ability to deny entry, though a crude instrument, would seem potentially potent.[98]

A particularly rich example helps to explain the policy adopted by Malesherbes. In order to defend the philosophes, Pierre Rousseau established the *Journal encyclopédique* abroad in 1756 (later moving it in 1760 to Bouillon, in Germany, just across the eastern French border). However, when the editor tried to secure entry for his paper, he found Malesherbes totally unsympathetic. Rousseau beseeched the director for a permission, claiming that many notables including Madame de Pompadour, Cardinal de Tencin and the keeper of the seals all supported him.[99] Malesherbes rather curtly replied that if such people really wanted the *Journal encyclopédique*, overall permission would not be necessary. Instead, suggested the director, use the special privileges allowed these individuals and mail it directly to them.[100] In late 1756, the impasse continued with Rousseau twice more imploring Malesherbes and promising to be satisfied if he could export only 200 copies to France.[101] But the head of the Librairie did not even bother to answer, scribbling across the last epistle, "I have not made . . . any response."[102]

Malesherbes apparently continued the same approach with the *Journal encyclopédique* through spring 1759, and seized several issues that year.[103] Although the archives yield no direct explanation for Malesherbes's resistance to Rousseau's pleas, a memo on foreign journalism likely explains why he posed these obstacles. The memo listed among reasons for opposing entry the financial advantages gained by foreign countries; the destruction of French commerce, specifically the privileges held by French periodicals; and the danger to religion and morality.[104] Malesherbes's reasoning essentially extended standards he had used on domestic journals to the foreign press. His reference to morality revealed his concern with ideological challenges that were already recognizable before distribution began. As such he adhered to his goals. Invoking economic questions suggests that he also had no interest in more publications. Procedural restrictions, censorship excepted, remained more intact than at home. All and all, those policies maintained a strong grip on the foreign discussion press.

Quite different were the policies on those papers specializing in formal politics. Responsible for this was the Ministry of Foreign Affairs. Inside the borders was the *Gazette de France*; but at issue here are the papers published outside the borders. The ministry allowed a much wider discussion of politics than its policy dictated, not to mention the requirements on the even more restricted *Gazette de France*. Although Malesherbes may have had little direct influence on these policies and his later actions showed some misgivings even about these recommendations, he did not hesitate to lay out his view. In a most revealing reminiscence, written in 1757, Malesherbes outlined his entire approach for handling the political fallout caused by foreign newspapers. The director noted that these organs posed a problem because they took money from the French economy and, more important, disseminated a spirit of "party" at home and abroad. For a long time, the French had allowed the practice of publishing foreign news in which each foreign ruler could plead his own case. So the issue became how to control the French news published in the foreign press. Toying with the possibilities, Malesherbes suggested refusing entry to foreign sheets that persisted in covering French political developments. The problem would be, he opined, that once eliminated, such papers would be free to make the most exaggerated claims and might broadcast the most radical critique throughout Europe. Moreover, such journals would discover a way to smuggle some issues into France. The better way was to admit them but threaten to reprint them, and thus destroy their markets.[105] This approach – allowing them only if they behaved – preserved the journals' economic rights, but gave the officials significant leverage. These ruminations occurred at a time in which significant changes were about to occur in all these matters.

Those in charge in the late 1750s were trying to deal with the very problems Malesherbes pointed out. On foreign affairs they maintained a standard below the norm set for French interactions abroad allowing a marketplace of ideas. In the most vulnerable situation, they accepted that other nations could, as Malesherbes suggested, distribute their own justifications. Although angered by viciously anti-French and distorted attacks, they generally permitted them to continue.[106] Such a response conceded control over criticisms, but it must be reiterated that the authorities did insist that there be a mix with alternate justifications whose exact nature at this stage of research remains unclear. Of course, all this represented a substantial departure.

On French domestic politics, authorities also accepted more vigorous reporting than the benchmark, though there were limits. Clearly, certain transgressions upset the bureaucrats at the Ministry of Foreign Affairs.[107] But defining the outlines of acceptability escapes currently available documentation. Likely goals existed. One might speculate that in general these officials had in mind tolerating extant debate among the national political elite. More specifically, this would seem to include not only the activity of the royal government, but also the magistracy, the actions of local governments relevant to the kingdom's politics, and celebrated court cases that played out before the public. What they seemed not to want was overheated commentary or information from individuals or groups beyond the major players' public pronouncements. By eliminating gossip, continued restrictions on personalities fed into this more staid reportage.[108] Officials might have been equally hostile to "popular" expression such as street rumors (*mauvais discours*) and pornography but, given the prejudices of the journalists and their interest in respectability,[109] this worry likely did not materialize to trouble the government. Evident so far is a desire to focus on "responsible" sources, although additional study may determine more specifics.

In this period of openness in all reporting, other features might be integrated into the governmental view. Because the structure of the press – its lack of editorials and desultory style – continued unchanged, it made sure that the press itself would not amplify negative reporting. In this context of laxity, the administration was likely to incorporate these factors into its policy, as a basic, probably unconscious, assumption which would limit the freedoms granted. Certainly, these same prohibitions reduced the ability to defend the monarchy as well, but likely this was a risk well worth taking. Ought this structure and this approach toward personalities be considered part of the governmental policy on political reporting in the standard, more restricted situation? In such circumstances, with an overall positive view of Versailles guaranteed, these other matters would seem ambiguous and not particularly instrumental.

One of the most curious aspects of all this was how often Versailles officials sought to further a complaint about coverage by asking for the source of a report.[110] One would imagine the government would assail first the periodical. Perhaps this other strategy may be explained first by considering the gazettes' common practice of relying on individual correspondents for reports. Officials considered this dependence inevitable. To excise undesirable remarks, just the matter that authorities were most anxious to rule out of bounds, meant going after correspondents who after all were much more vulnerable than presses on the soil of other countries.

161

Although the ministry of foreign affairs contemplated and accepted significant distortions of the rather restricted policy on political reporting on both foreign and domestic affairs, it did not simply rest with these measures. As indicated in the discussion about control of reporting, the French government tried to manage the news, in some cases by circulating its own version, in other cases by quashing troublesome correspondents. Measuring this effort and its success remains elusive, but it was weak enough so that the flow of reports continued effectively to allow the press to take advantage of the opening afforded it. Thus this practice of controlling information diluted reporting but did not eliminate all the valuable material. Such an approach proved a factor, not a prohibition, that future research may be able to present more precisely.[111] The most observable way that the government rolled back the opportunity offered to gazettes was to play a number of cards that changed both goals and procedures.

To greatly reduce the explosive reporting tolerated, the government allowed but five newspapers to enter the country. Seemingly, only two of these (from Amsterdam and Utrecht) carried the problematical reports at a high level of strength, and the government insured that these would have a limited circulation by charging enormous premiums for their distribution. Between profits for the designated distributor and enormous postal charges, periodicals that were priced below 25 livres ended up costing the French consumer 104 livres early in the 1750s and later in the decade 120 livres. Because of increased demand for news during the Seven Years War, counterfeiting and possibly other techniques lowered the price, as reprinting of the *Gazette d'Amsterdam* took place at least in Avignon, La Rochelle, Bourges, Bordeaux, and Geneva. In Bordeaux the price sank as low as 18 livres.[112] All these editions surely undermined but did not destroy the effect of raising prices so high in Paris. Furthermore, this policy had operated more effectively before the Seven Years War when counterfeiting spread. Such developments explain the existence of this complex system of pricing which had been far more effective in the very recent past.

Another endeavor that reversed to some degree the great openness in envisioned reportage was the provision of alternatives.[113] Indeed, the government experimented with establishing ostensibly private journals that would support French positions.[114] But these do not seem to have gotten off the ground. More successful was the promotion of the *Courrier d'Avignon* which after 1740 operated in extremely favorable circumstances. Kindly French regulation made it possible to sell this periodical at the bargain price of 18 livres.[115] This periodical certainly ranged far above the desired standards, with significant coverage of French domestic affairs. Nonetheless, because of its vulnerable location in an enclave entirely surrounded by France, it was quite constrained and became the most quiescent of the foreign gazettes. Such pricing led to a publishing rate around 3,000, thus wooing readers toward a less troublesome publication.[116] Also, attracting readers was the highly controlled *Gazette de France* which was selling for as little as 7 livres 10 sous.[117] It too attracted readers away from the more controversial press.

By such adjustments, the ministry of foreign affairs undermined some of the compromises it had made. Allowing only the two ambitious newspapers and greatly inflating their prices in the capital and elsewhere constituted a tight interpretation of the procedure desired by officials. Providing cheap alternatives, more subject to government control, reinforced this narrowness. And indeed, these same periodicals suggested a sliding scale for the government goals for the press in which some periodicals were simply more tightly defined than others. In this manner content was limited. Doubtless, controlling the flow of information possessed the same effect by diluting the problematic news available. This entire process, seen in its broadest perspective, still resembled to some degree the tight but hardly "despotic" policies envisioned more as a general guideline by authorities for political reporting.

Whatever changes the 1750s witnessed, more alterations were in store. In 1758 Choiseul came to the fore in the cabinet and began immediately altering the approach of the ministry of foreign affairs. Even before Malesherbes resigned in 1763, Choiseul, very influential at court as a protegé of Pompadour, expanded his influence into the regulation of the literary and philosophical press. Dominating affairs, this chief minister seemed more generous toward the press than his predecessors.

Unfortunately for our understanding of the new leadership and indeed every subsequent administration, insufficient evidence exists to produce systematic portraits. Henceforward, for these later periods this chapter first outlines the major known developments and, using previous periodicals as a base, broadly suggests some overall, rather than specific, directions.

Scholars have uncovered little on the Librairie during Choiseul's dominance. Nonetheless, he altered goals by allowing some political reporting and more radical philosophical speculation, though apparently not materialism, in the domestic press. Choiseul elected to widen policy to benefit the *Journal des dames*, which immediately took advantage of the new possibilities. Under the foreign minister's protection, this periodical published articles that went beyond the philosophes. A certain egalitarianism and sympathy for the poor graced these pages.[118]

The foreign discussion press may also have been liberated, as the one example available suggests. After several years of rejecting the *Journal encyclopédique*, the government unexpectedly announced the journal's entry in July 1761.[119] What effected this turn of events – which by implication lessened the procedural hindrances and reduced the need for ideological conformity – was doubtless the arrival of Choiseul, who six months earlier had become foreign minister. If the editor Rousseau owed something to Pompadour, Choiseul owed everything. A favor for the *Journal encyclopédique* may have been only a small return on the royal mistress's investment. Moreover, as we have seen with the *Journal des dames*, Choiseul was willing to take a lax stance toward troublesome ideas in the press.

A similar openness pervaded the efforts visible to us in the arena over which the minister of foreign affairs presided. Perhaps, the most significant area was procedural. Beginning in 1759, officials opened France's borders to the foreign press. From the first most of the significant newspapers flowed in, with the remainder following. The price was 36 livres. Although not as economical as before in some areas, this generally represented a drop of 84 livres. As the very cheap prices were of recent origin, this drop was more often measured against very high prices. From a policy of strong exclusion, the Choiseul government moved substantially in the opposite direction. Cheaper alternative domestic papers still existed, but they confronted a much more unchained foreign medium.[120]

On the treatment of "personalities," Choiseul continued the previous policy. The government was still willing to intervene on behalf of the *grands*. In a long internal memo about the *Gazette d'Utrecht*, an official of the foreign service complained about an article on the abbess, Madame de Clermont d'Amboise. The official accused this article of a "very reprehensible license" and "falsity and insolence." And concluded this memo, if the editor continued to write, "with as little discernment and truth as he often does," he would be denied entry. But more important, "he must know that personalities must be proscribed from his gazette, especially when it concerns subjects who are respectable by their birth and rank."[121] Interestingly, the minister apparently did adopt Malesherbes's openness on personalities when intellectuals were involved. In 1768 the philosopher La Harpe demanded the retraction of an article about him in the *Gazette d'Utrecht*, which accused him of publishing the *Café humain* under Voltaire's name. Wishing all to know of his innocence, La Harpe insisted: ". . . citizens are under the protection of the government, under you, Monseigneur, and a person in Holland has no right to defame them publicly." This author demanded a retraction to save his reputation from this serious attack because "such license is contagious if it is not repressed by the authorities."[122] Immediately and sharply, the government informed him that he would have to handle such problems himself.[123]

The content of the most adventurous foreign gazettes paralleled the Dutch gazettes of the previous decade, a development which suggests the continued willingness to tolerate hostile reporting of internal and external affairs. But only fragments exist on the policy of keeping freedoms

164

within bounds. When in 1765 the *Gazette de Leyde* printed a detail in the account of the rebellion by the parlement of Rennes, which the government saw as an unreliable commentary, it responded by inquiring into the source of the news and demanding a retraction.[124] In a later leak on Brittany, the government initially assumed that the paper was using a French source, and searched for the correspondent. Choiseul, the foreign minister, instructed his subordinate to demand to see the original copy of the report and to be given its author's name. The minister promised never to tell the correspondent how he had learned his identity. Eventually it turned out that the Leiden paper had used a non-French source. In such circumstances the authorities were particularly upset by such a source, likely because such correspondents, usually sensitive to pressure, proved difficult to attack. Yet caution governed, and they did nothing.[125] Another case indicates the effort to keep certain boundaries firm. When the *Courrier du Bas Rhin* published some anti-monarchical ditties in 1767, officials suppressed it for the "license and impiety which reigned in this work."[126] Evidently, the paper for publishing lyrics well outside the establishment's political discourse deserved suppression whether or not a correspondent could be located.

Illustrating Choiseul's general indulgence, however, was his treatment of the *Mercure historique et politique du Pays-bas*, (1759–61) whose editor was to be Maubert de Gouvest. The story, as we know it, began in late November 1759, after Choiseul's elevation to the ministry and with Malesherbes delaying a decision on the periodical. This periodical possessed literary/philosophical and political sections so both officials were directly involved in the case. Responding to the Duke de Belle-Isle, the director of the Librairie thanked him for his support of the *Mercure historique* and noted that it, along with the endorsement already received from Choiseul, would count on its behalf. Yet, Malesherbes continued, the principles of the journalist were a point of concern.[127] Even greater pressure came to bear down on the director, as one supporter of the *Mercure historique et politique* inquired if Choiseul might have the final disposition of this subject since he could guarantee the reliability of the desired editor. Leaving no stone unturned, this supplicant again wrote a few weeks later.[128]

Malesherbes, despite his liberal reputation and his seeming openness of 1757, likely already recognized that he had a more constricted definition of acceptable journalism than did the minister. Battling his superior, the director stuck to his guns and recruited a censor to evaluate the *Mercure historique*. The censor considered an article on seventeenth-century foreign relations and found it politically unacceptable on several points. In respect to bloody wars fought by supporters of the pretender to the seat of the Elector of Cologne, Malesherbes's subordinate commented: "Although the author apparently wished to observe a great circumspection, he has, however, included some remarks against France and her allies." This emphasis on a historical statement that criticized France though not by name indicated the enforcement of a high standard of political conformity. The censor's report elsewhere criticized other information "as seeming to be ironic." The censor also found other difficulties and recorded the prose of this *Mercure* on another subject:

> The manifesto of General Wolff published in Canada seems true, and also true to the character of this illustrious man, not less recommended by his civic virtues than by his military qualities. This would-be army [the French] which covered Quebec was not only badly organized but also in no position to undertake much. It was not only to the superiority of the British forces that one must attribute all these losses of France on other continents.

This remark, quite belligerent to someone hoping for tight limits, not surprisingly caught the eye of the censor who remarked, "The author appears to attribute the cause of the French's lack of success in America less to the superiority of the English forces than to a bad administration." Such was unacceptable as was a later comment in the periodical about seventeenth-century conflicts. In concluding his report, the censor summed up: "In all this number of the *Mercure* of Brussels, the author pretends to reveal all the foreign countries' animosity . . . and one cannot believe this a reason for tolerating the sale of this work in France."[129] Although some of the *Mercure*'s copy directly challenged the government, much that was very oblique likewise evoked the ire of the censor. In essence, this official's report imposed stringent controls on political reporting, even of historical events. Having ordered the report in order to contradict those who argued the *Mercure*'s harmlessness, Malesherbes likely would have agreed with it. In any case, he could have explicitly or implicitly dictated its contents. And at the least it certainly fit the high benchmark standards he had previously imposed on periodicals seeking permission.

Choiseul ignored Malesherbes's line on political reporting and, without the approval of the Librairie, allowed the periodical to circulate illicitly. Choiseul's initial reason lay in the government's wish to grant financial advantages to its northern neighbor. And he insisted the contents would remain acceptable.[130] Thus, Choiseul at first only widened the procedural gates, still claiming to insist on ideological purity.

The problem that definitively revealed Choiseul's greater tolerance of such papers erupted in late 1760 when the *Mercure historique* published news about the parlement of Paris that was detrimental to the government. In particular, the paper reported the judiciary's claims to act as sovereign courts.[131] The explosion over this article so inflamed the administration that continuing illegal circulation proved impossible. Permission to publish would either have to be granted or denied. Malesherbes sent a request to Choiseul that a formal decision be reached in the royal council.[132] Given Malesherbes's disapproval of the *Mercure*, he doubtless hoped that this pressure would yield a negative result. He was disappointed, for on December 14, 1760, Choiseul wrote curtly and informed him that the king had granted the permission.[133]

Such a conclusion in the *Mercure politique* case reinforces the image of Choiseul as a man willing to allow a broad range of political reporting who confronted an official who wanted to adhere more closely to the standard rules. Choiseul's actions went beyond simply a defense of open borders to an indifference to controlling tightly what was said. To be certain the head of the Librairie had advocated a policy of openness to the foreign gazettes, but he had also been extremely tough within his own jurisdiction.[134] That incident thus shows a contrast with Choiseul, whose goals on reportage by external gazettes resembled more the standards that his predecessors in the foreign ministry had imposed on the few foreign gazettes circulated. If essentially similar in this way, Choiseul departed in others; most significantly in procedures governing foreign gazettes. This last change is significant. Much wider circulation, linked to controversial ideas, really represented an enormous departure in the possibilities for foreign gazettes.

For all Choiseul's openness to widened reporting, he could support the contrary. Under the guidance of Edme-Jacques Genet, the father of the official who in the 1790s would so traumatize the Americans by violating American neutrality, Choiseul sought to set up propaganda organs to address current problems. Unlike the *Gazette de France*, their affiliation would remain covert in order to give them greater acceptability with the public. The creation of such papers not only contradicted Choiseul's other open policy but in fact propelled the government toward its goal regarding political reporting. Yet none of these papers lasted long, and they may be regarded a false start.[135] During Choiseul's period of ascendancy, the government undertook another effort that proved largely stillborn. The government hoped to establish a very imposing, brilliantly edited and written discussion journal, to be entitled the *Gazette littéraire*. Contemporary speculation seemed to envision it as a publication that would take advantage of the openness that existed in the standard governmental policy but go no further.[136] It too would reign in Choiseul's alternate approach in the area of literature. This journal like its political brethren lasted but a brief period.[137] Furthermore, Choiseul sponsored efforts to make the *Gazette de France* more appealing, but these quickly foundered.

These exceptions raise the possibility that the earlier assessment of Choiseul's expansiveness might be hyperbolic. With documentation comparable with the preceding decade, one might find significant control in the 1760s. Still the reticence common in the press created restraint. And clearly less expensive, more conservative newspapers (the *Gazette de France* and the *Courrier d'Avignon*), along with efforts to control the news, continued.[138] But the power of foreign gazettes, though in a muted style, surely eclipsed the effect of the *Courrier d'Avignon* and similar publications. And the weakness of all the more constricting innovations suggests that the expansive side of Choiseul informed those areas still closed off to us. Starting with the policy of his predecessors which seemed to take back with one hand what was given with another, overall he removed many remaining brakes. For now it might be best to regard this period as one in which periodicals had the opportunity to experience even freedom and financial opportunity. Another way of regarding the varied approaches of Choiseul is to see him as supporting the conflict of many views across the spectrum. Fulfilling this goal would be better supported by liberating genuinely private organs: hence his energy in that regard and his weakness on the government-sponsored media.

In contrast to the policy enforcement of Choiseul stand those of the Triumvirate. The French monarchy had endured virtually two decades of incessant controversy between king and parlement over sharing authority. In 1770–71 Louis XV established this new government, known as the Triumvirate, consisting of Maupeou as keeper of the seals, Terray as controller-general, and d'Aiguillon as secretary of state for foreign affairs. These men agreed that only the destruction of the parlements could solve current problems. In January 1771, Maupeou provoked a confrontation with the courts and exiled them for their recalcitrance. Unrelenting, he first sent the parlementaires to some very disagreeable locales, then abolished their offices without compensation, and finally set up new courts to replace them. The French people construed these acts as despotism, and a huge public outcry ensued.

From 1771 until its fall in 1774, the Triumvirate stifled discontent partly by attacking the press.[139] The slim evidence shows these three ministers focused on suppressing the most problematical parts of the press, although procedural matters seem unchanged from the relative openness of the previous regime. The focus was on reducing the freedoms they found upon entering office. Nonetheless, they left untouched Choiseul's and Malesherbes's shared policy on "personalities."[140] Interestingly, they tolerated the *Journal encyclopédique*, surely the most problematic of all the foreign literary magazines. This periodical only encountered troubles in 1774, and then not because of its own reports, but in a dispute over its sister newspaper, the *Gazette des gazettes*.[141] Here the important point is the government's willingness to tolerate the foreign literary press.

For domestic periodicals the government came to outlaw discussions both of domestic politics and of philosophical debates that either directly attacked the Church or experimented with more radical notions than the philosophes. Nina Gelbart has already shown how Maupeou, even before the "coup," crushed the *Journal des dames*, which had begun to discuss politics and had also been expanding the limits of philosophical discussions. Moreover, as she notes, no similar successor – akin to the very adventuresome papers that would pop up in 1775–76 – dared surface under the Triumvirate.[142] Doubtless, everyone quickly learned that the Triumvirate was in no mood to tolerate the *Journal des dames* and its kind of reporting. And all of the French-based papers that won the right to publish during the period were, indeed, relatively innocuous.[143]

But seemingly the Triumvirate made its most diligent efforts toward changing how foreign papers treated French domestic policies. The attack on the foreign gazettes began almost simultaneously with the assault on the parlements. Although the press had been able to cover the Maupeou "reforms,"[144] it soon found itself besieged. Because the archival trail remains most complete for the *Gazette de Leyde*, it is easiest to follow the story through that one periodical's experiences, with occasional outside excursions. This focus on the Leiden periodical seems warranted because all the others that had become accustomed to a substantial coverage of French domestic politics experienced a similar crackdown.

On January 31, 1771, the Duke de la Vrillière, head of the Maison du Roi, informed the embassy at The Hague on behalf of the Triumvirate that for some time the *Gazette de Leyde* had been experimenting with writing "with a more than indiscreet liberty, about the internal administration of the kingdom." Up to the present, he had been patient, this official continued, but:

> foreseeing that indiscretion could degenerate into license, it is necessary that you seriously warn the authors of this periodical henceforth to be more reserved in the articles about the administration. Be civil; be politic on France; be scrupulously attentive in the choice of correspondents in Paris for whose mistakes the publishers remain responsible to the public, and especially remove from their work all types of personalities and reflections created by passion and mischievousness.[145]

Wishing the publishers, the Luzac family, to know the seriousness of these complaints, the duke instructed his representative to express these doubts and to back them up with the threat of suppression. He concluded by asking for their response.[146]

Even Duprat, the Embassy official, was surprised by the sharpness of the attack. Forwarding the letter to Etienne Luzac, Duprat added a note that he hoped that the editor would believe that he had represented him to be conscientious on behalf of France. And Luzac was equally stunned by De la Vrillière's remarks, which caused as much "grief as surprise." Luzac then sought to refute the attack by defending his journalistic practices. Because of his respect for all the European governments he had never been indiscreet or indecent. The laws of the gazette, claimed Luzac, were those of "history, veracity and impartiality. Without being unfaithful to the public, one cannot pass over events which attract universal attention and one day will occupy a distinguished place in the annals of our century." If newspapers only announced births and deaths, all men of taste and knowledge would pay no attention. He admitted he added his reflections, but argued that he kept them to a minimum, using them only when related to the subject at hand. Without this commentary, the facts would lose coherence. He also rejected the notion that his mistakes had ever been motivated by a desire for mischief. Finally, averring that he had no choice but to credit his correspondents, he claimed to remain always willing to make retractions.[147]

These two letters reveal the crux of the government's intentions. The Duke was, in essence, demanding that the *Gazette de Leyde* avoid or downplay domestic conflicts. Surely he was considering the difficulties with the parlements. Although not yet forbidding all reporting on France as he later would, he was adding stricter demands by making the paper responsible for its correspondent. In the past authorities had obviously been willing to focus on correspondents. Luzac's reply promised discretion, in particular toward the court at Versailles. Yet this was only a partial answer to these demands, because it apparently did not exclude specific coverage of the parlements. Furthermore, Luzac seemed to backstep when he claimed the need for "veracity."[148] All in all, Luzac seemed to promise that he had followed and would continue to follow the rules regarding political reporting and personalities that had previously prevailed. Commentary he used only to impose some order. On other occasions where he had overstepped – by mistakes or by trusting unreliable correspondents – he did not see what he could otherwise do, except print retractions.

Thus, Luzac apparently wished to continue the system by which he had profited in the past. Impressed by him, Duprat informed his superiors that these statements should satisfy them. Mentioning the esteem that Luzac enjoyed among his countrymen, Duprat emphasized that the editor had attempted to please the French authorities.[149]

But what could satisfy Duprat became clearly insufficient for the Triumvirate which wished further to tighten the rules and altogether forbid foreign gazettes from reporting French controversies. Toward this end, the ministers kept up pressure on the *Gazette de Leyde* and its brethren through 1771, and briefly suspended the newspaper from Utrecht as an example for the others.[150] Indeed, the very restrained tone and content the Dutch gazettes adopted about conflict demonstrate the effectiveness of all this repression.[151]

But the ministers wanted no indiscretions, no matter how inadvertent, in the trivial matters still open for discussion. In spring 1772 they returned to the attack and complained about an item which mentioned that Choiseul in retirement was selling his paintings – evidently an indication of financial problems.[152] Even such an oblique comment might embarrass the government. In May officials decided to make absolutely certain their restrictive policy would be followed. An embassy official warned the already incredibly tame *Gazette de Leyde* that it was taking too many liberties, tolerating too many articles inimical to those in power. The letter closed with the threat that Luzac's journal might be suppressed.[153]

Luzac exploded. Arguing that these attacks completely lacked specificity, he stated that, given how careful he had been about reports on France, he could not imagine how he had offended. Although he had agreed to be discreet, Luzac once again complained that his readers expected accurate information about politics. Continued the publisher: "If one suppressed in a public newsheet all that the 'gens en place' in the different parts of Europe would wish not to be read, would this newspaper merit the confidence and esteem of the public? Could it keep any readers?" Why, queried Luzac, has the administration abandoned this reasoning which had earlier been so acceptable?[154]

As Luzac had already abandoned coverage of France's internal conflicts, his retort was mostly symbolic. Yet even this rejoinder drew a response. The embassy replied that the government had to be so rigorous because the gazettes published in French and could thus cause political convulsions in France. This government simply would not suffer any challenges.[155]

Having capitulated in practice, Luzac finally surrendered in principle to the administrator's logic. In a May 28, 1772 letter he promised that he understood the requirements and would do nothing to offend.[156] The Embassy reported success to the administration, and d'Aiguillon then expressed the hope that the example of the *Gazette de Leyde* would intimidate others.[157]

Indeed the Embassy worked to extend its victory and an official wrote d'Aiguillon in July 1772:

I hope, Monseigneur, that you will find less indiscretion touching our government in the Dutch gazettes since the execution of the last orders with which you have honored me. I will continue to watch over these writers, the most difficult of all; they can however be guided by the firm pressure of reason. It is certain that they did not have the least notion of the limits which separated license from political news. Their conversion was a true surrender.[158]

This eager beaver of an administrator, one Desnoyers, continued to busy himself, slapping down the *Gazette de la Haye*. Anyway, Desnoyers assured his superiors, the French government was far more successful than the Danes.[159]

Subdued, but restive, were the Luzacs and doubtless others in their position. After yet another correction of a minor point demanded by the government, the new editor Jean Luzac in his agreement to conform angrily retorted: "Thus permit me, sir, to say to you, while still observing the respect owed you, that if I were capable of going to the most discredited ends as you apparently believe, I would neither deserve your attention nor that of any other individual with values." Luzac claimed as had his predecessor that no one had ever written in such a way to him.[160] But even in his anger, Luzac did not reject – could not reject – the new rules imposed on the gazettes. He agreed that he would continue suppressing all sorts of information interesting to the public and sought an excuse for any mistakes that might still occur. Luzac noted: ". . . in the multitude of little facts which are presented every day, is it such an unpardonable fault to misunderstand once?" And he explained that if the government knew anything about the impossibility of his job, it would show greater sympathy. Even the *Gazette de France* written under the watchful eye of the government made such mistakes, argued Luzac. This line of justification would explain any independence, not as justifiable, but as a false step.[161]

Luzac's submissiveness, which powerfully testifies to the success of the Triumvirate's campaign against the press, still did not completely satisfy the administrators at Versailles. Even as the journalists obeyed the government, administrators were devising another strategy that would altogether undermine such periodicals. Clandestine newssheets were the key to this alternative. The underground quality of these papers breathed freedom and their reputedly wider range of information likely attracted readers from the gazettes. But these clandestine papers were not what they seemed, as they first were submitted to the government, and even the king read them before one single copy could be printed.[162] These newssheets, though actually agreeable to the government, could potentially take sales from the gazettes. Certainly the period of the Triumvirate represented a very difficult moment for political reporting of France's domestic situation.[163]

The Triumvirate further supplemented its repression of all adventurous reporting by permitting the growth of an open press with some vigor yet sure not to exceed the general standards on goals. In part they were pursuing strategies utilized to varying degrees by Choiseul and his predecessors in the Seven Years War. To accomplish this end, officials saw the wisdom in authorizing Charles-Joseph Panckoucke, who indicated conformity to the government, to publish in France two periodicals that focused on both politics and literary news, although the literary information was not initially included in the first paper. The two, almost identical in their general features – the *Journal de Genève* (begun in 1772) and the *Journal de Bruxelles* (1774) – were apparently approved to follow the officially defined policy which, while allowing openness on the Enlightenment, set relatively tight standards on domestic issues and somewhat looser ones on foreign affairs. Personalities were off limits. But what Panckoucke precisely promised remains unclear, though surely a large measure of cooperation. Nonetheless, the government hoped Panckoucke would attract readers, in part by the latitude allowed regarding philosophy and literature. Moreover, by indicating a foreign provenance, these papers could assert greater credibility than they would have otherwise enjoyed.[164] In yet another way, officials acted to increase the desirability of these publications. By relying on Panckoucke, they resorted to a proven success. And they were not to be disappointed as the publisher's efforts quickly brought a substantial following – over 2,000 subscriptions by 1774.[165]

In approving Panckoucke's proposal, officials meant to allow two attractive papers which might pull subscribers from other potentially more independent journals and thus reduce the likelihood of highly problematic information. If successful, Panckoucke's papers would add an economic volley to attacks on the foreign gazettes and help prevent any revival of frondeur papers. Furthermore, this strategy also permitted undermining the still tolerated diatribes against individuals and other excesses that did not conform to longstanding governmental goals. These papers provided continuity with the prescribed government approach to the periodical. One unfortunate result, from the ministerial point of view, of allowing political news to be easily published, was the economic damage sustained by the *Gazette de France*. But at least, through the subterfuge with Panckoucke, the government did not have to admit violating its principle of monopolizing domestic political reporting.

All these documented efforts by the Triumvirate, taken together, suggest that their policy was first an effort to cut off increased reportage in the domestic discussion papers that had been the case under Choiseul. On the foreign gazettes, the government crushed their independence in domestic reporting while the procedural right to circulate remained. Nonetheless some factors that did not seem particularly important in the 1760s, particularly competition from cheaper gazettes, might be more troublesome against rather tepid competition. Panckoucke's periodicals played a role here as well by presenting an interesting package near long-term standards. Yet leaving intact troublesome reporting in the foreign discussion paper, the *Journal encyclopédique*, and permitting the continued use of personalities in the literary press, the Triumvirate signaled some extra liberty. Thus regulations left significant freedoms beyond the standard policy of controls only in personal exchanges over literature. French men and women had generally to content themselves with the modest liberties left in that standard policy, whose main area of freedom – foreign policy – was diminished by the general quiet on these issues.

Even after the fall of Maupeou and his colleagues, whom Louis XVI ousted when he acceded to the throne, the new government, despite its liberal reputation, did not immediately change its approach to the foreign gazettes. This shift in administration signaled to the press a new freer regime, and within a few months it would beat down the administration. But the initial instinct of the new government was repression. In fact, the foreign minister nominally possessed the most control over these periodicals, and the new man in this position, Count de Vergennes, proved throughout his career no great admirer of independence in periodicals.[166]

That the new administration hoped to keep strong pressure on the gazettes appears obvious. When the *Gazette de Leyde* mentioned that Vergennes's wife had been born in Greece, he ordered that journal to indicate her French ancestry and birthright. Such a demand reveals the tight leash on any information that might stimulate opposition and, to ensure this strictness would be understood, the central administration insisted to the embassy:

> I restate, moreover, sir, the orders that have been given at different times to supervise closely all the gazettes of Holland and to employ all the means that you have to repress their penchant for misstatements and their facility to take up all the evils addressed to them from France. . . .

Desnoyers, the man on the scene in Holland, ever obedient, agreed and sought the appropriate retraction.[167]

But the rising tide of scintillating reporting in the gazettes continued, as these newspapers apparently put more stock in the government's liberal reputation than the efforts at rigid enforcement. In these circumstances Desnoyers became increasingly frustrated as he continued his efforts. He complained that he was unable to censor these gazettes, that reprimands only drew attention to the problem, and that the local governments proved intractable – all these contributed to the gazettes' increased indifference to his efforts.[168] His one success occurred when he showed up unexpectedly at the offices of the *Gazette de la Haye*, found an objectionable article, and demanded its suppression on the spot. But editors usually hid from him all their problematical articles.[169]

As far as may be determined, the administration gave repression one last attempt before apparently abandoning the policy. On January 11, 1775, the Marquis de Noailles, then ambassador to The Hague, wrote letters of rebuke to all gazettes of that country – The Hague, Amsterdam,

Leiden, and Utrecht. Their trespass lay in reporting an interchange between the king and the Archbishop of Paris about the refusal of sacraments and about the reaction to a curé being exiled. That these explosive stories on Church and state could be reported at all revealed how ineffectual the government was at that moment. But still Noailles demanded a retraction and a *return* to circumspection in the presentation of French news. To enforce this apology he threatened to suppress all the gazettes, and as an afterthought, he condemned another objectionable story.[170] Two days later Noailles was able to report at least some success to Vergennes.[171] But this incident likely ended the efforts of the government to enforce the Triumvirate's policy. During the Maupeou ministry, administrative correspondence frequently dealt with the disciplining of the press. The disappearance of this topic signaled a return to past more lenient regimes.

Simultaneously with the easing of the controls on foreign political papers, some French-based discussion periodicals began covering this most interesting of subjects. In fact, the government became tolerant enough that domestic political reporting became possible, though always under scrutiny. What apparently occurred was the appointment of ministers responsible for literary and philosophical periodicals, including Turgot, who, unlike Vergennes, were generally indifferent to these issues. In such circumstances, some liberally inclined censors allowed new subjects to be addressed. This same tolerance, however, permitted more censorious censors to remain strict. The frondeur papers led by the *Journal des dames*, which provided at least some political analysis, took advantage of this division.[172] Perhaps the most adventurous piece appeared in the July 1775 issue of this periodical. In this "Dream of a Citizen," the editor, Louis-Sébastien Mercier, gave his reactions to the coronation of Louis XVI. While the journalist insisted upon a spartan attitude and despised those who rejected law and work, such sentiments remained too vague to be very inflammatory. But then, Mercier provocatively noted that the coronation was of far less significance than the date of the return of the parlementarians, from which moment he and the virtuous could foresee a renewal, both in economic and human terms.[173] This article clearly reveals that, however briefly, the authorities not only sacrificed their resistance to political reporting but indeed were tolerating extremely incautious remarks. This greater tolerance possessed one certain limit, as the authorities banned the use of "personalities" against political figures. Finally, during this interlude of openness under the liberal ministers, a reduction in governmental restrictions on discussing religion and philosophy permitted the emergence of the *frondeurs*, if not the materialists. The papers also continued to include attacks on individuals who dealt with such intellectual debates.[174]

During this period of the general relaxation of controls, Vergennes tried to move the reporting of foreign gazettes on foreign affairs toward putting the best face on French initiatives with the American colonists. In order to prepare opinion for French involvement with the Americans, the foreign minister began to encourage favorable treatment of the colonists at the expense of the British.[175] From the cacophony of voices that remained available on this subject in the press, his stricture was obviously phrased more as a hint than a demand.[176] In the end, this tentative policy began to squeeze, ever so gently, foreign reporting into the desired mold. But by requesting a positive focus on America, which inevitably included her republicanism, the minister was also promulgating notions that indirectly undermined the Bourbons. This limited change did not much challenge the pattern of reduced regulation and a pattern which overall seems similar to, or more expansive than, the Choiseul regime.

Both Nina Gelbart and Suzanne Tucoo-Chala have noticed the more restrictive press policy begun late in 1776. Gelbart viewed this change as a reaction to the preceding administration's liberalism[177] and Tucoo-Chala as a function of the revolutionary war.[178] Yet another possible explanation relates to Vergennes. With the fall of Turgot, Vergennes, whose anti-press attitudes have already been documented, came to exercise a larger role in the administration. The principal problem with this third theory and with Gelbart's is that neither offers any explanation for the later relaxation that began late in 1784. More research may perhaps illuminate these matters.

At the end of 1776 and into 1777, a crackdown occurred with its main focus on a narrower reportage.[179] This new repression targeted the frondeurs. The Triumvirate had expended limited effort in doing this. Maupeou's position on the Council of State had so undermined Choiseul as to allow the suppression of the *Journal des dames* in 1769, even before the Triumvirate had fully grasped power.[180] Thus, Maupeou and his colleagues had only to intimidate the coterie of authors who worked on the *Journal des dames* from attempting another paper. But when the repression of 1776 came, a full panoply of frondeur papers were flourishing which the administration abruptly purged.[181]

The government also sought to make the foreign gazettes eschew French political difficulties, both domestic and foreign. Vergennes repressed the reporting of French conflict in the gazettes, but he apparently did not crush it as completely as the Triumvirate. Traces of controversy, but not much more, leaked out in most of the newspapers of the period.[182] Of course, the general decline in the kind of political turmoil that had been the staple of the press meant that the government's enforcement must have been relatively easy. Reporting on foreign affairs was also challenged. Continued even from the more liberal Turgot ministry was the intervention into foreign affairs, encouraging a positive view of

French efforts that led, serendipitously, to an abstract critique of France through spreading ideas of republicanism and British opposition thought. But this was only a suggestion, and critical reports endured, always moderated by the style and lack of editorials and personal attacks.

Complementing this crackdown were other prior efforts that took on renewed relevance. Government endeavors to control the flow of news operated best in this environment by increasing positive reports within the rather tame domestic side and functioned the same way with the less well regulated coverage of French foreign affairs.[183] Also, the *Courrier d'Avignon*, the *Gazette de France*, and Panckoucke's very well received papers (leaving aside for the moment their fate after 1778 when they merged with the *Mercure*) all contributed to lesser or greater extent to flooding the market with a less problematic media that, in effect, brought the controls on reportage toward the benchmark. This, of course, had procedural effects as well because competition attacked the viability of more adventurous organs.

But Vergennes was innovative. While other governments had in wartime set up papers expressly designed to serve government goals, that had largely failed. One of his efforts, the *Journal militaire*, seems to have generally taken the approach of the *Gazette de France*, possessing even less freedom than was normally reserved to private, or ostensibly private, papers.[184] This paper did not seem to locate a substantial audience. But he had great success with periodicals more subtly designed. This foreign minister imposed an interpretation of America generally serving his purposes during the life of the *Affaires de l'Angleterre et de l'Amérique*, and for all Panckoucke's papers from 1778 into the 1780s. He also accepted and encouraged the *Courrier de l'Europe* whose views on these matters conformed to his goals.[185] The fantastic circulation of these papers, especially the last, guaranteed the success of this plan. Specifically, the government deployed its past policy with a mix of reporting that would generate an image, as positive as circumstances would permit, of the American and French foreign policy. Critical to it was a managed examination of allies and foes which would turn out well. Here Vergennes turned to these periodicals to examine closely America and England, but with special attention to American patriots and British opposition. The wealth of information communicated guaranteed that these papers could not always control the message, but this does not seem to have often been a problem. Of course, the government paid a price here as before that ideas especially revolutionary in the French context became easily available.[186]

These innovations, along with earlier strategies, propelled the political press – like the literary periodicals – toward the standard policies.

Apparently a few extra cracks remained open as both foreign and domestic literary papers could discuss, despite the fate of the *frondeurs*, literature and philosophy with particular openness.[187] As noted, the foreign gazettes did maintain some freedom, particularly reporting on the war. And there would have been some liberty even under the guidelines. But the freedoms in the area of foreign reporting meant less because of the great successes of foreign policy. Indeed, the general cooperation domestically between the crown and its detractors and the spate of good news on foreign affairs made Vergennes's constrictive policies largely unnecessary. Yet this approach did exist, signaling the ministry's attempt to move the press toward the baseline goals and procedures.

The inclination toward the general policy regarding political coverage makes it difficult to understand how two periodicals – the *Courrier de l'Europe* and the *Annales politiques, civiles et littéraires* – found so much freedom to report what was elsewhere forbidden. Understanding how these papers were able to be relatively frisky may grant insights into the overall rigor of the ministerial effort. One should not overstate the independence of the *Courrier de l'Europe*, although at first this paper, published in England, had much problematic to say on French domestic politics. The *Mémoires secrètes* notation for August 18, 1777 gives some idea of this periodical's tone:

> The *Courrier de l'Europe* did not appear when last expected which has upset its subscribers and partisans. The abundance of matters that are treated there necessarily procure for it many more readers than the other gazettes in as much as it is permitted frequent excesses and a liberty that is infinitely greater than elsewhere. But also there is the continued fear that it will be suppressed. Already several issues have been stopped, in spite of the excessive indulgence of the ministry, doubtless because of its English nature, which supposes a particular independence. It is difficult to believe that its bad temper will not lead to its end and that paper, which in the end is too rare, too talkative, while having all the defects of this type of a periodical, will not be irrevocably proscribed.[188]

But the *Courrier* did survive by employing two tactics. First, it trimmed its sails, accepted a French governmental subsidy and censor, and had less and less negative to say about France. Second, the ministry was willing to tolerate some continuing indiscretions because the extremely negative, and comprehensive, reports on rival England's foreign policy made the overall venture appear quite worthwhile.[189] This evidently was a case about which even contemporaries must have wondered whether Vergennes's strategy about reporting the war was not causing additional problems for the monarchy.

Although it is relatively easy to believe that the general utility and docility of the *Courrier de l'Europe* was great enough for the government to allow it as an exception to its generally repressive tendencies, Simon-Nicolas-Henri Linguet's *Annales politiques* proves yet another matter. This journalist was definitely the most outspoken in the entire eighteenth century. In this journal, intermittently published from April 1777 until 1787 both in London and Brussels, Linguet continued the charges he had levied in the literary section of the *Journal de Bruxelles* from 1774 to 1776 (a period when Panckoucke's journal shook off some of its normal conformism). Both journals assailed the philosophes in terms little different than Fréron's. But Linguet's real departure from governmental norms lay in the political analysis of the *Annales*, which Darline Gay Levy has superbly summarized.[190]

Linguet envisioned world politics in total disarray with many parties squabbling over their claims to represent the nation, and France provided no exception. On the surface all appeared well with the arts ever more important; intellectual life never more vibrant; the times the happiest; luxuries or at least comforts well distributed. Yet beneath this veneer the producers of wealth existed in great despair and with depravities rampant. Because of the diseased state of the working class and because of the contrast with large numbers possessing great moveable wealth, an immense insurrectionary potential existed among those who either had little to lose or few obligations. The latter, these capitalists, would so oppress the former that their only reasonable response was rage and counterattack. Linguet believed that these two unalterably opposed forces had, indeed, arrayed themselves one against another and would drag Europe into an apocalypse. A revolution lay in the wings and would yield property for some of the poor and at least security for the rest. Otherwise the poor would sink into unspeakable oblivion.

With such a message, how could this periodical ever win entrance to France? In part the explanation rests on Linguet's reputation. Known to be violently anti-ministerial, he threatened that were he not allowed entry, he would unleash even more incredible bombast against royal officials in pamphlet form. Such an effort at intimidation likely would have remained ineffectual had Linguet not possessed powerful allies. In both earlier and present guises this author mixed his populism with a powerful monarchism, one might even say royal despotism. Harking back to these traditions, Linguet dedicated the *Annales politiques* to Louis XVI.[191] And this positioning seems also to have earned royal allegiance. When members of the Académie française, so often roasted by Linguet, sought to have his paper suppressed, one of the king's ministers rejected this request because the King and his family read the *Annales politiques* as their sole source of news and with "an inexpressible pleasure." Marie-Antoinette had her own reasons and no doubt appreciated Linguet's

179

animosity towards her enemy, D'Aiguillon.[192] Joining the royal family in this protectiveness was even Vergennes, though one suspects his support may have been more grudging. The *Correspondance secrète* in 1779 noted, "The King and Monsieur read carefully every page, and M. de Vergennes whom Linguet dared to mistreat about two years ago, has received him very well on his last trip to Paris. . . ."[193] Perhaps Linguet's anglophobia explains some of the foreign minister's growing good will towards the journalist.

A second explanation for the acceptance of Linguet's *Annales politiques* in the midst of a general attack on the most adventurous periodicals focuses on the difficulties of his position. In fact, the contradiction between the general situation of papers and that of Linguet lessens when one considers how tentative was the tolerance. His literary agent, Pierre Lesquesne, expended considerable time and effort to extract a *tolérance tacite*, a right to distribute in France that was unusual for periodicals. This required approval by a censor, but guaranteed no use of the postal system necessary to the distribution of any paper. Linguet was, however, assigned a sympathetic censor, Le Noir, the head of the Parisian police. And somehow Lesquesne acquired the right to send the *Annales politiques* through the mail.[194] Nonetheless, this proved to be no warm welcome, and in the end, the coolness never subsided. While avoiding attacks on the monarch, Linguet continued to assault previous targets, especially the parlementarians. In 1780 he especially pilloried a past enemy, the Duke de Duras. The Duke arranged for the issuance of a *lettre de cachet* so that when an unsuspecting Linguet returned to Paris for talks with Lesquesne, he was arrested and thrown in the Bastille on September 27, 1780. Enter the ministers. Duras's charge would not have long detained Linguet, but Vergennes and Le Noir, whatever their previous sentiments, had tired of the writer. Linguet's infernal, eternal critiques of the establishment probably wore out his welcome. Although the officials' precise motives remain uncertain, their actions were clear enough. With Linguet imprisoned, they sent police to Brussels to ransack his quarters to find a justification – a libelous writing or anything appropriate to their charge – for keeping him there. Even though they uncovered nothing, they evidently prevailed on the King to let the journalist cool his heels for some twenty months until his release on May 14, 1782.[195] By January 1783, Linguet had escaped from France and was writing an even more devastating political magazine, replete with stories of the injustices of the French legal system and the horrors of the Bastille. While Linguet penned these accounts, the ministers henceforward refused to authorize this journal's entry.[196]

This analysis of how the *Courrier de l'Europe* and the *Annales politiques* weathered the repression reveals, in the end, that only the second retained its independence and even it could not outlast government stringency. In addition, Linguet relied on many powerful friends and his own intimidating threats for the *Annales* to survive as long as it did. True, the *Annales politiques* continued to enter France after 1783 through smuggling and counterfeiting,[197] but that sort of distribution lay outside governmental policy. The journal was being published; the demand for it was incredibly great; and the borders were simply too porous to cut off its flow under such circumstances. Finally, over time Linguet reduced his level of invective.

Still the legal appearance of the *Annales politiques*, however shaky and brief, did constitute a partial exception to overall policy. This, coupled with the ability of some other gazettes to report French conflicts abroad suggests that the retreat from 1776 was not completely thoroughgoing. Official intensity also flagged a little in suppressing evidence of the intermittent domestic difficulties of this same period.

So little is understood about Versailles's relationship with the press after 1784 until the revolutionary crisis that only a coda may be now added. Clearly, the foreign newspapers regained their earlier vigor,[198] but simultaneously Panckoucke's efforts intensified as he continued much of his conformist approach, substituting the *Mercure*'s literary section for the remaining independent part of the *Journal de Genève*. Finally as the Revolution began in 1787, royal administrators tried to extend the reach of the official journals by hiring Panckoucke to operate the *Gazette de France* and thus inject some life in the ailing periodical. The only liberalization in these papers sprang from a general relaxation begun by the government after 1784 that Panckoucke somewhat extended to the *Mercure* and its clones.[199] These aspects suggest confusion, as elsewhere on the eve of the Revolution.

A great paucity in documentation makes difficult any attempt to integrate the government's control of the provincial affiches into this schema of successive expansions and contractions. Although the provinces saw a number of regional publications, the affiches, constituting the vast majority of these sheets, deserve special focus. Before their creation and even during their existence, some indigenous literary journals appeared and failed, both from lack of interest and from the enforcement of the monopoly held by the *Journal des savants*.[200] The affiches possessed no similar legal handicaps, as they emerged from the effort of the holders of the privilege of the *Gazette de France* to capitalize on the investment. From the late 1750s, Le Bas de Courment endeavored to lease out the right to establish affiches in localities all over France. Although locals and even Malesherbes contested Courment's right to create journals, in the end he and successive possessors of the privilege controlled this right and fairly successfully defended it throughout the century.[201] With this sort of journal already underway in Paris (the *Petites affiches* and the *Affiches de province*) for almost a decade, the government's expectations were clear that literature and politics must be minimized. Despite this stricture, some of these materials crept in, though always hemmed in by business and economic information.

Although the private individual who held the *Gazette's* monopoly could authorize the affiches which generally published only non-controversial materials, the administration still carefully watched the content of these papers. To be certain, in these matters local authorities competed with Versailles for power with the parlements among others involved. Gilles Feyel, whose work on this genre is fundamental and groundbreaking, cites a case of June 24, 1762, in which the procurer general of the Douai parlement complained about praise for Rousseau in the Lille paper. And at Bescançon, the parlement hoped to involve itself more generally. Elsewhere municipalities took a role although they seem also to have expected the central government's participation.[202]

For the most part, the central authorities set standards with little outside interference. In general, this proved a far easier task than for the rest of the press. First, officials had to allow a certain tolerance toward national journals that had international competitors. In addition, Feyel has argued that provincial journalists simply had fewer resources with which to deflect administrative oversight. In their cases, officials could afford to be demanding.[203] But at this point in our knowledge, it remains difficult to ascertain what standards the officials applied. The affiches' content suggests that they seldom, if ever, went beyond the limits for ideal reporting that informed the rest of the administrators' efforts. Nonetheless, variation from place to place, so typical of the Old Regime, may well have been a factor here as well.[204]

More information can be discovered about the regulatory procedures, which appear quite coherent. The government required prior censorship. In the case of Lille, Malesherbes named four censors: the procureur du roi at the Bureau des finances and three other similar officials. Later, the local head of the royal police force also provided surveillance and sometimes the only supervision. In the latter case, a lighter government hand was at work. Backing up this system was a Parisian checkpoint. Each editor sent his paper to Paris where an editor from either the *Petites affiches* or the *Affiches de province* named a censor who had the right to demand corrections.[205] Perhaps, further research into these intricate procedures can illuminate the administration's goals for the provincial press enough to provide at least the same kind of chronology constructed for the nationally distributed press.

In significant contrast to the present understanding of the affiches was the situation for the rest of the press. In part similar crucial gaps remain, yet enormously complex particulars have been uncovered. In this state of partial and complicated understandings, one might attempt a broad set of generalizations. Interestingly, at the very base, officials employed overall policies and procedures which tolerated some freedom in literature and, in the end, admitted something other than French political propaganda. And from Malesherbes to the Revolution, periodicals managed to expand that system episodically, most often with more permissions to publish granted, more personalities, and stronger foreign reporting. Attacks on the domestic activities of the crown and Church emerged quite successfully, though in the muted form of the political press, during the Choiseul era and the brief Turgot ministry. Overall this mix of approaches yielded a variety of results. When the government was vigilant, as during the Vergennes period (excepting Linguet of course), these ambivalent policies might generally be said both to minimize political problems while presiding over a more restive literary and philosophical press. Only the relatively short-lived Maupeou government was tougher, and Vergennes and his colleagues must have been pleased with their success, even if it was not total. At the other extreme under Choiseul and Turgot, official control significantly faded.

Surprisingly for those scholars who have envisioned an increasingly enfeebled regime, the last two decades of the Old Regime saw policies at the more restrictive end of a spectrum that ranged from largely controlled to its opposite. These controls, though certainly in contrast to other areas of weakness, revealed government resolution. This stronger effort also explains other events. An absence in publicly debated court cases during the Maupeou and Vergennes ministries seems to conform quite well to the regimen imposed on the press.[206] In addition, this newly achieved authority may throw light on another important event. In 1777 the government altered the copyright law to favor the individual over the publisher. This represented a sharp break from the Turgot position which had kept publishers' rights intact during its 1776 suppression of the guilds. The point in 1777 was to undermine an illicit trade in books by destroying publishers' rights and by releasing promising titles to provincial publishers. This last group would then turn from illegal to the newly opened legal forum.[207] This chapter links this effort to a very broad movement toward increased controls. Although this change in copyright was part of a fifty-year effort, its timing may relate to Vergennes's interest in moving toward constriction. Therefore, royal authority, weak in many areas and seemingly underestimated as well, needs to be part of any calculation about the public space created by publishing, especially in the decades just before the revolutionary crisis. Finally, in fashioning any new understanding, this chapter has also revealed that paying attention to changing ministries provides valuable insights and compelling detail to a chronology of the Old Regime. Even in these concluding paragraphs, with the emphasis on the longest-term trends, attention to this ebb and flow creates a clearer sense of what took place.

6

THE READERSHIP

In the study of the press – an ever-shifting and elusive terrain – no subject proves more difficult to pin down than the reader. By the 1970s, the influence of social history had led scholars to search, wherever possible, for the circulation figures and the social identities of subscribers.[1] Although such evidence continues to increase, it has remained quite skimpy. Furthermore, as many scholars have pointed out, the number and social class of subscribers do not answer the most important questions about how the audience approached the materials presented.[2] Exploring periodical readership requires connecting the available statistical configuration of the periodical audience to evidence about the relationship between readers and the press. A range of potential roles – from that of contributor to passive follower – remained conceivable and require examination. Understanding the reader's stance will allow a more general contribution to the broader literature on this subject.

To begin, who constituted the readership? As the introduction of this book has argued, a very much larger press – and by implication audience – emerged in the course of the eighteenth century. From a base at mid-century of ten to twenty thousand issues, sales tripled or quadrupled with issues commonly read by numerous individuals. Although sharing surely varied over time, nothing suggests a change large enough to have altered the growth of the press and its audience. This increase surely outstripped population expansion, even in the very dynamic middle class.

Unfortunately, such indicators actually say less than one would wish. For France, with 26 million inhabitants on the eve of the Revolution, the numbers remain far too fragmentary and unsystematically compiled to calculate the size of the audience, especially when one considers the impossibility of knowing how frequently copies were passed from hand to hand. And even if these figures became available, whatever they were in absolute terms, they would very likely remain small in relation to the size of France's population. And one would still be guessing about the identity of this audience.

Some documentation exists to allow generalizations. The most useful material comes from social analyses of six different periodicals' subscriber lists. Unfortunately, the categories in these data (see Tables 6-1 to 6-6) are not systematic and defy precise comparisons. In addition, the subscribers to one of the periodicals, the *Nouvelles de la république des lettres*, were mainly Swiss (Table 6-6). Because of the paucity of this sort of information, it is worth including this example despite whatever differences existed between the societies of Switzerland and France. Despite

Table 6-1 Journal étranger – 1755

Total subscribers	1521
Known subscribers	980
Nobles	148
Ecclesiastics	82
Women (mostly aristocrats)	42
Intellectuals	33
Finance	92
Wholesale merchants	72
Employees in the ministries	63
Military	47
Diplomats	45
Employees in justice	41
Parlementarians	40
Doctors	24
Engineers	8
Notaries	7
Architects	6
Booksellers	5
Unknown	225

Source: Jean Sgard, "Les Souscripteurs du *Journal étranger*" in Hans Bots, ed., *La Diffusion et la lecture des journaux de langue française sous l'ancien régime* (Amsterdam, 1987), pp. 89–100.

Table 6-2 Gazette de France – 12 page edition, 1756

Total known subscribers	199
Titled nobility (without function noted)	63
High finance	41
High administration	17
Sovereign court	17
Other professions	11
Court officials	8
Military	8
Lower robe	7
Employees of great nobles	5
Bankers	5
Lower administrator	1

Source: Gilles Feyel, "*La Gazette* au début de la guerre de sept ans. Son Administration, sa diffusion (1751–1758)," in Bots, *La Diffusion*, pp. 101–16.

Table 6-3 Année littéraire – 1774–76

Total known subscribers	169
Nobility	34
Women	32
Church	29
Liberal professions	28
Commerce	14
Other	5
Army	4
Unknown	23

Source: Harvey Chisick, *The Production, Distribution and Readership of a Conservative Journal of the Early Revolution: The "Ami du Roi" of the Abbé Royou* (Philadelphia, 1992), p. 216.

Table 6-4 Mercure de France – 1756

Total known subscribers	756
Nobles	200
Government functionaries	189
Women	117
Liberal professions	91
Church	49
Commerce	44
Unknown	66

Source: Daniel Mornet, "L'Intérêt historique des journaux littéraires et la diffusion du *Mercure de France*," *Bulletin de la société d'histoire moderne*, 22 (1910): 119–22.

Table 6-5 Journal helvétique – 1778

		Nobles
Total subscriptions	237	39
Anonymous	140	
Magistrature and functionaries	24	14
Booksellers	15	3
Ecclesiastics	13	2
Wholesalers/bankers	13	7
Military	6	6
Artisans	2	
Doctors	2	
Women	2	2
Intellectual	1	1
Circle	1	
Unknown	18	4

At least five of the *Journal helvétique* also were sent to a reading club.
Source: Michel Schlup, "Diffusion et lecture du *Journal helvétique* au temps de la Société de Neuchâtel, 1769–1782," in Bots, *La Diffusion*, pp. 59–72.

Table 6-6 *Nouvelles de la république des lettres et des arts (Paris) – 1786*

Total subscriptions	233
Nobles	52
Clergy	26
Intellectuals/professionals	25
Wholesalers	18
Military	10
Lawyers	6
Unknown	96

Source: Hervé Guenot, "Les Lecteurs des *Nouvelles de la république des lettres et des arts* (1782–1786)," in Bots, *La Diffusion,* pp. 73–88.

the lacunae and problems, what unmistakably emerges is the importance of the elite – both noble and common – and the relative weakness of the merchant and popular classes.

Although these data mainly focus on social categories, three single out women. In two cases women (the *Année littéraire* and the *Mercure de France*) provide between 15 and 20 per cent of all subscribers. The simultaneous emergence of a press self-consciously in search of a women's audience strongly indicates the women were important.[3] But these statistics cannot be more precise about the female subscribers.

More clearly, the noble and commoner elite predominated. Included with them are the mercantile groups of bankers and wholesalers, who by the great wealth that many had attained, would seem qualified for the highest layer of commoners composed of professionals, royal officers, and others clearly removed from commerce. The number of subscribers listed from the working and shopkeeping part of society proves exceptionally slight. The *Journal étranger*, the *Gazette de France*, and the *Journal helvétique* listed not a single one. Some of the working poor might, however, have been included in the "business" category among the subscribers to the *Mercure* and the *Année littéraire*. On the eve of the Revolution, the literary *Nouvelles de la république des lettres et des arts* went to two artisans. But this term may mislead, as artisans might be laborers, merchants or even manufacturers. Overall, the records reveal little more interest among the merchants and masters than among laboring classes. The only way the popular and merchant classes could amount to much is to assume that all subscribers with unknown social backgrounds came from these groups, and this seems too great a leap.

Although the social categories used to analyze subscription lists are quite imprecise, owing to the vagueness of the original recording, the presence of the nobility is most evident. Even if one takes as "noble" only those who were so recorded, discounting all those undoubtedly masked by such classifications as military and diplomatic, this social group occupies a significant space. But if one adds these other groupings in which nobles likely constituted all or almost all of a category, the numbers of the nobility mount substantially (see Table 6-7). Using a broad definition, the subscribers prove to be just under one-half noble. While the *Gazette de France* had a substantially higher percentage, these statistics were calculated for the more expensive of its two editions; the greater cost may explain a higher noble percentage. But for the entire sample, most of the other non-noble subscribers came from the wealthy commoners of all kinds including lawyers, governmental officials, intellectuals, bankers, and wholesalers. All these statistics may be somewhat high, since inflating one's social status, especially claiming nobility, was common in the Old Regime. Even allowing for this practice leaves a subscribership dramatically elite.

Table 6-7 The nobility as subscribers

Periodical	Nobility narrowly counted	Nobility broadly counted
	Number %	Number %
Journal étranger	148 (20)[a]	322 (43)
Gazette de France	63 (31)	113 (57)
Année littéraire	34 (23)	70 (48)
Mercure de France	200 (29)	317 (46)
Journal helvétique	N/A	39 (40)
Nouvelles de la république . . .	52 (38)	62 (46)

[a]Number in parentheses is the percentage of nobles in regard to the total number of subscribers with an ascertainable social category.

The different groups within the nobility and elite commoners seem to be well represented. Often scholars have asserted that those with commercial interests were only weakly attentive to intellectual life. But businessmen – bankers and wholesalers whose wealth and pretensions rivaled more elite commoners – seem to have subscribed as much as their peers. Consequently, the lack of support from the even lower ranks of commerce may relate to wealth, education, and status instead of any fundamental indifference among all those in business to the world of print.

The last group well represented was the clergy whose social status could vary considerably. Their presence may modify these findings about rank by including parish priests whose situation placed them among those commercial and laboring groups, otherwise virtually unrepresented here. At most, their numbers could only slightly shift the argument here about the dominance of elites. But the general predominance of the elite suggests that these ecclesiastics also hailed from the upper echelons of religious life.

These lists indicate the broad outlines of the subscribers. The some 23 million working poor in France and the one million merchants and masters figured little on subscription lists. To the contrary, the roughly

200,000 nobles, several thousand upper clergy, and 1,000,000 well-off commoners dominated,[4] and the nobles evidently greatly overrepresented themselves. Even dismissing my conjectures about the clergy and the tendency to inflate social status, one still finds very clear evidence on the pre-eminent role of wealthy commoners and nobles.

But can the broad patterns revealed by circulation records serve as a profile of subscribers? Even though the data remain sparse, their general contours are so uniform that aberrations seem unlikely. Also, because subscription lists, few as they are, are spread out reasonably well over the last half-century of the Old Regime press, such a pattern probably held up through the entire period under examination here. It would be desirable to locate more on the political press, but there is little reason to imagine a major difference between the public's reading of literary and political papers.[5] The single most obvious omission is the failure thus far to locate a subscription list for either Parisian or provincial affiches. Yet the content of these papers alone suggests that they too held limited appeal for the populace. Moreover, the quite low circulation figures reinforce that perception that the affiches attracted a narrow audience. Yet it may be that, because of the commercial focus of these periodicals, they appealed to the broader merchant community.[6] But much of the copy would also attract the highest strata of provincial society. These groups accepted the anti-aristocratic tone and would find much information (e.g., land sales, high office) to interest them. Thus, it seems likely only that the subscribers of the affiches would be more inclusive than radically different.

Other factors make convincing the almost complete invisibility of the bottom of the populace among the readership. The price of journals likely discouraged them. Affiches commonly cost just under ten livres; political papers ten livres more; and philosophical papers between 20 and 40 livres. For a family living on an annual income of 200 to 400 livres, such an expense would probably appear overwhelming.[7] Although Daniel Roche found books in numerous homes of the Parisian poor, periodicals rarely appeared.[8] In addition, a motive for buying a journal seems difficult to provide for the poorer classes. As already noted, even the affiches seldom discussed subjects that might have interested the poor. The discussion press usually operated at a very ethereal level, and the elliptical nature of news reporting in the political press must have been very problematical for uneducated readers.

But might, however, the contours of the general audience have differed from that of the subscribers? Doubtless, because other ways than subscription existed to read the press, a socially wide audience may have existed. But the most obvious contemporary way to expand readership – café perusal – infrequently existed in France. Although some retail establishments stocked periodicals for clients, this seems to be a very exceptional practice, especially when compared with contemporary England and Germany or Revolutionary France.[9] In fact, during this latter period, cafés came to provide papers; and their owners made up a significant part of the distribution. Conversely the failure of cafés to appear on Old Regime subscription lists indicates how restricted was their effort.[10]

Other practices surely enhanced readership, but without changing its social composition. France did have reading clubs, yet these were expensive, with annual fees often exceeding 20 livres.[11] In effect, what they offered was the opportunity to read several political and literary periodicals. For groups so uninterested in publications that their members scarcely subscribed, however, it is difficult to imagine that this still elevated price coaxed many new, more socially inferior participants. Thus, neither clubs nor cafés probably widened reading of periodicals. Another practice could have brought different kinds of people into the audience: the informal borrowing and sharing among family and friends. Nonetheless, the social barriers of the Old Regime largely separated inferior groups from the higher elites who purchased the lion's share of the press.[12]

Still other strategies may have recruited an appreciable following that was more diverse than subscribers. Although research remains very limited, some periodicals were sold by the issue. Though discouraged in some quarters, it continued anyway. One might presume that such a small expenditure would have encouraged some individuals. And, to be certain, public readings surely reached lower levels of society.[13] Also available was the likely prospect that commonly affiches were publicly posted. But until scholarship uncovers how common these methods were, their influence will remain cloudy.

But even if further research uncovers that these rentals and readings were quite significant, the editors and journalists would still see their main audience as the subscribers, composed most probably of elites. These groups, by subscribing, formed the main financial bulwark on which the press relied. Their steady support surely would guarantee them a sizable role in the eye of the publishing community. Subscribers might have occupied a lower rung for publishers if one imagines these latter to be a more aggressive band of entrepreneurs. The broader audience and a chance for expansion might have captivated them. But the little we know of them does not suggest such a mindset. Panckoucke, the press tsar who was surely the most active of this lot, mined already extant and neighboring veins of demand. He could not imagine jumping far beyond social groups with whom he had been already successful. It would take the Revolution to alter this perspective.[14]

The most likely social composition of periodicals' readership allows a conclusion about the availability of the press. One might suggest that their presence would certainly be significant among this top part of society. The circulation figures (see the Introduction) amplified by the mechanisms relevant for sharing with the elite, were surely large for a fairly small audience, whether or not women fully participated. Certainly by the end of the century, journals were sufficient in numbers to make periodicals common among the wealthiest. Even if one considers each sector of the press – the newspaper, the discussion journal, and the affiches – their numbers seem sufficient to serve this potential population of readers. Despite all the problems in calculating the distribution of the press it seems sufficient numbers of the first two genres of periodicals existed to reach their target group, no matter how its size may be reasonably construed. Greatest concern may be cast on whether the affiches blanketed the elite since these papers always had low circulations, and were most likely to be read across the whole spectrum of the educated nobles and commoners. Still, internal evidence in these periodicals – the broad base of advertisers – suggests this medium surely circulated among the elite.

If at least the upper echelons were familiar with the periodical as a part of daily life, what was their relationship to the press? What role did they expect the journalist to play? the reader? Examining these questions may indicate social expectations about how readers were, in fact, to read. The documentation available on this critical topic is characteristically minimal. Nonetheless, one might consider the views expressed by the journalistic community. One particularly rich source of journalistic insight into the audience are the prospectuses published to announce a paper's publication. Sometimes published separately, sometimes within issues, these announcements, also labeled "avis" and "avertissements," implicitly or explicitly defined the hoped-for relationship between audience and publication. Such opinions cannot necessarily be equated to a reader's view, but they did contain a powerful and perhaps persuasive language intended to convince readers. Unfortunately, prospectuses are difficult to obtain, because they have been erratically conserved either in runs of the periodical or sometimes separately bound and cataloged. Diligent combing of archives here and abroad has yielded for the Old Regime 139 prospectuses from 73 different papers.[15] Although the vast majority of these (see Tables 6-8 to 6-11) concern the period under examination here (1745 through 1786), the analysis gives some attention to even the earlier efforts as a backdrop.

Examining prospectuses for their view of the desirable rapport between journalists and readers reveals some uniformity from the 1660s to the Revolution. Publishers and editors almost always promised to be "useful." It would be interesting to speculate on the choice of practicality, as journalists evidently decided to avoid focusing on pleasure or stimulation as their centerpiece. Claiming to be helpful, advertisements did not

Table 6-8 Number of journals located
with prospectuses, 1660–1788

A. By location	
France	57
Foreign	16
B. By type of journal	
Political	6
Affiches	6
Discussion	63
Miscellaneous	2

Table 6-9 Number of prospectuses, 1660–1788

A. By location	
France	113
Foreign	26
B. By type of journal	
Political	13
Affiches	39
Discussion	85
Miscellaneous	2

Table 6-10 Number of journals located
with prospectuses by decades[a]

1660–1669	2
1670–1679	1
1680–1689	1
1690–1699	–
1700–1709	1
1710–1719	1
1720–1729	3
1730–1739	3
1740–1749	1
1750–1759	13
1760–1769	12
1770–1779	26
1780–1788	20

[a]The total here is higher than in Table 6-8 because
journals with multiple prospectuses in separate
decades would be listed for each decade.

Table 6-11 Number of prospectuses by decades

1660–1669	4
1670–1679	1
1680–1689	3
1690–1699	–
1700–1709	4
1710–1719	1
1720–1729	3
1730–1739	3
1740–1749	1
1750–1759	13
1760–1769	27
1770–1779	45
1780–1788	34

precisely define their target. Employed interchangeably were terms like "readers," "public audience," "citizens," "inhabitants," and "society." Probably the editors had in mind more the "public," which scholars have loosely defined as the literate elite, but the journalists in no way openly limited themselves. Consequently, this work does not attempt to resolve this question and instead uses the vague social language akin to the vocabulary of that time. Readers of this chapter confront the same lack of exact terminology that faced eighteenth-century readers.

These appeals to the public suggest two important problems. Here was an entrepreneurial openness that contradicted publishers' general lack of aggressiveness in this matter. This difference might be dismissed as a hopefulness that publishers simply suggested without much considera-tion. Yet if this discourse might be so easily contradictory with behavior, can it be seen to represent any reality at all? This is an important question that may be best taken up in the conclusion of this chapter after consider-ing the views of the journalists.

With the public somewhat defined, the "avertissements" turned to describe the relationship between periodicals and audience. Although the press generally promised to serve the reader, an approach which would appear to make the audience the master, many, even contradic-tory, options were pursued. The oldest prospectus uncovered was that of the *Journal des savants* (1665) which after listing its subjects, carefully noted how such topics might be helpful to readers. The appeal explained that anyone embarked on a large undertaking could use this information. Moreover, the reader might publicize his own work, even submitting *mémoires* for publication, and the journal in that way would directly assist readers.

Inevitably, this ad and others of this period recognized a role for the paper, but much more consistently they emphasized a place, not as an instructor or guide, but as a passive conduit for information that people desired. The prospectus promised to include many different contributions, so that it would contain neither passion nor partiality. A year or so later, after the publishing of the periodical had been interrupted, likely for ignoring the caution it advocated,[16] the paper once again appealed to readers by promising to avoid judgments, which it called "a form of tyranny." Reporting remained necessary but this time without criticism, and everyone would be pleased at such an agreeable and useful work.

The *Mercure de France*, founded shortly after in 1672, agreed with the *Journal des savants*'s publicity and primarily justified itself as a service organ whose goal was meeting the needs of readers as they themselves understood them. And so the prospectus stated: "Thus, one must consider this volume as the design of a work to which one may add a great deal and not as a finished work." Moreover, continued the advertisement, if you have some information, this is the periodical to spread it. In a later advertisement of the same year (vol. 2), the editor attributed the paper's overwhelming success to the variety of its contents. In this way, this magazine could respond to the demands of a wide readership. Such appeals clearly cast this journal in a similar light to the *Journal des savants*.

Much the same appeal – information publicly deemed useful and delivered without opinion – dominated Pierre Bayle's 1684 prospectus of *Nouvelles de la république des lettres*. Once again a journal stressed its desire to serve, promising both long and short reviews to gratify different attention spans. The paper also would include obituaries since everyone wished to read them. Likewise the *Nouvelles de la république des lettres* offered to publish its readers' manuscripts. In one way, this literary journal's claims proved slightly more adventurous than others. As usual, the paper guaranteed impartiality and in the most controversial area of religion planned to offer no opinions at all. Yet the paper did admit that, even with such restrictions, disagreement remained possible and even desirable. This statement did at least contemplate that the paper's views might not always be congruent with readers' wishes, but this proved the only break with an approach which promised only to reinforce extant values.

Only a few months later the *Nouvelles de la république des lettres* was issuing a second "avertissement," this time falling completely into line with the *Journal des savants* and the *Mercure*. The editor here apologized, a disarming tactic designed to indicate his interest in immediately satisfying the public. He argued that his goal had been to instruct and satisfy the curious, but he had been forced to admit many mistakes. And he stated:

When one is docile enough to publish the errors that have been pointed out, there's surely the appearance that one is inclined to reform one's manner that has displeased. The public may rest assured that this work will become better daily because its composer is sincerely aware that he has not pleased and he'll do all he can to correct matters. He clearly understands that people don't want him to take sides in the matters of which he speaks, and everyone will like it better if he keeps himself within the limits of a disinterested historian who spares his reflections. People will remark henceforward that he has profited from this advice.

The editor had retreated to avowals of simply letting his materials speak for themselves. Of course such neutrality was impossible, as some editorial intervention was inevitable, but it announced a particular direction.

It would seem this renewed promise, however ineffectual, does at least help overcome some of the lacunae in the seventeenth-century data. Indeed, what apparently brought forward this second "avertissement" was a negative public reaction to strongly stated opinions. And the editor apparently believed the public preferred journalists appear impartial. Consequently, one might expect such an opinion to be present in most publicity campaigns and shared by other editors.

Indeed, the dominant image in the prospectuses available from the reign of Louis XIV is that of the editor prostrate before the public. Surely, such a relationship flattered readers and encouraged them to provide judgments. Although historians have been debating when society began to recognize public opinion as a court that had or ought to be consulted, scholars have placed the beginning for this in the eighteenth century. That seventeenth-century editors implicitly advanced this view may reflect earlier origins than expected. Because advertising methods usually depend on already accepted values, it seems likely that public opinion acting as a court was already afloat when the editors used it.

By the mid-eighteenth century, the prospectuses depicted a greater variety of interactions and consequent roles for the public. Indeed, simply the greater array of prospectuses creates a more nuanced picture of what "avertissements" proclaimed. Some of the new prospectuses continued earlier traditions. An "avertissement" for the *Censeur hebdomadaire* in 1760 promised careful attention to the tastes of the public, stating, "Journalists must cede to the will of the greatest number." The public wants extracts and "the public is our master; the surest way is to make new efforts to satisfy it." Once again, the advertisement reminded readers that "the desire to render ourselves agreeable in the eye of the public energizes our vigilance."

This approach promised that these papers would serve the entire public by catering to its various goals. But as the eighteenth century progressed, few others came to share this vision of the periodical simply as a supplier of information desired by the audience. A second, yet still a minority, approach might generally be described as imperious. Perhaps this new confidence emerged as the medium matured and gained greater certainty, at least enough to change the balance in the relationship deemed appropriate between the public and the journalist. Here periodicals expected to be useful by guiding readers, by preparing that news designated significant by the journalists. In many cases they relied on the findings of others or on the dictates of a universal reason or morality and thus might reduce their own significance. But, as they accepted this dependence, the knowledge they contained most often remained quite unattainable to the audience they often simultaneously deprecated. Of course, they served readers, but the latter's main role was to listen and obey. Regardless of the tack, the distinguishing feature was the dominant stand of the journalist. But the other journals, clearly the majority, embarked on a middle path not entirely unconnected to earlier traditions. Journalists were arbiters of taste, but of a broadly acceptable taste. Most often advertisements in this genre promised to provide information connected to generally desired social norms. These claims proved rather modest. Such publicity also stated an interest in public collaboration and public wishes. This approach proclaimed a more restrained journalistic liberation that would give them a share of center stage with the public.

Surprisingly, given the *Censeur hebdomadaire*'s later abject subservience, this paper had in an earlier prospectus strongly asserted its independence, making it typical of the imperious "avis." Despite an initial disclaimer of any intention to criticize, the "idea of this journal" claimed that its main goal was to impose the rules of literature. "We propose for ourselves the example of those severe judges with integrity, who in condemning the guilty, only read the laws to them. We do not share the doubts of those who wonder what the rules of literature are. For violators, we'll rake them over the coals. Reason, duty, and public interest require this." Here the editors also promised, of course for all the best reasons, to improve society through literary uplift. Although reading laws made by others to offenders somewhat reduces journalistic independence, the tone of the remarks reestablishes more than sufficient power.

Even before mid-century, periodicals advocated journalistic independence and dedication to educating the audience. For example, this approach characterized the Jansenist paper, the *Nouvelles ecclésiastiques*. The clandestine organ of a beleaguered movement, this periodical predictably viewed its role as changing, not reinforcing, public opinion. Writing in 1728, the editors noted that simple people needed the *Nouvelles* to instruct them as it remained unreasonable to ignore ecclesiastical developments. And the editors also proclaimed that the paper elevated the "good people" who because of sound reasons wished to know what was transpiring. Others, who remained ignorant, accepted the terror of the worldly life. By recording and disseminating reasoning and facts not available to the audience, the *Nouvelles* would warn of possible retribution and thus would restrain those who did not sufficiently fear God. Making themselves the master of the audience, these editors found surprising company among French imitators of Addison and Steele's *Spectator*, who were part of a new wave of such publications. These periodicals shared format and content but not necessarily outlook with their English brethren. One of these – *Le Spectateur français* edited by Marivaux in 1727 – sought readers by claiming to be a non-systematic author eschewing careful logic. Eschewing any promise of analysis, the editor instead focused upon the inspiration of the imagination and reiterated: "I would prefer all the fortuitous ideas that chance allows to what the most ingenious research involving great labor would furnish me. Although sometimes I react erratically to similar situations, I usually find I am right. I hope that reflections from this vantage point might be useful to the readers." From a personal and hidden Mount Olympus would come notions necessary to the audience.

Others besides the *Censeur hebdomadaire* followed this didactic relationship consisting of omniscient journalists who instructed passive readers. No matter how much the periodicals claimed to serve the audience, the activity of the latter, other than acceptance, remained minimal. Those familiar with the passions of Elie Fréron would scarcely be surprised to find that his successors adopted a style elevating the journalist and preaching to a public in need of their guidance. In the 1786 announcement soliciting renewals for *Année littéraire*, the editors promised to provide "matters of taste solidly discussed," and new works evaluated by the rules of the relevant art form. Despite a vow to avoid animosity and bitterness, the announcement stated that the *Année littéraire* would "courageously sustain . . . the course of religion, morality, and reason; the criticism will be severe, but honest and well motivated, as far from bitter satire as from lazy and fatal indulgence." Coupled with this vision of a strong journalistic role was a very low opinion of the public. More often imperious prospectuses treated, directly or indirectly, the audience as a passive recipient, but here the journalists deprecated the audience, noting: "The more one departs from the true principles of morality as in literature, the more the public shows itself credulous and easy to persuade, the more a periodical work like this one, becomes useful and even necessary." While the editors did go so far as to allow the potential readership to submit articles, they reserved the choice to themselves.

Another periodical that followed the approach of the *Année littéraire* was the far more obscure *Journal de Monsieur dédié à Monsieur, frère du roi*. In an announcement published in 1776, this periodical promised that it would not be content simply to tell a reader where to search, but would indicate "the most precious riches," and the most extensive materials. A specialty of this periodical was to republish and revitalize old articles, currently sunk in oblivion. For this a grateful public ought to be thankful. But here as well the audience was not only a passive recipient of the bounties of the journalists but also a somewhat incompetent body that could be led astray to make bad judgments "by an imposing cabal."

Closely related to these didactic publications and at least as numerous were journals that on the whole elevated the journalist above the public yet allowed a greater role for the latter. For example, the 1765 prospectus of the *Gazette d'Agriculture* made bold promises for the articles it would publish and highly rated the expertise of its journalists. In addition to elevating the staff, the announcement downgraded the role of the people to mere recipients of knowledge. Noted the prospectus: "It is then useful and even necessary that a people who wish to acquire the degree of forcefulness to which nature has called it, be instructed about the best agricultural methods. . . ." Here the "people" were empty vessels waiting for the education that the journal would provide. Nonetheless, positive remarks reduced this condescension. After noting that various luminaries would find satisfaction in the *Gazette d'Agriculture*, the editors remarked: "The proprietor of land, the wholesaler, and in a word all the orders of citizens will find here some details, sometimes agreeable and always useful." Such statements, in the context of showing how the public would approve the periodical, allowed some, admittedly minimal, critical judgment for the heretofore silent reader.

Not dissimilar was the relationship defined by the *Journal des sciences et beaux-arts* by abbé Grosier in 1779. This journalist elevated his role by promising much:

> To speak with method and precision on each science, to publish discoveries and new inventions, to recall or defend the principles of good literature, to encourage the spirit of warriors with the information essential to them, to give the wisest lessons of morality to the young by choice examples, to ameliorate the condition of the poor, to provide support to children lacking it, to be personally useful to subscribers, such is . . . the proposed end that we put forward. . . .

Such claims evidently prescribed an interaction in which the periodical was to provide useful goods to passive receivers. Nonetheless, this promise appears less imperious because of the banality of the claims, especially when compared to the paper's more didactic kin. The general acceptability of the claims, in a sense, lowered the pedestal on which the journalist stood bringing Grosier closer to the public. In addition, envisioning some readers as warriors credited the public, and the term "personally pleasing" seemed to imagine a relationship with a reader who already possessed needs. As if to emphasize some respect for the reader, the prospectus noted, though admittedly in a footnote: "He [Grosier] will receive with recognition the morsels, of whatever sort that one would wish to send, and authors will remain anonymous unless they desire otherwise." Although the personnel of the periodical still retained the guiding hand, they exercised it less autocratically and entertained a notion of general participation, that surely included readers.

Virtually all those publications that defined the relationship between periodical and reader in such a way as to elevate the former and denigrate the latter were discussion journals; political newspapers and advertisers rarely employed such justifications. Rather they tended, along with even the majority of discussion periodicals of the period, to accept a greater role for the broad public while continuing a place for the journalists.

The most common approach – in its balance between journalist and public – may be found in the announcements of the *Affiches du Poitou*. It simultaneously adhered to a point of view and pandered to readers. Part of the 1773 appeal for subscribers included a vision of what the paper would pursue. The prospectus positioned the editor, Joyneau-Desloges, to decide what would be published in the journal and listed his credentials – previous public acclaim, local origins, and respect for the government. But whether from his pen or that of others, the items published would satisfy curiosity, spark conversation, inspire patriotism, or narrate the history of religion. Moreover, not only history, but agricultural matters and belles-lettres would be listed as well as legal information included, so that criminal acts and their subsequent prosecution would not spring from ignorance of the laws. Here was a commitment more specific than filling the whims of readers. Yet such promised materials could hardly have been meant to disturb eighteenth-century tastes. Indeed, unlike Marivaux, Joyneau-Desloges's prospectus consisted of appeals vague enough to gain almost universal approbation. Although many imperious prospectuses also claimed to rely on universals, often their appeals proved more contestable than the banalities here and in other similar "avis." By listing such values, these goals left more room for a competent public. But more important in differentiating itself from imperious prospectuses, the *Affiches du Poitou* was also specific in its positive view of the public. The prospectus utilized many strategies to align the paper with society. First the editor noted "our charge and first goal is to serve men in all possible ways." Only that agreeable to the inhabitants would be published. Continued the periodical:

> Honest and educated citizens will have the willingness to relate all curious and important events around them. We invite all the good citizens who can interest themselves in the success of a *feuille* for their instruction and amusement to tell us about their discoveries, reflections, remarks, and advice.

Not only did this quotation flatter the public but, interestingly, it bears witness to the assumed unity of the social order. Although the invitation to honest citizens dismisses the less reputable members of society, it bespeaks more the fundamental fusion of all well-meaning people. By elsewhere asking that submissions concern only that which was honorable and based on good morality, it presupposed agreement upon those questions. Finally, its policies on book reviewing indicated how undivided was to be public opinion. Joyneau-Desloges assured readers that no outlandish opinions would penetrate into book reviews since only the judgments of the most distinguished writers would be used. Such a statement rested, as Keith Baker has often asserted for this period, on the belief that pluralistic opinion resulted from malicious intent or ignorance. Decent people entertained no reasonable differences. One other sidelight worth noting is the use of the term "citizen" before the Revolution definitely categorized members of the body politic. This item, as opposed to "subject," further raised the importance of the reader.

Not dissimilar from Joyneau-Desloges' vision – at least in its significant place for both journalists and audience – was that of the *Journal de littérature française et étrangère*. Its prospectus (written in the 1780s) specifically claimed a limited independence for its writers. Renouncing past high-handedness, the announcement promised:

> We will no longer with a bold cynicism claim the right to degrade with one stroke of the pen the most esteemed works, or while incessantly decrying the loss of morals and taste, give an example of one and the other while ripping the best writers with a bitter and pedantic style.

Instead, the editors offered honest criticism which would avoid "personalities" and be sprightly and short. Against such reduced claims for its writers, the *Journal de littérature* granted respect to the reader. Analyses were there to allow the "reader to judge for himself, as much as one can do so by such a review." By this remark, the prospectus reinforced its own humility by noting the limits of its efforts, while simultaneously accepting the audience's ability to judge. Underlining this point was another promise that "general opinion" would play a significant role in the paper's coverage.

Yet another prospectus evoked the same strategy. The *Journal de Monsieur dédié à Monsieur, frère du roi* (a revival of the aforementioned *Journal de Monsieur* under entirely new management) issued an announcement in August 1778 which offered to find the most interesting, useful, and agreeable articles from other journals. No endeavor "would be more appropriate for spreading enlightenment and knowledge, the precious sources of virtues and happiness." These avowals paralleled the innocuous ones common to this genre of prospectus. Against lowered claims of expertise for the journalists, the flier greatly elevated the public. First, the prospectus claimed that its goal in collecting information was, in the final analysis, to aid the reader whose powers of judgment would be able to evaluate at a glance the justice of the journalistic opinions. While accepting the importance of a critical role for the public, this editor raised it still further. The *Journal de Monsieur* justified its offer of space to authors to rebut the negative reviews of journalists by pointing out that the debate would lead to an appeal to the public – "a tribunal both surer and more impartial." Confronting a tentative journalist was an able audience.

This balancing act between independence for the journalist and a role for the public elicited a variety of approaches, especially when journalists described their importance and its limits. The prospectuses relied on a wide range of claims that bespoke expertise but of a kind widely accepted and thus not high-handed. One editor promised variety; another, clarity.[17] Papers advertised their interest in helping people earn more money or avoid high prices, in uncovering little-known books or sticking to famous works, or in avoiding untruths, rumors, and political subjects in general.[18] There was some agreement as more than one planned to assist farmers and businessmen, to illuminate science, to improve taste, to support patriotism, and to address complex questions.[19] Even among this group of cautious advertisers, a few ventured potentially problematic claims. In its 1782 prospectus the *Annales politiques, civiles, et littéraires* gave its guarantee to speak freely and frankly, and in 1733 the *Bibliothèque britannique* agreed to cover disputes, at least those which were not personal. Yet such isolated examples should not obscure the fact that, however diverse these advertisements, their various assertions shared a common acceptability to any reader. Who would oppose either clarity or variety? Or aiding farmers? Or any of the other commitments offered? Just as the *Affiches du Poitou* had charted a tranquil course, the other periodicals with similar advertisements tried not to offend any segment of society. First, even the statement of independence was again a mark of their dependence. Providing such banal choices excluded no one and appealed to everyone.

Related to the limited claims were the various ways that announcements deliberately sought to reduce the authority of the periodicals' staffs. Prospectuses proclaimed their limits by deprecating their authors. Pointing out the many problems of publishing a magazine, they would make no overreaching claims. In this way they lowered their stature vis-a-vis their intended audience. Journals also promised discretion.[20] In 1755 the *Année littéraire* and the *Bibliothèque des sciences* dedicated themselves to reining in their passions, though of course Fréron had far to go in this respect. The *Ephémérides du citoyen* (1765) likewise provided a long diatribe on how journalists existed not to display themselves but to serve the public interest. Perhaps the *Journal de Bruxelles* (1774) stated the doctrine of weakness as starkly as possible:

> Our writer is persuaded that a journalist is no judge; that he is permitted to present the decisions of the public, and to let everyone perceive the motifs; but if he prevaricates, if he lightly hazards an opinion then he becomes very culpable; if he goes yet farther, then the laws must punish him severely so that he'll forget how to lend himself to calumny.

Already in 1733 the editor of *Le Pour et le Contre* had not been able to imagine how he would displease anyone.

Even though this form of pleading predominated throughout the eighteenth century, a new view began very hesitantly to appear from the 1760s. More tightly linked to the public than those in other eighteenth-century periodicals, even more obeisant than those in seventeenth-century papers, this new approach promised readers even greater control. These prospectuses begged readers to fill the papers with their own publications. Publishers were to provide no more than a form where articles would be received, then printed. Such procedures also embellished the vision of the public, since no attempt would be made to regulate this body. This plan never affected a large number of journals since it was often proposed only tentatively by a few provincial advertisers and to some extent, the women's paper, the *Journal des dames*.

The advertisement for *Annonces, affiches, et avis divers de la haute et basse Normandie*, founded in 1762 by Etienne-Vincent Machuel, indicates the characteristics of this new paradigm. To be certain, the initial prospectus made some claims of information to satisfy curiosity and inspire health and fortune. But, more evidently, the public was supposed to assist the editor who had left his staff little room to operate. The prospectus began by arguing that purchasing the *Affiches* was necessary, since placarding this periodical simply had not made it sufficiently available. For example, "if this same information had reached all those who inhabit the countryside or neighboring villages, sellers of lands, of houses, etc. would have received better prices for their goods." And continued the announcement:

> Gentlemen secluded in their châteaux, curés of the countryside, people working at their desks, wholesalers and others, whose business consumes all their time and prevents them from leaving, and all those who live far from the cities, would doubtless love to find at their offices the paper we announce since it will provide them all the news of the province.

From whom is this news to come, if not from the journalists? The editor mused that at first he thought a professional correspondent so expensive as to defeat the project; he then proposed the following solution:

> We want to instruct people: this sheet will do it by becoming the object of a general and public correspondence on all sorts of objects and all sorts of affairs, among all the cities of Normandy, and one will envision it as the daily depository [*dépositaire journalier*] of all that happens and of all the facts that can be useful to the public.

And, indeed, he extended an invitation to everyone who could assist in providing such material. To be sure, the editor set up various rubrics but nothing imaginably of interest was lacking.

Thus the *Affiches de Normandie* forged a new approach for selling its product. Like its seventeenth-century ancestors, the *Affiches de Normandie* specified little and proved anxious to meet whatever needs the public expressed. But the greatest departure from the seventeenth century is the utter dependence of the advertiser on the public for copy. As Machuel noted, the paper aspired to be a "daily depository." And throughout its existence, he continued his reliance on the community for material. The annual "avertissements" in the *Affiches de Normandie* reiterated this desire that inhabitants of the region contribute.

Of the advertisements I located, no others exactly shared the inclinations of the *Affiches de Normandie*. Yet after simply revising and publishing the prospectus of the *Affiches du Poitou*, the advertiser from Orléans gradually shifted its stance toward that adopted by its Norman counterpart.[21] In addition, the *Journal des dames* assumed a parallel position. Passing through the hands of many different editors and publishers, this periodical offered numerous prospectuses. Although the themes varied, the concept that the journal depended on contributions from women in its audience persisted. This one clarion call among the welter of claims aligns its publicity campaign with that of the Normandy paper. Promises of editorial responsibilities waxed and waned, the relationship to the public varied, but the need – repeatedly proclaimed – for women to contribute remained the main characteristic of the *Journal des dames*'s advertisements. Thus, in such a way, could this new approach to promoting the periodical press leave, at least tentatively, the confines of the provinces.[22]

This last possibility, combined with the other appeals, represented the flowering of various specific relationships between the audience and the press. Although the diversification might be a deceptive artifact of increased data, it certainly seems that readers provided a variety of possible roles – from passive, easily misled recipients to principal contributors. But it does suggest that, if the prospectuses' view of the audience's role declined somewhat from the reign of Louis XIV, it was improving in the decades immediately preceding the Revolution. Both the political papers and the affiches paid great obeisance to the public, far more unreservedly than the discussion papers. And it was these two genres that were surging during the 1770s and 1780s. Such trends remain extremely difficult to chart for many reasons including the fragmentary circulation figures available; the question also exists whether to regard prospectuses as indicators of opinion or individual attempts to persuade. Nonetheless, one should not overlook the overwhelming inclination of periodicals, when issuing their prospectuses, to recognize positively their potential audience.

Did the readership share the aspirations outlined for them? One surely must doubt that these "avis" systematically granted insight into the actual calculations of journalists who sometimes held a much higher opinion of themselves and a lower view of the public than allowed in their own announcements.[23] As we have seen, the appeal to a broad public was not always matched by the journalists' products. Nonetheless, prospectuses might best stand as an assessment, not of their own goals, but of the goals of their readers. In a prospectus, designed to promote and ultimately sell a product, editors were astute enough to know what readers wanted to hear. These documents seem to address clearly the wider viewpoint. They appear to bear trustworthy witness to the typical view of the audience. But what of those prospectuses that adopted the minority view? If anything, because the logic of the "avertissements" emphasized the purposes of the editor and drew discussion away from the role of the public, even those editors who praised readers found that this format constrained their claims for the public. Furthermore, while a considerable number of prospectuses rated journalists above the public, these imperious pieces may not have been testifying to a division of opinion among journalists. Because such prospectuses all hailed from the discussion press where the writers might be playing the intellectual role with which they closely identified, they may have tried to attract readers by proclaiming their expertise. Sharing with the other prospectuses the same motive of finding readers, these "avertissements" may simply have stressed a line that somewhat inadvertently rather than deliberately downgraded the public. Perhaps, the largest seeming contradiction to the image of the independent reader is the expanding circulation of the very didactic journals of Linguet and Fréron. Even more than their aggressiveness, their public acceptance would seem to argue for readers accepting the status of underling. But their popularity may attest far more to the pleasure of reading hyperbole than to a willingness to subordinate judgment.

But could readers, if they held the positive view of themselves expressed in the prospectuses, act in such a light? Whenever a reader perused a periodical, he or she became both dependent on the journalist and involved in the independent act of interpreting the words. Many milieus conspired to control the reader. Yet nothing could stop readers, if imbued with a sense of self-importance, from some exercise of their critical judgment, even when journalists made opinions overly evident. Overall this understanding of the reader combined with the social makeup of the audience suggests a picture of an educated elite which drew on its own assumptions to joust with a press that inevitably also played a part in what readers understood. This mixed situation marks an early stage in press history, prior to modern media in which the balance of power seems to have tipped much farther toward journalists.

The approach to eighteenth-century readers framed by Robert Darnton may be refined and supported by these findings. His work stressed that the eighteenth-century reader was an "intensive one" who very carefully pored over texts. The basic image of the reader in this chapter is of one with a self-image as a critical reader perusing texts that were more or less didactic. Such a confrontation would lead, it would seem, to careful reading, compatible with Darnton's findings. Yet his subjects practiced careful reading less to strike an independent view, than to understand and accept, rather dutifully.[24] So these portraits of readers both portray laborious reading but the interpretations differ on the purpose of this activity. Yet the divergence still supports Darnton's strongest argument, for, no matter what the purpose, intensive reading provided the technique. Not only for religious instruction or absorbing a lionized author, this kind of interaction with texts prevailed.

CONCLUSION

Coming together in this volume has been a picture of a press whose message occupied something of a middle ground between conformism and challenge. This study also has sketched these periodicals' milieu – educated editors serving an elite audience under variable governmental controls. It is now time to connect these parts with an eye to explaining the content of this medium. Such a general approach can, of course, explicate only the broader outlines of reporting, in part because sporadic or exceptional attributes stem from particular rather than structural explanations. The second part of this conclusion tries to relate the findings to important historiographical debates that help to assess what role the press played in the coming of the Revolution.

The gazettes and other political papers of the day produced a complicated record of France. To a very large extent, the reporting of domestic and foreign affairs followed like trajectories. Through most of the 1750s, a rather limited number of foreign gazettes treated France rather harshly; counteracting this tendency were journals that took a more cautious and pro-French view. With the end of the 1750s, the point of view enunciated earlier in the gazettes became rather widespread. Nonetheless, most of the seventies and eighties (1774–76 and 1785–86 excepted) witnessed generally positive treatment of news regarding both home and abroad. Yet one subtext in all this was an abstract critique of France that emerged over the century simply from presenting more open political systems. It should be recalled that the style of reporting ensured that all these points were made without editorials to drive them home forcefully or gossip to reinforce points made viciously.

Explaining such a mixture of reporting begins with the staff of the periodicals. With careers and interests as intellectuals, they fitted into that milieu. Yet anxious to turn a profit, the journalists sought to please their audience. To be sure, annoying the government might destroy the business, but without purchasers there could be no enterprise at all. Thus, the editors turned toward their intellectual roots and their public.[1] Both groups held grave reservations about the monarchy. At many levels and in many ways, French elites, while not imagining an alternative to kingship, lost faith in their government and longed for an accountable kingship.[2] Although Panckoucke's papers prove that the public did not desire fragmentary reporting, trumpeting opinion was widely considered improper. For reasons other than the demands of the audience, editors presented many specifics that they did not regret if they led to negative conclusions. Of course, it was partly this expectation about the reserve of the gazettes that allowed the government to experiment so much with laxity in policies of control. In this context the papers pursued their shared interests with the audience.

But an effort to report the facts, coupled with the government's requirement to omit personalities and thus eschew a salacious approach, led to a press obsessive about detail, although ideology inevitably intruded. This observation explains the tone of the press but not its viewpoints. It would have been difficult for most elite observers of what took place in the 1750s and 1760s not to find the monarchy wanting at home and abroad. A hostile public surely would have shared this opinion in the 1750s, but only a few newspapers communicated such a message. Direct and indirect influence took its toll, though it was less a factor under the more tolerant Choiseul. Under his aegis, newspapers largely printed what the elite would have perceived. The major effort at control seems to have been an insistence on focusing upon elite formal politics, a control with little impact because of the extraordinary public interest in these subjects. Furthermore, governmental influence and its absence go far to explain the reporting during the Maupeou and Turgot ministries.

The most interesting case is the largely positive reporting during the hegemony of Vergennes. Although he certainly was quite resourceful in this regard, other factors helped him achieve positive coverage. Formal politics, the major focus of reporting, calmed down, drying up much problematic news at its source. In addition, most of the French saw their government's involvement in the revolutionary war as a great success. Even democratic and near-democratic upheavals, the source of problematic information, also appeared because of a coalescence of public, publishers' and minister's views. Generally sympathetic to such upheavals, press and public saw them positively, also encouraging coverage of anti-government activities in England. All these circumstances generally created less challenging periodicals, but Vergennes's efforts were also useful, though probably less important, as domestic flareups occasionally occurred but were scarcely covered. His controls made it impossible for gazettes to amplify other information to replace the absent political news. Moreover, his state-encouraged publications supported the war effort even more firmly than others. But the press appeared largely as it would have wished with some government assistance. Fully prepared to crush other problems, Vergennes found few, with the important exception of Linguet. This journalist and the period after 1784 still defy explanation.[3]

Two important points emerge regarding the efforts of Vergennes who fought to control a medium that was already extremely likely to be favorable. While generally, positive press coverage of France depended on governmental repression, here the connection was not nearly so necessary. This unusual event possesses another significance. During this ministry, peace broke out in the domestic public sphere, including especially the parlements.[4] Success in war overshadowed and reinforced this. Even though the war ended somewhat badly for the French, this represented a sharp collapse of a long euphoria. Considering the press in this political milieu thus indicates a more widespread political dominance by the government in the twilight of the Old Regime. While an investigation of this era falls outside the bounds of this study, certainly all these coincidental occurrences in French politics owe something to state intervention, though the balance between repression (possibly the parlements) or willing compliance (support for the war) remains unclear. Points of weakness – particularly budgetary struggles and the publication of pornographic diatribes – remained.[5] Probably a deeper level of discourse – that concerning political theory as well as public assumptions – remained untouched, but the daily level of contestation noticeably slackened. Nonetheless, under Vergennes, the monarchy achieved a measure of strength through war and domestic control, some of which the administration engineered.

That the affiches printed what they did was more predictable. In their substantive articles praise emerged for a society based on restraint.[6] Primarily indicted was the aristocracy. Advertisements, too, generally expanded this critique to other areas of the Old Regime. The main way that the ads diverged from the articles was including notices placed by domestics in the papers.[7] Such a different voice doubtless emerged from the ability of advertisers to use the language they wished when placing an announcement. But the overall perspective of articles in the affiches critiqued the aristocracy and promoted an alternate ideal often labelled *bourgeois*. The attitudes reveal Rousseauian influence tempered by the papers' particular commercial purpose. Thus, editors shared the views of their time but were also swayed by their papers' special niche. Even the highest portions of the elite, doubtless believing themselves personally meritorious whatever the disposition of their class, seemed to proclaim affinity with the notions that seemingly opposed them. Only the positive emphasis on commerce might have rubbed them wrong, but their own hubris about their productivity and the mildness of these charges encouraged indifference. In practice these people were far more cautious, continuing in general to harness new notions to more traditional goals.[8]

The ads, which related very much to practice, still did not overall support traditional social interests because of the happenstance of publicizing everything together, undermining any preeminence of older notions of the good. Furthermore, the advertising strategies for land, compatible as they were with class society, may have been used because of attitudes that fell outside the more conscious avenues to social advancement that the elite followed.

While a presumption of generally shared intellectual cultural values between the journalists and the elites seems best to explicate the content of the affiches, this union of values alone will not suffice to explain the discussion journals' view of the High Enlightenment.[9] The press did not wholeheartedly embrace Encyclopedism. It broadly advocated the idea of the Enlightenment but certainly did not include the philosophes' precise views of Church and state; future research may uncover other exclusions. Furthermore, the press lent little support to the philosophes as individuals. Perhaps, the general commitment to the beliefs reflects a consensus of the journalists and public,[10] though constrained by the government which, as far as we know, protected Church and state.[11] But why did the papers have so little positive to say about the Encyclopédistes themselves. Perhaps these journalists restrained themselves regarding the philosophes as individuals for differing reasons. While covering ideas, they were reporting on what they themselves believed and would have had a difficult time extricating themselves. But on the intellectuals, they held no such commitment and likely thought of them as equals. And the journalists had good reason in vying with their subjects. If they could only blindly support these intellectuals and the High Enlightenment, their value to themselves and others would seem reduced. Possibly, this need to compete explains their attitude regarding these individuals. Also, most of the ideas had a more venerable heritage than any particular individuals. Many Enlightenment notions were updated versions of a long-term secular ideology while the philosophes individually had a more slender pedigree. This mixture of motives perhaps indicates why ideas received better treatment than the fellow intellectuals who enunciated the ideas.

Fitting this enormously complex system of papers into the broader historiographical battles concerning the Old Regime and the French Revolution provides the remaining subject for this work. No better place to start exists than with the famous hypothesis Jürgen Habermas developed in *The Structural Transformation of the Public Sphere.*[12] His book demands attention because it more than any other general interpretation gives pride of place to the press.

Habermas formulated that in the seventeenth century kings completely dominated public space, representing themselves to their subjects and permitting nothing but obedience from the latter. But, with the rise of capitalism, civil society began to form, particularly within the bourgeois family. Inside these nests a new family ethic developed which, dominated by the harsh rules of capitalism, emphasized rationality instead of religion as its core belief. One important means forming these families into something of a coherent class was the literary press. It was a perfect vehicle for the bourgeoisie to move from its private sphere to an "authentic" public sphere that reflected its, not the king's, values. Literature accommodated the private origins as well as burgeoning public claims. Prior to 1789, the French were more or less arrested in their effort to develop an "authentic" space because they could not make their claims openly political. Despite certain foreshadowings, it was the Revolution that gave birth to political discussion and claims of participation.

The discoveries in this book provide much sustenance and some modification to Habermas's conceptualization. Almost every recent study of the private/public sphere as it developed in France would convert his bourgeoisie into a notability that included the wealthy, both noble and common.[13] This study certainly supports such a modification as the main audience for the press possessed these higher characteristics. According to Habermas, the discourse of the private sphere, intruding increasingly on the public as the eighteenth century wore on, supported rationality. Indubitably, the literary and philosophical press, as the German philosopher predicted, served these goals, as it did manage, although without directly attacking the pillars of Church and state, to disseminate Enlightenment thinking with its strong rationalistic patina. The affiches, by supporting open trade and a society based on merit, contributed just as much as the discussion papers. Furthermore, prospectuses directly called upon the "public" to form opinions. Despite this general agreement with Habermas's expectations for the press, this study shows that the press's restrictions on certain kinds of content reduced the role it played.

But the existence of a political press, completely unanticipated by Habermas, compensated for some of the failings of the affiches and the literary press. Clearly, if evidence for Habermas's political public space demands open discussion of public participation, the press supplied substantial servings. In the 1750s and especially the 1760s, parlementary constitutionalism was available and suggested an ideology in which the monarch remained beholden to the French. Later, the democracy from America, oppositionism from England, and Linguet's outcries schooled Frenchmen in a more radical, if far less concrete form of involvement. And, as others have shown, the press was not the only medium providing a direct political forum for the public.

Although the public sphere was far more precocious than Habermas projected, it was not without its wrinkles. In the last two decades of the Old Regime, the newspapers' treatment of home affairs was dampened.

Similar efforts also contracted elite politics, generally the basic source of news, so that the press's coverage of domestic matters sharply declined. Although news from turbulent England and Revolutionary America possessed implications, they were less immediate. Only on the eve of the Revolutionary crisis did events in domestic politics and their coverage simultaneously rise.

This information on the political press tends to reshape considerably Habermas's system. While he envisioned a continuous, but limited expansion of the bourgeois public sphere that culminated in a cataclysmic opening into politics in 1789, this evidence reveals a much earlier rise and deceleration along with other areas of political involvement. By underestimating the extent of politics, Habermas miscalculated the chronology of the second half of the eighteenth century.

This critique of Habermas's theory, based as it is on his blindness to politics and a failure to chart it, may also be used when considering François Furet's theory of the Revolution.[14] This immensely influential approach, which has often been revised by its author, argues that the emerging private sphere had two possible choices to guide its development – the inequalities embodied in the Old Regime and partially championed by the parlementarians or the commitment to equality trumpeted by Rousseau. The King had so elevated himself as to remove the monarchy utterly from any equation. In fact, in Furet's account, over the course of the century, Rousseauianism came to predominate and such inclinations led, in the power vacuum of the Revolution, to the ideal of equality. To some extent, Furet considers the Revolutionary situation itself as calling for this ideology, but the weight of his argument suggests roots in the Old Regime. Finally, the triumph of egalitarianism, Furet believes, resulted in the Terror. In the course of defending his position, Furet has increasingly emphasized contingency in these developments, yet has not abandoned Rousseauianism as a key factor.[15] Thus, his belief in an intellectually stunted rebellion confronts Habermas's more optimistic view.

Influenced by Furet, Keith Michael Baker too believes the private space deeply troubled. But unlike Furet, he accepts the emergence of a political discourse in the private sphere. Yet France never gained a political culture with the clear give-and-take, so characteristic of the English. Even the Anglophile Montesquieu distrusted open debate, which to him appeared so chaotic. Instead the French yearned for a unified public space in which one true opinion might hold sway. Even though these circumstances surely bespoke a royal vision, monarchical efforts to capture it proved vain.

Mona Ozouf and Ran Halévi, among the many others generally favoring Furet's approach, have slightly different versions of the nature of

211

rising political culture, but they too perceive both defects and monarchical impotence. Studying the press contradicts this view by indicating the continued significance of discourses supporting the monarchy and official efforts – some necessary, others not – to sustain that positive coverage. Furthermore, although Furet personally argues that an over-emphasis on Rousseau lies at the root of the problem, the political press in any case did not share such a preoccupation. Rather than acting as the Rousseauist organs necessary to Furet's explanation, they focused most upon democratic upheavals. More research is necessary to understand Rousseau's place in the discussion press, but clearly he had to vie for attention with other matters. Furet, along with Halévi, has differentiated the Americans from the French, in the latter's purportedly Rousseauist experiences.[16] While this book does not disprove Furet's contention, it suggests that the press went in a different direction.

Finally, this depiction of the press under Vergennes addresses the general emphasis on a defective political culture. By connecting the positive view of the monarchy in the press to the military and diplomatic successes and a kind of political truce, this study suggests not only the strength of the king but a substantial satisfaction. This is a far cry from Furet's alienated body politic, continuously suffering from an overdose of Rousseauianism. As noted above, Rousseau was there among much else. More precise analysis can ascertain if this peace also undermines Baker's, and indeed, Ozouf's interpretation which finds a hostile, un-compromising public. Neither the king's successful efforts at control nor his probable popularity prove active collaboration among king, inter-mediate bodies, and society. Only an investigation of this political quiet can ascertain whether collaboration and accommodation or temporary acquiescence were involved.

Although the press – especially its emphasis on politics under Ver-gennes – may raise questions for Furet's interpretation, interestingly it finds a very similar fault among his competitors, the Marxists.[17] Of course there are many variants of this view, but they also overlook the revival of the monarchy virtually on the eve of the Revolution. In their accounts, a weak king confronted a recalcitrant selfish aristocracy, but they found the real focus of the Revolution centering on the aristocracy as the Revolution arraigned itself against the social elite of the Old Regime. The king, who receives little attention, by implication possessed no power.

Evidently then, this work strongly suggests an approach to the Old Regime that would incorporate royal power. But overall, the emphasis on royal revival has also to be seen as an important, though short-term, phenomenon in a book that also reveals a press that provided theoretical assaults on some aspects of the Old Regime. The discussion press and a lower octave of the political press offered indirect, abstract attacks. Even the most moderate of these genres, the affiches communicated through its pages a modest rebuke of the aristocracy, surely identified with the status quo. Added to these critiques was the general din provided by the network of criticism, discussed intermittently throughout this work but most relevant here. That the most acerbic language came from a supporter of the monarchy (Linguet) and that others were so much more restrained created an upper limit to the aggressiveness of this time. Partially accounting for permission for such assaults, however tepid, was the governmental regulation of the press that focused on immediate problems while tolerating general indirect criticisms.

Integrating such points into a broader schema can suggest how to understand the causes of the Revolution and how to isolate and evaluate the role of the press. The press's assaults against and its defenses of the Old Regime may be incorporated in a structure that once had great appeal, but presently has few users.[18] Roger Chartier has recently indirectly deployed this, and I follow but more explicitly.[19] What I have in mind is understanding Revolutions in various temporal stages: preconditions, precipitants, and triggers. Such a framework explains that Revolutions occur because long-term dissatisfactions rise to the surface when new elements give older complaints particular moment. Periodicals surely contributed, if only modestly, to the accumulation of grievances. But the reticence of the newspapers, from 1776 to 1784, certainly seems to make them poor candidates as precipitants. But what the press, combined with the limits elsewhere on the public sphere, does suggest is that the precipitants must have been short term. A king buoyed by a popular war and dominant domestically through whatever means was surely not in great jeopardy, even if problems loomed. With the monarch riding high until 1785, precipitants and triggers in this case virtually merge. One might describe the mounting problems of 1785–86 as the factors that led into the trigger period of 1787. The press's awakening late in 1784 and into 1785 and 1786 makes it a precipitant, perhaps necessary but not sufficient, as its more vigorous reporting of the 1760s had certainly not led to Revolution. Surely newspapers played a part, but inevitably one must turn to other factors, including of course the fiscal crisis to which the periodicals themselves contributed little. The great moment of the press may have been the largely reinvented Revolutionary periodical, as Pierre Rétat has already laid claim to "trigger" status for the medium.[20] Yet this rise in the newspaper from 1784 on, with its criticisms of the monarch, is not enough to salvage visions of a political culture that was consistently problematic for the king, since they generally argue that difficulties dated from at least 1770.

In short, this study suggests an interpretation in which the press assists a general, gradual loss of faith in monarchy, which might never have come to anything without shorter term activating agents. Indeed, from this perspective the Revolution appears far away during the halcyon days of Vergennes, even despite problems clouding the horizon. The press surely contributed to this stability, in conjunction with the political and military circumstances. But when periodicals revived in the winter of 1784–85, they had numerous massive problems to fill their pages. Some of those came from the murmur of discontent under Vergennes; others hailed from structural difficulties, political and otherwise, kept alive in the press. Consequently, one may speculate about the periodical as a medium that both forestalled and hastened change, just at different times and circumstances and as part of a process.

Inscribing the press in this last theory, as well as describing its implications for earlier interpretations, is also a beginning attempt to explain the moderate and contradictory way periodicals functioned in eighteenth-century France. The eighteenth-century press constituted an important episode in the development of this medium. During the Revolution a heavily ideological, political press emerged with few links to most of the Old Regime press.[21] Although the style of the press has not been systematically explored in this work, it registers as a subtheme in each chapter on content. And in fact, the political press generally was given to reticence. Examples from the discussion press reveal considerable hesitation, and the affiches were primarily collections of assorted information. Of course, the prerevolutionary periodical had its own way of making a point, but its general indirection, though less marked in the discussion press than in the political press and the affiches, gave the impression of a lack of *parti pris*. Though the pre-1789 periodical bequeathed such a legacy, the Revolution seemingly took little interest in its birthright. Such concepts had to wait for substantial resonance as the next century evolved different notions of objectivity. While no analyst has examined the French press in the way that Michael Schudson has the American, his categories may be usefully transferred. Nineteenth-century journalists would come to define unbiased reporting as that which represented the public instead of a political party's interest.[22] Perhaps the Old Regime press ought to be seen as a precursor of the tradition in the press which downgraded analysis and commitment in favor of providing more neutral writings.

Appendix I

Publication estimates for periodicals that existed during the years 1745–86

While new figures are emerging all the time, what follows here is a conscientious effort to assemble what is presently available.

POLITICAL PRESS

Gazette de France[1]
1638	1200
1670	3400–4800[2]
1749	6800–8800
1758	15,000–17,000
1780	12,260
1785	6500
1787	6000
1788	6250
1789	15,000

Courrier d'Avignon
1733	1300
1734	2000
1745	2500[3]
1747	2800
1751–58	9000[3]
1758	6000–8000
1760	2800[3]
1776	3000
1778	4000
1784	3100
1789	6000

Courrier du Bas-Rhin
1767	1000
1793	1340

Journal de Bruxelles[4]
1775	5000

1780   5000
Courrier de l'Europe
1776   3000–4000
1778   6000
1784   7000
1787   1300
Journal militaire et politique[5]
1778–79   200
Mercure de France (considered here as a political journal because its surge in circulation related to its political section)
c.1780   6500
1788   15,000
Journal de Genève[6]
1780   4800
1782   8000
1788   4000
Annales politiques, civiles, et littéraires[7]
(c.1780)   20,000
Gazette de Leyde[8]
mid-1780s   4200–9000

LITERARY–PHILOSOPHICAL JOURNALS

Bibliothèque britannique
1733   1500
Entretiens historiques sur les affaires présentes
1744   300
Lettres sur quelques écrits de ce temps
1749   2500
Bibliothèque impartiale
1750   200
after 1750   400
Journal britannique[9]
c. 1750   500
Tablettes dramatiques
1752   2000
Journal étranger
1755   2000 (1521 subscriptions)
Journal encyclopédique[10]
1756   1200
(?)   2000
Année littéraire[11]
c. 1760   over 2000
1778   1250

1779   850 subscriptions
1780   960 subcriptions
Journal des dames[12]
1760s   300–1000
Europe littéraire
1762   159
Mercure de France
1763   1600
1764   1778
Ephémérides du citoyen
1769–72 - 500[13]
Journal helvétique[14]
1769   401 subscriptions
1772   234 subscriptions
1778   237 subscriptions
1778   500
1781   220 subscriptions
1782   under 200 subscriptions
Le Glaneur (Lyons)
1772   under 200
Journal de Provence
1776   300
Journal français
1778   900[15]
1778   261[16]
Nouvelles de la république des lettres et des arts[17]
1779   500
1780   300
1781   188
1782   313
1786   400
Journal de Monsieur[18]
1781   100
1782   470–750
Journal de Paris
1782   5000[19]
1789   11,000–15,000
Journal des savants
(?)   1000
Mémoires de Trévoux
(?)   1000

AFFICHES

Affiches de Reims
1776   250
Affiches d'Angers
1776   220
Affiches du pays chartrain[20]
1781–82   300–350
1782   400–450

Appendix II

Sampling the press 1745–86

THE JOURNALISTS

The enormous outpouring of periodicals over the course of the eighteenth century, as described in the introductory chapter, necessitates sampling, and in certain instances systematic samples. In particular, a desire to understand the journalistic community proved to be a case in which studying significant individuals still could not easily lead to generalization. Locating representative individuals proved similarly problematic.

To create a sample for studying journalists, I first had to select periodicals, not journalists, because very complete lists exist for the first, not the second. Through the periodicals one could find the journalists. To identify the appropriate periodicals, I used the same rule, indicated in the introduction, of looking at those periodicals that lasted three years, eliminating the ephemeral as the most important limit employed. This was also a strength because it led to a list of periodicals in which a high percentage of editors might be identified. Also, I then chose not to sample randomly various periodicals and then examine their personnel. Rather this work relies on a stratified sample to ensure that particularly important characteristics be fairly represented. In particular, I hypothesized that the most important internal divisions among these individuals would emerge from geographical differences and chronological shifts. Along with selecting representative papers and thus journalists from such categories, I included another special subgroup for comparison. The French government authorized three papers (the *Gazette de France*, the *Journal des savants*, and the *Mercure de France*); I selected by random sample one of these for the entire period involved. Omitted from this effort to produce a sample substructure was establishing extra categories where the journalists of different kinds of periodicals – gazettes, affiches, and discussion publications – were specifically isolated. This omission resulted mainly from my view that a profile of the journalistic community would not vary according to the purposes of papers. Different kinds of periodicals in the same location seemed to emerge from the same stratum of editors so relying on this variable to subdivide the sample further seemed fruitless. It should also be noted that adding categories generates high costs. The more subdivided becomes the sample, the more individual subgroups (created by matching two or more characteristics) have few, or even no, candidates. Such a sample becomes increasingly less meaningful with all those empty categories. These practical problems, combined with the apparent characteristics of the press, thus led to abandoning the kind of journal as an additional category. Also, some of these same circumstances rendered another potential problem inconsequential. As noted in the introduction, uncertainty exists about the actual circulation within France of some foreign periodicals, particularly literary ones. Yet I concluded that they probably entered so I kept them in the sample. However, the similarity among editors of different genres of periodicals indicates that substituting for them periodicals absolutely known to have circulated – far more political than literary – would not have altered the social makeup.

In order to describe the journalistic community, this study thus relies upon sampling periodicals to uncover those who worked on them; furthermore this sample is largely structured to see if important chronological and geographic differences emerge. Specifically, how was this all operationalized?

First, the press of the last forty years of the Old Regime was geographically divided: Parisian, the provincial, and foreign. Within each geographical subgrouping, one paper that could span a great deal of the entire period was randomly selected. Then for each of four decades (1745–54, 1755–64, 1765–74, and the extra-long 1775–86), I listed the available papers whose entire run was over three years (defined by beginning and ending *years*, in order to compensate for many periodicals where the precise date is not listed, e.g., 1754–58). I took a random sample from these subgroups, selecting two papers, but disallowing any repeats. For the first decade, only one year of one provincial paper remains to us and that paper was already employed in the rest of the sample. To these were added one governmental representative, the *Gazette de France*, which was selected by lot.

Some of the decisions made in defining the sample, beginning with the geographical divisions, are not self-evident. As the introductory chapter explains, the press located first in Paris, then along the northern and eastern borders of France, and finally after mid-century in the provinces. These separate centers might potentially generate different kinds of participants. And selecting a group of papers based on duration could provide another angle on chronological change. By focusing on a few such case studies, one obtains a microcosm to compare with the broader shifts in the wider sample. Of course, this effort tended to weight equally, and perhaps unfairly, each arm of the press, but the overall findings as revealed in the chapter do not seem to suffer from this. In particular, the final conclusion locates sufficient similarity among categories to suggest that variable weights would make no difference.

The results of the sampling technique follow. The dates are those for which copies of the periodical have been located.

Paris
Long term
    Petites Affiches, 1751–86
Decade 1 (1745–54)
    Nouvelles ecclésiastiques, 1745–54
    Journal économique, 1751–54
Decade 2 (1755–64)
    Affiches de province, 1755–64
    Annales typographiques, 1758–62
Decade 3 (1765–74)
    Journal des dames, 1765–68, 1774
    Année littéraire, 1765–74
Decade 4 (1775–86)
    Journal de lecture, 1775–79
    La Nature considérée, 1775–81
Foreign
Long term
    Courrier d'Avignon, 1745–86
Decade 1
    Cinq Années littéraires, 1748–52
    Nouvelle Bibliothèque germanique, 1745–54
Decade 2
    Gazette de Cologne, 1759–64
    Gazette de Bruxelles, 1756–64
Decade 3
    Bibliothèque des sciences et des beaux arts, 1765–74
    Gazette universelle de littérature aux Deux-Ponts, 1770–74
Decade 4
    Nouveau Journal helvétique, 1775–80
    Gazette de Leyde, 1775–86
Provincial
Long term
    Affiches de Lyon, 1750–86
Decade 1
    Nothing available
Decade 2
    Affiches de Nantes, 1757–64
    Affiches de Bordeaux, 1758–64

Decade 3

> *Annonces, affiches, et avis divers de l'Orléanais, 1765–74*
> *Annonces, affiches, et avis divers de Normandie, 1765–74*

Decade 4

> *Affiches du Poitou, 1775–86*
> *Annonces, affiches, et avis divers de Flandre, 1781–86*

THE AFFICHES

The chapter examining the affiches also required a systematic examination of content. The volume of these was too large to tackle in its entirety. In this case, a sampling shortcut was used and indeed proved desirable. The sample drawn for the provincial press was largely retained for the affiches. As the provincial papers turned out to be affiches, the sample for the first, with its recognition of both stability and diversity, could be employed for the second. Using the same group of affiches for two purposes allowed closer attention to a smaller number of papers than would have resulted if two separate samples had been drawn. And fortuitously all those selected did last long enough in the relevant decade to provide data sufficient for the examination described below. But three alterations were necessary. The *Affiches de Nantes* in Decade 2 was replaced by the *Annonces, affiches, et avis divers de province* because during this early period containing relatively few provincial papers, the message of this latter paper was likely to have been widely circulated. This advertiser certainly contributed heavily to the notions advanced in the affiches. Another problem emerged from the use of the *Affiches de Lyon*. Although it was the first provincial affiches and lasted the longest, I could only locate a few early issues and a run of 1759 to 1772. To supplement this, I added the *Annonces, affiches, et avis divers de l'Orléanais* as a paper in the last decade, a period for which no copies of the Lyons paper could be located. There was nothing suitable to fill the early lacuna. To compensate further for chronological gaps I joined the *Petites Affiches* to the sample. This affiches was begun very early, because it served the Parisian basin, and doubtless was the most widely circulated. It gave a completeness otherwise unavailable. Thus, with these changes, the sample for the provincial press stands here as the sample for the affiches.

Even focusing on a sample of seven affiches left too much for a single researcher to consider completely. The approach adopted here was to read every tenth issue of each paper in order to discover what re-emerged over the entire run. But to examine how this part of the press could respond to problems over several weeks, I rigorously read one randomly selected, three-month period. For those papers consulted for more than a decade, one three-month period was included for *each* ten-year span.

NOTES

INTRODUCTION: THE PERIODICAL PRESS

1 Ensuing chapters explain most of the assertions of this paragraph. The footnoted items are those not developed in the course of this book.

2 For an attack on the aridity of the press, see Louis Petit de Bachaumont, *Mémoires secrets pour servir à l'histoire de la république des lettres en France depuis MDCCLXII jusqu'à nos jours. Ou Journal d'un observateur* 36 vols. (London, 1778), 22: 242. For the opposite opinion, see Michel Gaulin, "Le Concept d'homme des lettres, en France, à l'époque de l'Encyclopédie d'après quelques représentants du groupe des philosophes." (Ph.D. diss., Harvard University, 1973).

3 Jeremy D. Popkin, *News and Politics in the Age of Revolution: Jean Luzac's "Gazette de Leyde"* (Ithaca, 1989), pp. 99–114.

4 For the development of a journalistic ethos, see Thelma Morris, *L'Abbé Desfontaines et son rôle dans la littérature de son temps* (Geneva, 1961), pp. 106–8.

5 Many different definitions have been employed. For a recent definition and deployment of the term, see Jean Sgard, "Journales und Journalistes im Zeitalter der Aufklarung," in Hans-Ulrich Gumbrecht, Rolf Reichardt, and Thomas Schleich, eds., *Sozialgeschichte der Aufklärung in Frankreich* 2 vols. (Munich, 1981), 2: 3–33.

6 On newspapers, see Popkin, *News and Politics*, 57–60. For more on this genre, consult Jean Sgard, ed., *Dictionnaire des journaux*, 2 vols. (Paris, 1991), pp. 826–35; and Robert S. Tate, Jr., *Petit de Bachaumont: His Circle and the "Mémoires Secrets"* (Geneva, 1968). See also Frantz Funck-Brentano, *Les Nouvellistes* (Paris, 1905). Little is known about the periodicals that at most compiled narrow sorts of data. For some material on commercial lists, consult Christopher Todd, "French Advertising in the Eighteenth Century," *Studies in Voltaire and the Eighteenth Century* 266 (1989), p. 528.

7 Any dates selected would to some extent remain arbitrary but the thinking that went into this selection may be succinctly summarized. One goal of this study was to see if the press significantly changed as the Revolution approached. Although historians have pushed the origins of the late eighteenth-century crisis deeper and deeper into the past, preconditions became strikingly more evident in the 1750s with the blow-up between the King and parlement over Jansenism. The starting date for this book was thus selected to pre-date this mid-century conflagration. Furthermore as I began to focus more on the press as an Old Regime rather than a pre-Revolutionary phenomenon, a starting point of 1745 allowed for a long, substantial look at the press during decades of very important expansion in its numbers of titles. Any thought of

223

extending this work to include the Revolution, a possibility already rendered problematic by the many discontinuities between the pre- and post-1789 papers as well as the increased numbers of papers, disappeared with the recent publication of two syntheses on the revolutionary press: Hugh Gough, *The Newspaper Press in the French Revolution* (Chicago, 1988); and Jeremy D. Popkin, *Revolutionary News: The Press in France, 1789–1799* (Durham, N.C., 1990).

8 For a more complete survey of this literature, see Jack R. Censer and Jeremy D. Popkin, "Historians and the Press," in Jack R. Censer and Jeremy D. Popkin, eds., *Press and Politics in Pre-revolutionary France* (Berkeley, 1987), pp. 1–23.

9 Eugène Hatin, *Histoire politique et littéraire de la presse en France,* 8 vols. (Paris, 1859–61); Charles Ledré, *Histoire de la presse* (Paris, 1965); and Claude Bellanger *et al., Histoire générale de la presse française,* vol. 1, *Des Origines à 1814* (Paris, 1969). One major exception to this critique is Georges Weill, *Le Journal. Origines, évolution, et rôle de la presse périodique* (Paris, 1934) which provides a coherent account. Nonetheless, the section dedicated to the press from 1745 through 1786 consists of only a few pages.

10 For a longer treatment of this subject, see Censer and Popkin, "Historians and the Press."

11 Consult *ibid,* and the chapters which follow. Some very important titles that are not included in either of the above are: Claude Labrosse and Pierre Rétat, *L'Instrument périodique. La Fonction de la presse au XVIIIe siècle* (Lyons, 1985); Pierre Rétat, ed., *La Révolution du journal, 1788–1794* (Paris, 1989); Roger Chartier, ed., *The Culture of Print: Power and the Uses of Print in Early Modern Europe,* trans. Lydia Cochrane (Princeton, 1989); Henri Duranton, Claude Labrosse, Pierre Rétat, eds., *Les Gazettes européennes de langue française (XVIIe-XVIIIe siècles)* (St.Etienne, 1992); and Sgard, *Dictionnaire des journaux.*

12 Historians can no longer deal as confidently with journals' content as they could a short while ago. The advent of critical theory in its many manifestations has raised the sensitivity of scholars to the malleability of the text. Throughout this work I have endeavored to treat the press with these considerations in mind, seeking to read papers with contemporary eyes and endeavoring to cut through the fluctuations of specific meanings between then and now. Nonetheless, the understandings inevitably remain my own and the voice used in this book remains the traditional one of the historian-narrator. For greater discussion on these points, see Dominick La Capra, "Rethinking Intellectual History and Reading Texts" in Dominick La Capra and Steven L. Kaplan, eds., *Modern European Intellectual History* (Ithaca, 1982), pp. 47–85, and Wolfgang Iser, *The Act of Reading: A Theory of Aesthetic Response* (Baltimore, 1978).

13 Jürgen Habermas, *The Structural Transformation of the Public Sphere: An Inquiry into a Category of Bourgeois Society,* trans. Thomas Burger (Cambridge, Mass., 1989), p. 67.

14 Jack Censer, "Die Presse des Ancien Régime im übergang – eine Skizze" in Rolf Reichardt and Eberhard Schmitt, ed., *Die Französische Revolution als Bruch des gesellschaftlichen Bewusstseins* (Munich, 1988), pp. 127–52.

15 For definitions of these terms, see below pp. 91–2, 116–17.

16 Daniel Roche, *Le Siècle des lumières en province. Académies et académiciens provinciaux, 1680–1789* (Paris, 1978).

17 Sarah Maza, *Private Lives and Public Affairs: The Causes Célèbres of Prerevolutionary France* (Berkeley,1993).

18 Robert Darnton, *The Great Cat Massacre and Other Episodes in French Cultural History* (New York, 1984), pp. 215–56.

19 This count is based on the list of journals provided in Sgard, *Dictionnaire des journaux*. Using the *Dictionnaire* meant accepting its definition of a periodical. Many organs transmogrified, changing titles repeatedly. Settling on which were continuations and which constituted independent entities is no easy matter, but the *Dictionnaire* must be regarded at this time as definitive. For a more global effort to count the entire French language press up to 1789, see pp. 1131–40.

20 See, for example, the works noted by Nina Gelbart in *Feminine and Opposition Journalism in Old Regime France* (Berkeley, 1987), pp. 207–47.

21 Among the problems, a few do stand out. The assumption here is that periodicals published near the French border, with appeal to the French audience, ought to be included. But their place remains difficult to determine. Although little is known about foreign participation in the French market, the available information suggests that literary and philosophical periodicals mailed very few issues to France and found most subscribers elsewhere. See the data reported in Michel Schleys, "Diffusion et lecture du *Journal helvétique* au temps de la Société typographique de Neuchâtel," in Hans Bots, ed., *La Diffusion et la lecture des journaux de langue française sous l'ancien régime* (Amsterdam, 1988), p. 71; and, for contrast with a French journal, Jean Sgard, "Les Souscripteurs de *Journal étranger*," in *ibid.*, p. 99. See also Sgard, *Dictionnaire des journaux*, p. 190. Thus, while domestic periodicals that lasted seem to justify the label of substantial, such foreign counterparts might have achieved longevity without an important French presence. Also it is possible, that the government simply did not allow many of these to circulate, at least at certain times. But as Table Intro-3 indicates, all these speculations concern but a relatively small group of periodicals except for the 1745 and 1750 census. Removal or reduction of these, however, amplify the tendencies described below with general conclusions needing little adjustment.

Much the same argument as above may be made about the foreign political press, except that we do know for the first three censuses a nearly exact total of periodicals circulating (counterfeiting aside). The work of Gilles Feyel ("La Diffusion des gazettes étrangères en France et la révolution postale des années 1750," in Duranton, *Les Gazettes*, pp. 82–9) does give exact details for that period when most were suppressed, but seems to account only for newspapers, with little to say at all on political magazines with a lower periodicity. Scattered evidence suggests, however that all of these were forbidden from France. So for this period, the number of foreign papers seems adequately calculated. Furthermore, enough statistics and references in memoirs exist to presume that the political press along the border did penetrate successfully after 1759. This discussion of suppression gives yet one more reason to imagine yet a lower total for the foreign literary philosophical press. A few of these possessed political sections, and in the early period with widespread suppression the order of the day, this must have further encouraged their prohibition. But these were so few that, regardless of one's assumptions, they barely nuance the figures.

It must be added that this mixing of genres in a single periodical will be discussed later in the text (pp. 9–10) in those cases with more serious implications. But the remarks do not overlap as the periodicals that become important to those reflections come from a later period than relevant here. The overlap that does exist seems to add little to the results and the complications already discussed.

22 The total number of periodicals apparently available in France lasting three or more years from 1745 to 1788 was 139. The analysis focuses here upon

availability for selected years, but many other possible options might be pursued, for example, investigating life span by genre. It should also be noted that, because inventories of periodicals may only give publication dates by years, ensuring a three-year run meant in practical terms considering those that appeared over five years (e.g., 1774–78). This test guaranteed three years. Often more exact data exist, but to be consistent I simply stayed with the five-year span.

23 See Chapter 5 below; and Raymond Birn, "Le Journal des savants sous l'ancien régime," *Journal des Savants* (1965): 27–31.

24 Suzanne Tucoo-Chala, *Charles-Joseph Panckoucke & la librairie française, 1731–1798* (Paris, 1977), pp. 191–252.

25 Gilles Feyel, "La Diffusion," pp. 82–9.

26 Tucoo-Chala, *Panckoucke*, pp. 191–252. See also Peter Ascoli, "American Propaganda in the French Language Press during the American Revolution," (unpublished paper, 1977); and Bernard Faÿ, *The Revolutionary Spirit in France and America*, trans. Ramon Guthrie (1927; New York, 1966), pp. 54–6, 87–91.

27 On the *Journal de Paris*, consult, Sgard, *Dictionnaire des journaux*, pp. 615–27.

28 Likewise the *Annales politiques* of Linguet could have been placed in the literary press, but for the same reasons as the *Mercure*, it was placed in the political.

29 Jean Daniel Candaux, "Batailles autour d'un privilège. La Réimpression genevoise des gazettes de Hollande," in Duranton, *Les Gazettes*, pp. 47–8. Even newspapers denied official entry rights might be the subject of counterfeit editions. See Sgard, *Dictionnaire des journaux*, p. 714.

30 Feyel, "La Diffusion," pp. 89–94.

31 Candaux, "Batailles," p. 49. Counterfeiting never completely vanished, however. See Sgard, *Dictionnaire des journaux*, p. 287.

32 Feyel, "La Diffusion," p. 96. Here because of his seeming indifference to politics not carried in the gazettes, he has probably underestimated the circulation (a few hundred copies?) of foreign political magazines.

33 *Ibid.*, p. 98.

34 *Ibid.*

1 THE POLITICAL PRESS

1 Howard Solomon, *Public Welfare, Science, and Propaganda in Seventeenth Century France: The Innovations of Théophraste Renaudot* (Princeton, 1972), pp. 100–22.

2 Gilles Feyel, "La Diffusion des gazettes étrangères en France et la révolution postale des années 1750," in Henri Duranton, Claude Labrosse, and Pierre Rétat, *Les Gazettes européennes de langue française (XVIIe–XVIIIe siècles)* (St. Etienne, 1992), pp. 89–98.

3 Claude Bellanger *et al.*, *Histoire générale de la presse française*, vol. 1, *Des origines à 1814* (Paris, 1969) pp. 143–57 and 285–98.

4 Patricia Howe, "The Pre-Revolutionary Press: Pierre Le Brun of *Journal général de l'Europe*, 1785–1789" (Paper, Consortium for Revolutionary Europe, 1991). I thank the author for sharing her paper with me.

5 Jeremy Popkin, *News and Politics in the Age of Revolution: Jean Luzac's "Gazette de Leyde"* (Ithaca, 1989), pp. 215–48.

6 See Gilles Feyel, "Nouvelles du Temps," in Jean Sgard, ed., *Dictionnaire des journaux (1600–1789)* (Paris, 1991), p. 950.

7 For the definitive work on this subject, see Suzanne Tucoo-Chala, *Charles-Joseph Panckoucke & la librairie française, 1736–1798* (Paris, 1975), pp. 191–251.

8 On earlier efforts by the foreign minister Choiseul, consult Madelaine Fabre, "Edme-Jacques Genet," in Jean Sgard, ed., *Dictionnaire des journalistes (1600–1789), Supplément II*, ed. Anne-Marie Chouillet and François Moureau (Grenoble, 1983), pp. 80–6.

9 Two superb papers by Peter Ascoli provide the best analysis currently available on these journals. Peter Ascoli, "The French Press and the American Revolution: The Battle of Saratoga," in *Proceedings of the 5th Annual Meeting of the Western Society for French History*, ed. Joyce Duncan Falk (Santa Barbara, Calif., 1977), pp. 46–55, and "American Propaganda in the French Language Press during the American Revolution" (unpublished paper, 1977). I thank the author for sharing it with me.

10 There exists a substantial bibliography on Linguet but the analysis in this chapter depends on Darline Gay Levy, *The Ideas and Careers of Simon-Nicolas-Henri Linguet: A Study in Eighteenth Century French Politics* (Urbana, 1980), pp. 172–224, and Jeremy Popkin, "The Pre-Revolutionary Origins of Political Journalism," in Keith Michael Baker, François Furet, and Colin Lucas, eds., *The French Revolution and the Creation of Modern Political Culture*, vol. I, Keith Michael Baker, ed., *The Political Culture of the Old Regime* (Oxford, 1987), pp. 203–23.

11 For an interesting study on the question of temporality, consult J.G.A. Pocock, *The Ancient Constitution and the Feudal Law: A Study of English Historical Thought in the Seventeenth Century* (New York, 1967).

12 Those who have found the political press to be conservative have generally not considered the circulation of the foreign press. See Robert Darnton, *The Literary Underground of the Old Regime* (Cambridge, Mass., 1982), p. 113. But the historical profession as a whole, by searching for the roots of the Revolution without ever consulting the periodical press, has largely implicitly rendered its view of the conservative nature of eighteenth-century journalism.

13 For two hypotheses in that very direction, see Jack R. Censer, "*Die Presse des Ancien Régime im Übergang – eine Skizze*" in Reinhard Kosselleck and Rolf Reichardt, eds., *Die Französische Revolution als Bruch des gessellshaftlichen Bewusstseins* (Munich, 1988), pp. 127–52; and Jeremy Popkin, "Pre-Revolutionary Origins of Political Journalism."

14 On the postal service, consult Eugène Vaillé, *Histoire générale des postes françaises*, 6 vols. (Paris, 1951–53).

15 See Chapter 6 below.

16 See Louis-Sébastien Mercier, *Tableau de Paris* (Paris, 1853), *passim*.

17 There exists a very substantial literature on the French view of English politics, including Richard M. Leighton, "The Tradition of the English Constitution in France on the Eve of the Revolution" (Ph.D. diss., Cornell University, 1941); Frances Acomb, *Anglophobia in France, 1763–1789* (Durham, N.C., 1950); Gabriel Bonno, *La Constitution britannique devant l'opinion française de Montesquieu à Bonaparte* (1931, New York, 1971); Josephine Grieder, *Anglomania in France, 1740–1789* (Geneva, 1985); and Jack R. Censer, "English Politics in the *Courrier d'Avignon*" in Jack R. Censer and Jeremy D. Popkin, eds., *Press and Politics in Pre-Revolutionary France* (Berkeley, 1987), pp. 170–203.

18 Popkin, *News and Politics*, pp. 71–7.

19 The analysis of the *Gazette de France* relies upon its unabridged edition. On its shorter version, see Gilles Feyel, "La Gazette au début de la Guerre de Sept Ans. Son Administration, sa diffusion (1751–1758)," in Hans Bots, ed., *La Diffusion et la lecture des journaux de langue française sous l'Ancien Régime* (Amsterdam, 1988), pp. 101–16. For a parallel analysis, see Shelly Charles, "Sur

l'Ecriture du présent. La *Gazette d'Amsterdam* et la *Gazette de France,*" in Duranton, *Les Gazettes européennes,* pp. 177–85; and Jean Sgard, "On dit", in Harvey Chisick, ed., *The Press in the French Revolution* (Oxford, 1991), pp. 26–7.

20 For an interesting comment by Panckoucke on the purpose of gazettes, consult Christopher Todd, *Political Bias, Censorship and the Dissolution of the "Official" Press in Eighteenth-Century France* (Lewistown, N.Y., 1991), pp. 4–5.

21 See Chapter 6 below.

22 See Jean-Louis Lecercle, "L'Amérique et la guerre d'Indépendence," in Paul Jansen *et al., L'Année 1788 à travers la presse traitée par ordinateur* (Paris, 1982), pp. 17–42. In this excellent and helpful article, the author argued that this style inspired confidence. But it is very difficult to imagine that an editor would sacrifice so much clarity to authenticity alone. More factors need to be offered. And as a corollary to this explanation of the gazettes' style: the fact that periodicals later in the eighteenth century achieved more certainty for readers explains how they could modify this strategy of reportage.

23 When the *Journal de Bruxelles* absorbed the *Affaires de l'Angleterre et de l'Amérique* in 1779, it absorbed parts of its style which persisted into the early 1780s.

24 Slowing down the "Brussels" and "Geneva" papers were their once weekly appearances. Furthermore, even though they published in France, they kept throughout this period the fiction of a foreign location.

25 Omitted from this analysis are those stories of a few paragraphs, but these appear to be relatively few in number in the *Journal de Bruxelles.* Further scrutiny should include these as well.

26 Tucoo-Chala, *Panckoucke,* p. 210.

27 Ascoli, "American Propaganda"; and Sgard, *Dictionnaire des journaux,* pp. 6–7.

28 See Durand Echeverria, *Mirage in the West: A History of the French Image of American Society to 1815* (New York, 1960), pp. 3–115; and Philippe Roger, "Liberté vs. Liberty: Two Heads under the Same Bonnet," in Jack R. Censer, Daniel Shumate, Josephine Pacheco, eds., *An International Perspective on Human Rights* (Fairfax, Va., 1992), pp. 17–45.

29 Popkin, "Pre-Revolutionary Origins of Political Journalism," pp. 216–20.

30 See Appendix I.

31 For parallel and very illuminating discussions, see three articles by Claude Labrosse, "L'Apport de l'étude des journaux de 1789 à la réflexion sur l'événement," in Robert Chagny, *Aux Origines provinciales de la révolution* (Grenoble, 1988), pp. 260 and 267; "Le Récit d'événement dans la presse de 1789," *Dix-huitième siècle,* no. 20 (1988): 101–8; and "Le Temps immédiat dans la presse parisienne de 1789," in *L'Espace et le temps reconstruit. La Révolution française, une révolution des mentalités des cultures* (Aix-Marseilles, 1990), pp. 109–20. For comparison's sake, consult Joel Saugnieux, "Le Temps, l'espace et la presse au siècle des lumières," *Cahiers d'histoire* 23 (1978): 313–34. For more on the relationship between the presses of the Old Regime and the French Revolution, see the debate among Pierre Rétat, Jeremy Popkin, Hans-Jürgen Lüsebrink, Daniel Roche, Rolf Reichardt, and Jack Censer in "Revolutionpresse und Strukturwandel der politischen Offentlichkeit," in Kosselleck and Reichardt, *Die Französische Revolution,* pp. 127–82. Consult also Hugh Gough, *The Newspaper Press in the French Revolution* (Chicago, 1988), pp. 1–14; and Jeremy D. Popkin, *Revolutionary News: The Press in France, 1789–1799* (Durham, N.C., 1990).

32 For the change in the regimen governing the press, consult Alma Soderjelm, *Le Régime de la presse pendant la révolution française,* 2 vols. (Paris, 1900–1).

33 Jack Richard Censer, *Prelude to Power: The Parisian Radical Press, 1789–91* (Baltimore, 1976), pp. 73–91.

34 Jack R. Censer, "La Presse vue par elle-même. Le prospectus et le lecteur révolutionnaire," in Pierre Rétat, *La Révolution du journal, 1788–1794* (Paris, 1989), pp. 117–26.

35 Popkin, *Revolutionary News*, pp. 89–90.

36 Bellanger *et al.*, *Histoire générale* pp. 451–2. See Pierre Rétat, "Forme et discours d'un journal révolutionnaire. Les *Révolutions de Paris* en 1789," in Claude Labrosse and Pierre Rétat, eds., *L'Instrument périodique. La Fonction de la presse en XVIIIe siècle* (Lyons, 1985).

37 Censer, *Prelude to Power*, pp. 73–91.

38 Popkin, *Revolutionary News*, p. 91.

39 Popkin, "Prerevolutionary Origins of Political Journalism," pp. 216–20.

40 For a long discussion of this subject, see Todd, *Political Bias*, pp. 261–308.

41 The history of suppression of problems is long. For a 1711 case, see *ibid.*, p. 5.

42 June 5, 1751.

43 See, for example, June 19, 1751.

44 July 17, 1751.

45 Cited in Ascoli, "American Propaganda," and Echeverria, *Mirage in the West*, pp. 36–7.

46 For example, see October 18, 1782, and especially November 8, 1782, concerning Florence.

47 This transformation suggests another chronology for the coverage of foreign policy. The early focus on monarchies should generally have decreased negative coverage of foreign countries on non-military matters. Without so much opposition to report, it was more difficult to make a critique. There were thus in the early *Gazette* additional limits on the malleability of the news on the behalf of France. While the case, these viccissitudes do little more than slightly alter the overall pro-French manipulation.

48 See this tendency tracked in Hans Rosenberg, *Bureaucracy, Aristocracy, and Autocracy: The Prussian Experience, 1660–1815* (Boston, 1958).

49 René Moulinas, *L'Imprimerie, la librairie et la presse à Avignon au XVIIIe siècle* (Grenoble, 1974), pp. 300–45. On the *Courrier d'Avignon*, see also Charles F. Hinds, "The *Courrier d'Avignon* in the Reign of Louis XVI" (M.A. thesis, University of Kentucky, 1958).

50 Moulinas, *L'Imprimerie*, pp. 372–9; and Chapter 5 of this volume.

51 For a comparative assessment of the content of the *Courrier d'Avignon*, see René Moulinas, "Du Rôle de la poste royale comme moyen de contrôle financier sur la diffusion des gazettes en France au XVIIIe siècle" in *Modelès et moyens de la réflexion politique au XVIIIe siècle*, p. 394.

52 Echeverria, *Mirage in the West*, p. 43n; and Bernard Faÿ, *The Revolutionary Spirit in France and America*, trans. Ramon Guthrie (New York, 1927), p. 54.

53 *Courrier d'Avignon*, December 17, 1779.

54 *Ibid.*, September 21, 1779.

55 *Ibid.*, July 13, 1779.

56 See for example, *ibid*, March 21, 1775.

57 *Ibid.*, May 17, 1776.

58 *Ibid.*, November 8, 1776.

59 *Ibid.*, July 4, 1775.

60 For an exceptional criticism of the monarch, consult *Ibid.*, May 9, 1777.

61 *Ibid.*, December 26, 1777.

62 *Ibid.*, July 28, 1775.

63 *Ibid.*, November 14, 1775, November 29, 1776.

64 *Ibid.*, October 24, 1775.

65 *Ibid.*, July 14, 1775.

66 *Ibid.*, June 12 and July 10, 1781.
67 *Ibid.*, November 5, 1782.
68 *Ibid.*, January 8, 1782.
69 For typical reporting from America, see *Ibid.*, September 8, 1775.
70 For the exceptional report on the monarch, see *Ibid.*, January 7, 1777.
71 To understand the American view of the British constitution, see Caroline Robbins, *The Eighteenth-Century Commonwealthman* (Cambridge, Mass., 1959), especially pp. 356–77 and 385–6; and Bernard Bailyn, *The Ideological Origins of the American Revolution* (Cambridge, Mass., 1967).
72 Supplement to the *Courrier d'Avignon*, July 23, 1779.
73 Acomb, *Anglophobia in France*, pp. 51–68.
74 Popkin, "The *Gazette de Leyde* and French Politics under Louis XVI," in Censer and Popkin, *Press and Politics*, p. 82.
75 Popkin, *News and Politics*.
76 For insights into the broad intellectual milieu, see Hans Erich Bödeker, "Enlightenment in the German and French Provinces: Kassel and Grenoble" (Paper presented at History Department Colloquium, George Mason University, 1984). And consult Elizabeth L. Eisenstein, *The Printing Press as an Agent of Change* (Cambridge, 1979), 2 vols.
77 Popkin, *News and Politics*, pp. 137–87.
78 *Ibid.*
79 Pierre Rétat, "Les Gazetiers de Holland et les puissances politiques au 18e siècle. Une Difficile Collaboration," *Dix-huitième siècle* no. 25 (1993), pp. 319–35. For another comparative treatment which envisions the *Gazette de Leyde* as a very aggressive paper but just slightly more so than several others, see Pierre Rétat, ed., *L'Attentat de Damiens. Discours sur l'événement au XVIIIe siècle* (Paris, 1979), pp. 15–46.
80 Popkin, *News and Politics*, pp. 137–57.
81 For the general reaction of the press regarding this attempt on Louis XV, consult Rétat, ed., *L'Attentat de Damiens*, pp. 15–46.
82 Popkin, *News and Politics*, pp. 139–40 and 149–50.
83 For an excellent comparative account, consult Lecercle, "L'Amérique et la guerre d'Indépendence."
84 Ascoli, "American Propaganda," and "The French Press and the American Revolution."
85 Frances Acomb, *Mallet du Pan (1749–1800): A Career in Political Journalism* (Durham, N.C., 1973), pp. 158–209.
86 Suzanne Tucoo-Chala, *Panckoucke*, pp. 205–6; and Acomb, *Mallet du Pan*, pp. 158–209.
87 These views on the *Affiches d'Angleterre et de l'Amérique* depend heavily on Sgard, *Dictionnaire des journaux*, pp. 7–10. For the *Courrier de l'Europe*, see Gunnar and Mavis von Proschwitz, *Beaumarchais et le "Courrier de l'Europe,"* 2 vols. (Oxford, 1990); and Hélène Maspero-Clerc, "Une 'Gazette anglo-française' pendant la guerre d'Amérique: Le *Courrier de l'Europe* (1776–1788)," *Annales historiques de la révolution française* 226 (1976): 572–94. For another interesting analysis, consult Eugène Hatin, *Les Gazettes de Hollande et la presse clandestine aux XVIIe et XVIIIe siècles* (Paris, 1865), pp. 39–42. My assessment of the *Courrier de l'Europe* follows the magisterial study by the von Proschwitzes who see a school for the French in the coverage of the British opposition. However, Keith Baker in "Politics and Public Opinion" questions this possibility by arguing that the French were especially wary of their across-the-Channel neighbors. My own view is that caution surely did affect the use of the English system as a blueprint. Yet it still would suggest that the Bourbon

monarchy needed radical overhaul. The French admired enough about the English surely to see their political structure as a rebuke to absolutism and as a source for speculating about a better government. Evidently this is an area requiring greater consideration.

88 Levy, *Linguet*, pp. 172–80.

89 Popkin, *News and Politics*, p. 62.

90 François Metra, *Correspondence secrète, politique, et littéraire. Ou Mémoires pour servir à l'histoire des cours, des sociétés et de la littérature en France, depuis la mort de Louis XV*, 16 vols. (London, 1787–89) 3: 276.

91 *Ibid.*

92 Levy, *Linguet*, pp. 172–225; and Jeremy Popkin, "Un Journaliste face au marché des périodiques à la fin du dix-huitième siècle. Linguet et ses *Annales politiques*," in Bots, *La Diffusion*, pp. 11–19.

93 Louis Petit de Bachaumont, *Mémoires secrets pour servir à l'histoire de la république des lettres en France, depuis 1762 jusqu'à nos jours*, 36 vols. (London, 1777–89), 25: 95.

94 Popkin, *News and Politics*, p. 62.

95 Miriam Yardeni, "Paradoxes politiques et persuasion dans les *Annales* de Linguet" in Chisick, ed., *The Press in the French Revolution*, pp. 211–19 comes to largely similar conclusions.

96 Perhaps this conclusion may be modified by the decline in the circulation of Panckoucke's journals after the American Revolution, but so may have the numbers of many others. See Tucoo-Chala, *Panckoucke*, p. 243.

2 THE AFFICHES

1 For interesting analyses of the world of the provincial affiches, see Jean Quéniart, *L'Imprimerie et la librairie à Rouen au 18e siècle* (Paris, 1969); and Louis Trénard, *Lyon de l'Encyclopédie au préromantisme*, 2 vols. (Paris, 1958). On the origins of the affiches see Gilles Feyel, *La "Gazette" en province à travers ses réimpressions, 1631–1752* (Amsterdam, 1982), pp. 177–81. And consult the invaluable collection of essays on this subject: Jean Sgard, ed., *La Presse provinciale au XVIIIe siècle* (Grenoble, 1983).

2 See the directions in the *Affiches de Lyon*, March 8, 1769 and the *Petites Affiches*, December 30, 1779.

3 Prices were often listed at the end of each issue. When the *Petites Affiches* became a daily paper in the last decade of the Old Regime, it raised its price to 30 livres for Paris, 37 livres 20 sous for the provinces. See *Petites Affiches*, October 1, 1782.

4 See, for example, *Annonces, affiches, et avis divers de l'Orléanais*, July 15, 1768 and June 15, 1770.

5 See Chapter 1.

6 June 7, 1771.

7 See Robert Harris, *Necker: Reform Statesman of the Ancien Régime* (Berkeley, 1979), pp. 217–35.

8 *Affiches du Poitou*, March 29, 1781 and *Annonces, affiches, et avis divers de province*, February 9, 1757.

9 *Annonces, affiches, et avis divers de Normandie*, July 1, 1768.

10 *Annonces, affiches, et avis divers de l'Orléanais*, February 10, 1769.

11 The *Annonces, affiches, et avis divers de l'Orléanais* broke form by publishing a story on a curé in its September 28, 1787 issue.

12 For the relationship between the monarch and king in mid-century and beyond, see Dale K. Van Kley, *The Damiens Affair and the Unraveling of the*

"Ancien Régime," 1750–1770 (Princeton, 1984); Carroll Joynes, "The *Gazette de Leyde*: The Opposition Press and French Politics, 1750–1757," in Jack R. Censer and Jeremy D. Popkin, eds., *Press and Politics in Pre-Revolutionary France* (Berkeley, 1987), pp. 133–69; and Dominique Julia, "Les Deux Puissances. Chronique d'une séparation de corps," in *The French Revolution and the Creation of a Modern Political Culture*, 3 vols; Vol. 1, *The Political Culture of the Old Regime*, ed. by Keith Michael Baker (Oxford, 1987), pp. 293–310.

13 See also on this, François Lebrun, "Une Source de l'histoire sociale: La Presse provinciale à la fin de l'ancien régime. Les 'Affiches d'Angers' (1773–1789)," *Le Mouvement social* (1962): 62–4.

14 For a similar view, consult Michel Marion, "Dix Ans des affiches, annonces, et avis divers (1752–1761)," in Jacques Godechot, ed., *Regards sur l'histoire de la presse et de l'information. Mélanges offerts à Jean Prinet* (St.-Julie-du-Sault, 1980), pp. 29–31.

15 *Petites Affiches*, August 21, 1760.

16 *Petites Affiches*, April 15, 1762, and *Annonces, affiches, et avis divers de Flandre*, February 15, 1782.

17 *Petites Affiches*, May 6, 1765.

18 For example, see *Petites Affiches*, January 1, 1756, and *Affiches de Lyon*, December 22, 1750.

19 *Annonces, affiches, et avis divers de l'Orléanais*, December 21, 1775.

20 *Annonces, affiches, et avis divers de Normandie*, September 1, 1769.

21 On moderation, see *Annonces, affiches, et avis divers de Normandie*, September 9, 1768; on observing Christian limits, *Annonces, affiches, et avis divers de l'Orléanais*, December 4, 1767; and on securing the happiness of the population, see *Annonces, affiches, et avis divers de province*, February 9, 1757, and *Annonces, affiches, et avis divers de l'Orléanais*, January 6, 1775.

22 A massive literature exists on constitutional thinking about the French monarchy. Among these works, see Roger Mettam, *Power and Faction in Louis XIV's France* (Oxford, 1988), pp. 34–41; William Farr Church, *Constitutional Thought in Sixteenth-Century France: A Study in the Evolution of Ideas* (Cambridge, Mass., 1941), and J. H. Shennan, *Government and Society in France, 1461–1661* (London, 1969).

23 Stephen Botein, Jack R. Censer, and Harriet Ritvo, "The Periodical Press in Eighteenth-Century English and French Society: A Cross-Cultural Approach," *Comparative Studies in Society and History* 23 (1981), 464–50.

24 Cissie C. Fairchilds, *Poverty and Charity in Aix-en-Provence* (Baltimore, 1976), pp. 18–37; Harvey Chisick, *The Limits of Reform in the Enlightenment: Attitudes to the Education of the Lower Class in Eighteenth-Century France* (Princeton, 1981); and Michel Foucault, *Discipline and Punish: The Birth of the Prison* (New York, 1977).

25 *Affiches du Poitou*, April 6, 1786, and *Affiches de Bordeaux*, January 15, 1761.

26 For example, consult the issues of *Annonces, affiches, et avis divers de Normandie*, March 20, 1772 and October 16, 1772.

27 October 9, 1772. For a story with a very similar moral, see the *Annonces, affiches, et avis divers de Normandie*, October 16, 1772.

28 For an important articulation of the role of money in the workplace, see Michael Sonenscher, *Work & Wages: Natural Law, Politics & the Eighteenth-Century French Trades* (Cambridge, 1989). On domestics in particular, see Cissie Fairchilds, *Domestic Enemies: Servants & Their Masters in Old Regime France* (Baltimore, 1984).

29 December 22, 1750.

30 *Affiches de Lyon*, March 17, 1759 and October 13, 1759.

31 *Ibid.* October 13, 1759 and May 26, 1763.

32 *Ibid.* October 13, 1759.

33 *Ibid.* October 3, 1764.

34 *Annonces, affiches, et avis divers de Normandie,* August 17, 1772, and *Affiches de Lyon,* July 25, 1764.

35 *Affiches de Lyon,* September 18, 1765.

36 *Ibid.* February 18, 1761, January 20, 1762, March 16, 1763.

37 *Ibid.*

38 *Affiches de Lyon,* January 2, 1772.

39 *Annonces, affiches, et avis divers de Normandie,* February 28, 1767.

40 *Affiches de Lyon,* August 1, 1759.

41 *Ibid.* June 26, 1766.

42 *Ibid.* January 2, 1772.

43 *Ibid.* June 9, 1762.

44 *Annonces, affiches, et avis divers de Normandie,* October 25, 1765.

45 *Affiches de Lyon,* April 13, 1767.

46 *Ibid.* May 7, 1760.

47 *Ibid.* July 25, 1764.

48 *Annonces, affiches, et avis divers de Normandie,* September 25, 1767.

49 *Affiches de Lyon,* November 12, 1766.

50 *Ibid.* February 18, 1761.

51 *Affiches de Lyon,* September 19, 1770.

52 *Ibid.* January 28, 1767.

53 *Ibid.* July 29, 1772; October 7, 1772; supplement to October 7, 1772 edition; and December 16, 1772.

54 Daniel Roche, *The People of Paris: An Essay in Popular Culture in the Eighteenth Century* (Berkeley, 1987).

55 February 28, 1767.

56 *Affiches du Poitou,* July 16, 1778.

57 *Annonces, affiches, et avis divers de province,* October 12, 1763. *Affiches de Lyon,* May 1, 1765.

58 *Annonces, affiches, et avis divers de l'Orléanais,* September 23, 1768.

59 *Petites Affiches,* July 8, 1785.

60 *Annonces, affiches, et avis divers de l'Orléanais,* December 4, 1767.

61 *Petites Affiches,* April 29, 1785.

62 My vision of male/female relationships in eighteenth-century France has been greatly influenced by Joan B. Landes, *Women and the Public Sphere in the Age of the French Revolution* (Ithaca, 1988); Suzanna Van Dijk, *Traces des femmes. Présence féminine dans le journalisme français du XVIIIe siècle* (Amsterdam, 1988); and Samia Spencer, ed., *French Women and the Age of Enlightenment* (Bloomington, 1984). Also, shaping my view has been Joan Wallach Scott, *Gender and the Politics of History* (New York, 1988). For a more positive understanding of the relationship between Rousseau and feminism, see the fascinating work by Nina Rattner Gelbart, *Feminine and Opposition Journalism in Old Regime France: "Le Journal des Dames"* (Berkeley, 1987).

63 *Affiches de Bordeaux,* February 5, 1761.

64 *Annonces, affiches, et avis divers de province,* May 9, 1764; see also, in the same periodical, the issue for January 20, 1762.

65 *Affiches du Poitou,* July 16, 1778.

66 See also, *Annonces, affiches, et avis divers de province,* May 9, 1764.

67 *Affiches de Lyon,* May 18, 1765.

68 *Affiches de Bordeaux,* November 19, 1761.

69 *Petites Affiches,* March 29, 1759.

NOTES

70 *Annonces, affiches, et avis divers de province*, May 6, 1761.
71 *Petites Affiches*, July 8, 1785.
72 See, for example, *Annonces, affiches, et avis divers de l'Orléanais*, November 18, 1785 and *Annonces, affiches, et avis divers de province*, September 22, 1756.
73 *Annonces, affiches, et avis divers de l'Orléanais*, December 19, 1782.
74 *Affiches de Lyon*, November 11, 1761.
75 *Affiches de Bordeaux*, September 17, 1761.
76 *Annonces, affiches, et avis divers de province*, May 5, 1756.
77 *Annonces, affiches, et avis divers de Flandre*, March 11, 1783.
78 *Annonces, affiches, et avis divers de Normandie*, October 10, 1773. See also *Affiches du Poitou*, December 11, 1783.
79 *Annonces, affiches, et avis divers de province*, March 16, 1763.
80 *Annonces, affiches, et avis divers de l'Orléanais*, December 3, 1773.
81 *Annonces, affiches, et avis divers de l'Orléanais*, February 11, 1774.
82 *Petites Affiches*, July 8, 1785.
83 *Annonces, affiches, et avis divers de province*, September 22, 1756.
84 *Petites Affiches*, December 9, 1765.
85 No one has been more influential in documenting this conception – often labelled "commonwealthman theory" – through the Western world than J. G. A. Pocock. See especially his *Machiavellian Moment: Florentine Political Thought and the Atlantic Republic Tradition* (Princeton, 1975); and *Virtue, Commerce, and History* (Cambridge, 1985). Caroline Robbins in *The Eighteenth-Century Commonwealthman* (Cambridge, Mass., 1959) provides the classic treatment of the development of this point of view in England. Scholars have been very busy locating this ideology in their particular countries. For America, see Bernard Bailyn, *Ideological Origins of the American Revolution* (Cambridge, Mass., 1967); Sean Wilentz, *Chants Democratic: New York City and the Rise of the American Working Class* (New York, 1984); and J. William Harris, *Plain Folk and Gentry in a Slave Society: White Liberty and Black Slavery in Augusta's Hinterland* (Middletown, Ct., 1985). Actually, French historians have been tardy in this effort, finding hostility to the court and its power more in natural law than anything else. Recently, however, Dale Van Kley, in his *The Damiens Affair*, and "The Estates General as Ecumenical Council: The Constitutionalism of Corporate Consensus and the *Parlement*'s Ruling of September 25, 1788," *Journal of Modern History* 61 (1989): 1–52, has pointed to parlementary opposition as a source of hostility to the concentration of authority in the court. And finally, Keith Michael Baker has begun to document the arrival in France of Commonwealthman theory in his important "A Script for a French Revolution: The Political Consciousness of the Abbé Mably," *Eighteenth Century Studies*, 14 (1981): 235–63. For an interesting study that provides much evidence on this court/country dichotomy, see Nannerl O. Keohane, *Philosophy of the State in France: The Renaissance to the Enlightenment* (Princeton, 1980). Although Keohane finds French thinking alien from the English, much that she locates suggests that "Commonwealthman theory" was dispersed through France.
86 *Annonces, affiches, et avis divers de province*, September 22, 1756; and *Annonces, affiches, et avis divers de Flandre*, December 21, 1781.
87 *Affiches de Bordeaux*, December 17, 1761.
88 *Affiches du Poitou*, December 18, 1777.
89 Jack R. Censer, "La Presse vue par elle-même. Le Prospectus et le lecteur révolutionnaire," in Pierre Rétat, ed., *La Revolution du journal, 1788–1794* (Paris, 1989), p. 119.
90 *Annonces, affiches, et avis divers de Normandie*, February 28, 1767.

91 *Affiches de Lyon*, June 10, 1761.
92 Keith Baker, "A Script for the French Revolution"; and Pierre Gaxotte, *Louis the Fifteenth and His Times* (New York, 1934).
93 For this vision of Rousseau, see Carol Blum, *Rousseau and the Republic of Virtue: The Language of Politics and the Republic* (Ithaca, 1986), pp. 27–107.
94 Robert Darnton, *The Great Cat Massacre and Other Episodes in French Cultural History* (Cambridge, Mass., 1984), pp. 215-56.
95 Eugène Hatin long ago found this quote and pointed attention to it. See his *Histoire politique et littéraire de la presse en France*, 8 vols. (Paris, 1859–61), 2: 125.
96 Pointing out this division between theory and practice are Michael Sonenscher, *Work and Wages*; Hilton L. Root, "Challenging the Seigneurie: Community and Contention on the Eve of the French Revolution" *Journal of Modern History* 57 (1985): 652–81; and Jonathan Dewald, *Pont-St.-Pierre, 1398–1789: Lordship, Community, and Capitalism in Early Modern France* (Berkeley, 1987).
97 Colin Jones, "Medical Entrepreneurialism in the Enlightenment" (unpublished paper). I thank the author very much for sharing this with me. See also Michèle Gasc, "Le Rôle des *Affiches de Lyon* dans le développement de la lecteur et la diffusion des idées," *Etudes sur la presse* 3 (1978): 61–80.
98 *Annonces, affiches, et avis divers de province*, October 27, 1762.
99 *Petites Affiches*, March 12, 1767; and *Annonces, affiches, et avis divers de province*, February 9, 1757.
100 *Petites Affiches*, June 15, 1778.
101 *Ibid.*, May 13, 1751.
102 *Ibid.*, August 21, 1777.
103 The state was having a great deal of trouble in any case working out what to do about venality. Though it had sold offices, it was beseiged by office holders. For new, exciting understandings of the relationship between the monarchy and those holding venal positions, see David D. Bien, "Offices, Corps, and a System of State Credit: The Uses of Privilege under the Ancien Régime," in Keith Baker, ed., *The Political Culture of the Old Regime*, pp. 89–114 and Gail Bossenga, "City and State: An Urban Perspective on the Origins of the French Revolution," in Baker, *The Political Culture of the Old Regime*, pp. 115–40. See also William Doyle, "The Price of Offices in Pre-revolutionary France," *The Historical Journal*, 27 (December 1984): 831–60.
104 Each advertisement was evaluated to see if it contained any appeals for each subcategory. If it had two or more appeals that could fit a single subcategory, the subcategory was still noted only once. This procedure was followed because so often specific appeals worked together to create a single impression that giving double, triple, or more credit seemed to violate the overall message generated by an advertisement.
105 Simon Schama, *Citizens: A Chronicle of the French Revolution* (New York, 1989), pp. 183–5; Peter Gay, *The Enlightenment: An Interpretation*, vol. 2, *The Science of Freedom* (New York, 1969), pp. 319–68; and Kingsley Martin, *French Liberal Thought in the Eighteenth Century: A Study of Political Ideas from Bayle to Condorcet* (New York, 1962), pp. 228–35.
106 Keith Michael Baker argues that, in fact, by the second half of the eighteenth century, progressives had really gained control of the debate. See his "French Political Thought at the Accession of Louis XVI," *Journal of Modern History*, 50 (1978): 279–303.
107 See the assertions in Jürgen Habermas, *The Structural Transformation of the Public Sphere: An Inquiry into a Category of Bourgeois Society*, trans. Thomas Burger (Cambridge, Mass., 1989), pp. 1–102.

108 For the efforts of the monarchy to move beyond tradition, see among many valuable accounts, Schama, *Citizens*, 51–60; and Daniel Roche, *Le Siècle des lumières en province. Académies et académiciens provinciaux* (Paris, 1978). That the king had in no way completely escaped the past is revealed by his reluctance to abandon its principles. For example, although much elite opinion advocated free trade, the monarchy never could firmly grasp the nettle there. See Steven Kaplan, *Bread, Politics and Political Economy for the Reign of Louis XV*, 2 vols. (The Hague, 1976); and Douglas Dakin, *Turgot and the Ancien Régime in France* (London, 1939).

109 In general, contemporary opinion did associate Old Regime society with its government. For the major exception to such a linkage, consult Peter Gay, *Voltaire's Politics: The Poet as Realist* (New York, 1965), pp. 309–33.

3 THE LITERARY–PHILOSOPHICAL PRESS

1 For a good example of this interchange, see Henri Duranton, "Un Usage singulier des gazettes. La Stratégie voltairienne lors de la parution de *l'Abrégé d'histoire universelle* (1753–1754)," in Hans Bots, ed., *La Diffusion et la lecture des journaux de langue française sous l'ancien régime* (Amsterdam and Maarssen, 1988), pp. 31–8. For another effort to link periodicals broadly, see Claude Labrosse, "Réception et communication dans les périodiques littéraires (1750–1760)," in Bots, *La Diffusion et la lecture*, pp. 263–77.

2 Eugène Hatin, *Histoire politique et littéraire de la presse en France*, 8 vols. (Paris, 1859–61), vol. 3, p. 15.

3 Nina Rattner Gelbart, *Feminine and Opposition Journalism in Old Regime France: "Le Journal des Dames"* (Berkeley, 1987). The *Journal des Dames* has received a great deal of attention. See also Suzanna Van Dijk, *Traces des femmes. Présence féminine dans le journalisme français du XVIIIe siècle* (Amsterdam and Maarssen, 1988), pp. 134–85, and Caroline Rimbault, "La Presse féminine de la langue française au XVIIIe siècle," in Pierre Rétat, ed., *Le Journalisme d'ancien régime. Questions et propositions* (Lyons, 1982), pp. 203–4. For a broader perspective, see also Evelyne Sullerot, *Histoire de la presse féminine en France des origines à 1848* (Paris, 1966).

4 This analysis relies only on the issues of 1775, according to Gelbart, *Feminine and Opposition Journalism*, pp. 236–7.

5 The following analysis relies on *ibid.*, pp. 224–5.

6 See, in general, the magisterial study by Daniel Roche, *Le Siècle des lumières en province. Académies et académiciens provinciaux, 1680–1789* (Paris, 1978).

7 The materialist text, *De l'Esprit*, did receive favorable treatment in the *Journal encyclopédique*, a rare enough occurrence. For the favorable treatment of Helvétius, consult Claude Bellanger et al., *Histoire générale de la presse française*, 3 vols. (Paris, 1969), 1: 275. But see Raymond F. Birn, *Pierre Rousseau and the Philosophes of Bouillon* (Geneva, 1964), pp. 170–3 for the general rejection of these notions.

8 John N. Pappas, *Berthier's "Journal de Trévoux" and the Philosophes* (Geneva, 1957), pp. 204–6.

9 *Journal de Trévoux*, October, 1758.

10 *Ibid.*, November, 1758.

11 *Ibid.*

12 *Ibid.*

13 *Ibid.*, September, 1758.

14 *Ibid.*, October, 1758.

15 *Ibid.*, November, 1758.

16 See, for example, the description of intellectual life in Remy G. Saisselin, *The Literary Enterprise in Eighteenth Century France* (Detroit, 1979). For a good general background to all these matters, consult also Michel Kerautret, *La Littéraire française du XVIIIe siècle* (Paris, 1983).

17 This description of the High Enlightenment depends on understanding this movement in the context of other intellectual developments. Readers of this volume will grant indulgence for a long list of those studies that have most influenced the creation and deployment of this category. See Norman Hampson, *A Cultural History of the Enlightenment* (New York, 1968); Peter Gay, *The Enlightenment: An Interpretation*, 2 vols. (New York, 1967–69), vol. 2, *The Science of Freedom*; Margaret Jacob, *The Radical Enlightenment: Pantheists, Freemasons and Republicans* (London, 1981); and Gelbart, *Feminine and Opposition Journalism*. But no one has been more important than Robert Darnton in explaining this whole field. See, in particular, *The Literary Underground of the Old Regime* (Cambridge, Mass., 1982); *Mesmerism and the End of the Enlightenment in France* (Cambridge, Mass., 1962); and "Trade in the Taboo: The Life of a Clandestine Book Dealer in Prerevolutionary France," in Paul Korshin, ed., *The Widening Circle: Essays on the Circulation of Literature in Eighteenth Century France* (Philadelphia, 1976), pp. 11–83. See also several important articles by Sarah Maza, "Le Tribunal de la nation. Les Mémoires judiciares et l'opinion publique à la fin de l'ancien régime," *Annales, E.S.C.* 42 (1987): 73–90; "'The Faith Placed in Covenant': Adultery and Politics in Prerevolutionary French Culture," in Peter McPhee, ed., *Proceedings of the Fifth George Rudé Seminar in French History* (Wellington, N.Z., 1986), pp. 172–87; and "Domestic Melodrama as Political Ideology: The Case of the Comte de Sanois," *American Historical Review* 94 (1989): 1249–64. It is thanks to Dale K. Van Kley that the immense intellectual storm surrounding Jansenism and the parlements has been brought into view. See, among many works, "Church, State and the Ideological Origins of the French Revolution: The Debate over the General Assembly of the Gallican Clergy in 1765," *Journal of Modern History* 51 (1979): 630–64, *The Damiens Affair and the Unraveling of the Ancien Régime* (Princeton, 1984), and "The Estates General as an Ecumenical Council," *Journal of Modern History* 61 (1989): 1–52. See also Carroll Joynes, "The *Gazette de Leyde*: The Opposition Press and French Politics, 1750–1757," in Jack R. Censer and Jeremy D. Popkin, eds., *Press and Politics in Pre-Revolutionary France* (Berkeley, 1987), pp. 133–69. On yet another competing notion – commonwealthman theory – see Keith Michael Baker, "A Script for a French Revolution: The Political Consciousness of the Abbé Mably," *Eighteenth Century Studies* 14 (1981): 235–63; and Michael Sonenscher, *Work & Wages: Natural Law, Politics & the Eighteenth-Century French Trades* (Cambridge, 1989). Most all the above cited works, by focusing both on ideas and their circulation, allow an understanding of these categories of new ideas and their breadth of dissemination. For a series of important insights, consult Roger Chartier, *The Cultural Origins of the French Revolution* (Durham, N.C., 1991).

Of course, alternative ways exist to understand the categories of thought possible for contemporary use. Keith Michael Baker has argued that after the 1750s, the intellectual struggle, at least in politics, focused on debates over will, justice, and reason ("French Political Thought at the Accession of Louis XVI," *Journal of Modern History* 50 [1978]: 279–303). Additionally, one may use the evaluation of various intellectuals as a series of litmus tests for the acceptance or rejection of the new ideas. See, for example, Pappas, *Berthier's "Journal de Trévoux"*, pp. 65–196. See also, Pierre Peyronnet, "L'Actualité dramatique (Théatre-français, Théatre Italien)," and Sylvette Milliott, "La Vie musicale à Paris pendant le printemps et l'été 1778," in Paule Jansen et al., *L'Année 1778 à travers la presse traitée par ordinateur* (Paris, 1982) pp. 183–221 and Robert Favre, "Montesquieu et la presse périodique," *Etudes sur la presse au XVIIIe siècle* 3(1978): 39–60.

18 Simon Schama, *Citizens: A Chronicle of the French Revolution* (New York, 1989), pp. 19–199.

19 Robert R. Palmer, *Catholics and Unbelievers in Eighteenth Century France* (Princeton, 1939).

20 Gelbart, *Feminine and Opposition Journalism*, *passim*.

21 Birn, *Pierre Rousseau*, pp. 19–34.

22 Michel Gaulin, "Le Concept d'homme de lettres, en France, à l'époque de l'Encyclopédie d'après quelques représentants du groupe des philosophes," (Ph.D. diss., Harvard University, 1973).

23 Jean Sgard, "Les Souscripteurs du *Journal étranger*," in Bots, ed., *La Diffusion et la lecture*, p. 95. On the *Gazette universelle de littérature aux Deux-Ponts*, see Jean Sgard, ed., *Dictionnaire des journaux* (Paris, 1991), pp. 463–4. Also possible to include in this list is the *Mercure de France* from 1771 to 1778 under the tutelage of La Harpe. See Christopher Todd, *Political Bias, Censorship, and the Dissolution of the Official Press in Eighteenth-Century France* (Lewiston, N.Y., 1991), p. 53.

24 Birn, *Pierre Rousseau*, *passim*; Bellanger, *Histoire générale*, 1: 312–13; and Gay, *The Science of Freedom*, pp. 344–68.

25 *Ibid.*, pp. 52–5.

26 Sgard, *Dictionnaire des journaux*, p. 134. For an interesting study of a journal that closes too early to be included here, see Jean Sgard, *Le "Pour et contre" de Prévost* (Paris, 1969).

27 Jacques Wagner, *Marmontel journaliste* (Paris, 1975); and Gelbart, *Feminine and Opposition Journalism*. See also Eugène Hatin, *Histoire politique et littéraire de la presse en France*, 8 vols. (Paris, 1859–61), 3: 30–40.

28 For more, see Thelma Morris, *L'Abbé Desfontaines et son rôle dans la littérature de son temps* (Geneva, 1961), pp. 106–8.

29 Wagner, *Marmontel*, pp. 255–306, for an assessment of Marmontel's editorship.

30 *Ibid.*, pp. 218–28.

31 Gelbart, *Feminine and Opposition Journalism*, pp. 38–169.

32 Nina Rattner Gelbart, "The *Journal des dames* and Its Female Editors: Politics, Censorship, and Feminism in the Old Regime Press," in Censer and Popkin, *Press and Politics*, p. 29.

33 For all its evident links to the High Enlightenment, this work did not take the form later outlined by Louis-Sébastien Mercier as appropriate for a novel. However, Mercier was far more involved in the radical phase, and it may be that what has been designated the Enlightenment novel belongs to critics of the philosophes.

34 Gelbart, *Feminine and Opposition Journalism*, pp. 133–69.

35 *Ibid.*, pp. 151–2.

36 Bellanger, *Histoire générale*, 1: 284.

37 Pierre-François Guyot Desfontaines's papers were *Le Nouvelliste du parnasse ou réflexions sur les ouvrages nouveaux* (1731–32); *Observations sur les écrits modernes* (1733–43); and *Jugements sur quelques ouvrages nouveaux* (1744–46). On this journalist, see the excellent work of Morris, *L'Abbé Desfontaines* and Paul Benhamou, "Les Lecteurs des périodiques de Desfontaines," in Bots, *La Diffusion et la lecture des journaux*, pp. 139–51. Fréron's publications included *Lettres sur quelques écrits de ce temps* (1749–54); *Journal étranger* (1755–56), and *Année littéraire* (1754–75). There exists a very substantial bibliography on Elie-

Catherine Fréron. Among the most interesting works, consult Jean Balcou, *Le Dossier Fréron* (Geneva, 1975), and *Fréron contre les philosophes* (Geneva, 1975); François Cornou, *Elie Fréron, trente années de lutte contre Voltaire et les philosophes du XVIIIe siècle* (Paris, 1922); Robert Myers, *The Dramatic Theories of Elie-Catherine Fréron*; and Paul van Tieghem, *L'Année littéraire comme intermédiare en France des littéraires étrangères* (Paris, 1907). The papers of Simon-Nicolas-Henri Linguet were *Journal de Bruxelles* (1774–76) and *Annales politiques, civiles, et littéraires du dix-huitième siècle* (1777–92). See, in particular, Hatin, *Histoire politique et littéraire*, 3: 324–400; and the excellent biography by Darline Gay Levy, *The Ideas and Careers of Simon-Nicolas-Henri Linguet: A Study in Eighteenth-Century French Politics* (Urbana, 1980), especially pp. 172–224.

38 Bellanger, *Histoire générale*, 1: 263.
39 Balcou, *Fréron*, p. 270 for a good example.
40 Pappas, *Berthier's "Journal de Trévoux,"* pp. 142–3.
41 Balcou, *Fréron*, pp. 83–9.
42 As cited in *ibid.*, p. 243.
43 *Ibid.*, p. 343. For earlier attacks, see Cornou, *Elie Fréron*, pp. 159–252.
44 Balcou, *Fréron*, pp. 340–65.
45 *Ibid.*, p. 342.
46 *Ibid.*, pp. 342–3.
47 *Ibid.*, pp. 345–6.
48 Cornou, *Elie Fréron*, pp. 422–7, and Balcou, *Fréron*, p. 350.
49 Balcou, *Fréron*, pp. 350–2.
50 *Ibid.*, p. 353.
51 *Ibid.*, pp. 354–5.
52 *Ibid.*, p. 355.
53 *Ibid.*, pp. 355–6. On the salons, see Dena Goodman, "Enlightenment Salons: The Convergence of Female and Philosophic Ambitions," *Eighteenth Century Studies* 22 (1989): 329–50.
54 See the account in Morris, *L'Abbé Desfontaines*, pp. 21–147.
55 Balcou, *Fréron*, pp. 257, 270.
56 *Ibid.*, pp. 370–401.
57 Robert Lancelot Myers, *The Dramatic Theories of Elie-Catherine Fréron* (Geneva, 1962), pp. 196–200; and Balcou, *Fréron*, pp. 392–401. See also the mixed picture in the long review of the *Almanach des muses*, in *Année littéraire*, January 10, 1771.
58 Gay, *The Science of Freedom*, pp. 216–48.
59 *Année littéraire*, January 20, 1771.
60 Hampson, *Cultural History*, pp. 76–7.
61 *Année littéraire*, January 30, 1771.
62 Balcou, *Fréron*, pp. 150–5.
63 *Ibid.*, pp. 405–6 and 429–30.
64 *Ibid.*, p. 413.
65 There are three monographs, all of value on the *Journal de Trévoux*: Alfred Desautels, *Les "Mémoires de Trévoux" et le mouvement des idées au XVIIIe siècle, 1701–1734* (Rome, 1956), Gustave Dumas, *Histoire du "Journal de Trévoux," depuis 1701 jusqu'en 1762* (Paris, 1936), and Pappas, *Berthier's "Journal de Trévoux."* Also see the extended discussion in Bellanger, *Histoire générale*, 1: 219–40, and more recently the first two volumes of *Etudes sur la presse au XVIIIe siècle*, 3 vols. (Lyons, 1973–1978) both of which are dedicated to the *Journal de Trévoux*. Three articles are of particular interest: in vol. 1, Henri Duranton, "Les *Mémoires de Trévoux* et l'histoire. L'Année 1757," pp. 5–37, and Robert

Favre, "Les *Mémoires de Trévoux* dans le débat sur l'inoculation de la petite vérole (1715–1762)," pp. 39–57; and in vol. 2, Pierre Rétat, "Les Jésuites et l'économie politique. Les *Mémoires de Trévoux*, 1750–1762," pp. 117–63. See also Pascale Ferrand, "Notes pour le traitement informatique de dix années des *Mémoires de Trévoux*" in Rétat, *Le Journalisme d'Ancien Régime*, pp. 27–31.

66 Bellanger, *Histoire générale*, 1: 225–8; and Pappas, *Berthier's "Journal de Trévoux,"*, pp. 36–3.

67 Joseph Daoust, "Les Jésuites contre l'*Encyclopédie* (1751–1752)," *Bulletin de la société historique et archeologique de Langres*, 153(1951): 29–44, and Pappas, *Berthier's "Journal de Trévoux*," pp. 170–96. For a broader contextualization of this controversy, consult Raymond Birn, "The French Language Press and the *Encyclopédie*, 1750–1759," *Studies on Voltaire*, (1967): 263–86; and G. D. Zioutos, "Le Presse et l'*Encyclopédie*," *Etudes de Presse*, 8(1953): 313–25.

68 Jean Ehrard and Jacques Roger, "Deux Périodiques français du 18e siècle: *Le Journal des savants* et *Les Mémoires de Trévoux*. Essai d'une étude quantitative," in Genevieve Bollème *et al.*, *Livre et société dans la France* (Paris, 1965), pp. 43–4.

69 Pappas, *Berthier's "Journal de Trévoux*," pp. 48–9.

70 *Journal de Trévoux*, November, 1753.

71 *Ibid.*

72 Pappas, *Berthier's "Journal de Trévoux*," p. 48.

73 *Journal de Trévoux*, April, 1761.

74 *Ibid.*, April, 1757.

75 Pappas, *Berthier's "Journal de Trévoux*," p. 180.

76 *Ibid.* p. 221.

77 *Ibid.* p. 69.

78 Ehrard and Roger, "Deux Périodiques," p. 48.

79 *Journal de Trévoux*, April, 1761.

80 Pappas, *Berthier's "Journal de Trévoux*," pp. 197–8.

81 *Ibid.*, pp. 143–52.

82 *Ibid.*, pp. 198–99.

83 *Journal de Trévoux*, April, 1761.

84 Pappas, *Berthier's "Journal de Trévoux*," *passim*, supported by Bellanger, *Histoire générale*, 1: 233–4.

85 Cited in Pappas, *Berthier's "Journal de Trévoux*," p. 200.

86 *Journal de Trévoux*, April, 1761. For more on the progressive notions in the *Journal de Trévoux*, see Rétat, "Les Jésuites et l'économie politique," pp. 117–63.

87 The omission most desirable to fill is a new study of the *Nouvelles ecclésiastiques*. However, the very size and complexity of this work will be daunting. Such an investigation can receive significant help from the indispensable work of Dale Van Kley as well as two older monographs: J.C. Adolf Haringan, *Les Nouvelles ecclésiastiques dans leur lutte contre l'esprit philosophique* (Amersfoort, 1925); and Françoise Bontoux, "Paris janseniste au XVIIIe siècle, 'Les Nouvelles ecclésiastiques'" *Paris et Ile-de-France* 7 (1955): 205–20.

88 Samples of the following journals were consulted: *Journal des savants; Nouvelles ecclésiastiques; Journal économique; Annales typographiques; Journal de lecture; La Nature considerée; Cinq Années littéraires; Nouvelle Bibliothèque germanique;* and *Gazette universelle de littérature*.

89 Most works cited in note 17 consider at least in part this phenomenon. See also Paul Hazard, *European Thought in the Eighteenth Century: From Montesquieu to Lessing*, trans. J. Lewis May (Cleveland, 1967), pp. 353–90.

90 Again consult the general works listed in note 17 above.

91 For the reception of Rousseau's *La Nouvelle Héloïse*, see Claude Labrosse, *Lire au XVIIIe siècle: La Nouvelle Héloïse et ses lectures* (Lyons, 1985). See also Balcou, *Fréron*; and Pappas, *Berthier's "Journal de Trévoux."*

92 But even systematic studies have elevated this view. See the classic work by Daniel Mornet, *Les Origines intellectuelles de la révolution française, 1715–1787* (Paris, 1967).

4 EIGHTEENTH-CENTURY JOURNALISM AND ITS PERSONNEL

1 *Encyclopédie ou dictionnaire raisonné des sciences des arts et des métiers* (Paris, 1757), vol. 7, p. 535.

2 *Ibid.*

3 *Ibid.*

4 J.-B.-C. Delisle de Sales, *Essai sur le journalisme depuis 1735 jusqu'à 1800* (Paris, 1811).

5 Denis François Camusat, *Histoire critique des journaux* (Amsterdam, 1734).

6 *Encyclopédie méthodique, ou par ordre des matières* (Paris, 1782–1832).

7 For the general run of opinions, see Michel Gaulin, "Le Concept d'homme de lettres en France, à l'époque de *L'Encyclopédie* d'après quelques réprésentants du groupe des philosophes" (Ph.D. diss., Harvard University, 1973), pp. 122–60.

8 Jean Sgard, ed., *Dictionnaire des journalistes (1600–1789)* (Grenoble, 1976).

9 For the last general survey of the Old Regime press, see Claude Bellanger *et al.*, *Histoire générale de la presse française*, 3 vols. (Paris, 1969), 1: 83–402. The most comprehensive list of such journals is Jean Sgard, ed., *Dictionnaire des journaux (1600–1789)*, 2 vols. (Paris, 1991), pp. 1131–40 and 1179–90. For a complete discussion of the sampling technique, see Appendix II: The Journalists.

10 Because eighteenth-century periodicals generally did not name their editors, it proves impossible to construct an all-inclusive list of these people. However, other researchers have compiled lists, and memoirists mentioned these individuals. From dozens of sources then, I offer the following people as holding the position of editor. Future research will doubtless produce additions and deletions from this group. Some editors served on more than one paper so instead of 68 listed here, one finds 66 individuals.

The biggest disagreement from two highly informed sources concerns the *Journal des dames*. While Nina Gelbert makes Maisonneuve an editor after 1765 and does not include Sautreau de Marsy (*Feminine and Opposition Journalism in Old Regime France: "Le Journal des dames"* (Berkeley, 1987), pp. 141–6), Suzanna Van Dijk (*Traces des femmes. Présence féminine dans le journalisme français du XVIIIᵉ siècle* (Amsterdam, 1988), pp. 144–6) takes the reverse position. I compromised by including both editors. Another questionable call worth mentioning is my inclusion of Etienne Luzac after 1775. Despite his relinquishing daily control after 1772, he was nominally editor until 1783 and was clearly involved in daily affairs after 1775 (Jeremy Popkin, *News and Politics in the Age of Revolution: Jean Luzac's "Gazette de Leyde"* (Ithaca, 1989) p. 20).

11 See Table 4-1 for deletions.

12 The immense diversity of sources that provided these data and all the composite results reported hereafter prove impossible to cite. However the general procedure utilized to gather this information is worth describing to inform readers of the nature of the material. The most useful of many

dictionaries and encyclopedias that provided general information were: Sgard, *Dictionnaire des journalistes;* Sgard, *Dictionnaire des journaux; Dictionnaire des lettres françaises,* 2 vols. (Paris, 1960); *Biographie universelle ancienne et moderne,* 45 vols. (Paris, 1854-n.d.); *Nationaal Biografisch Woordenboek,* 9 vols. (Brussels, 1964–81); and Eugene Haag, ed., *La France protestante,* 10 vols. (Paris and Geneva, 1846–59). The most complete list of editors' publications was usually located in either Alexandre Cioranescu, *Bibliographie de la littérature française du dix-huitième siècle,* 3 vols. (Paris, 1969), or J. M. Quérard, *La France littéraire ou dictionnaire bibliographique,* 12 vols. (Paris, 1828–1864). The Cioranescu volumes also provided a bibliography of studies of many editors. These references and those found in the general dictionaries sometimes cited modern articles and books. More often, however, such bibliographies pointed to nineteenth-century provincial dictionaries and eighteenth-century obituaries. Several editors were eulogized in the eighteenth-century periodical, *Nécrologe des hommes célèbres* (1764–82), and others had a pamphlet dedicated to them.

13 For the most comprehensive statement of the St. Malo-Geneva thesis, see François Furet and Jacques Ozouf, *Reading and Writing: Literacy in France from Calvin to Jules Ferry* (Cambridge, 1982). For a good assessment of the relationship between urban areas and intellectual life, consult Daniel Roche, "Urban Reading Habits During the French Enlightenment," *British Journal for Eighteenth Century Studies* 2 (1979): 138–49, 220–31.

14 For an interesting comparison, see Robert Darnton's analysis of the makers of the *Encyclopédie méthodique* in *The Business of Enlightenment: A Publishing History of the Encyclopédie, 1775–1800* (Cambridge, Mass., 1979), pp. 437–47. To compare with members of provincial academies, consult Daniel Roche, *Le Siècle des lumières en province. Académies et académiciens provinciaux, 1680–1789,* 2 vols. (Paris, 1978), 1: 189–210.

15 For more on women's education, consult Carolyn Lougee, *Le Paradis des Femmes: Women, Salons, and Social Stratification in Seventeenth-Century France* (Princeton, 1976).

16 Willem Frijhoff and Dominique Julia have provided a very insightful study of the functioning of the educational system in their *Ecole et société dans la France d'ancien régime* (Paris, 1975).

17 Jean Balcou, *Fréron contre les philosophes* (Geneva, 1975), pp. 11–13.

18 Charles Franklyn Zeek, *Louis de Boissy, auteur comique (1694–1758)* (Grenoble, 1914), pp. 18–19.

19 Antoine Ricard, *Une Victime de Beaumarchais* (Paris, 1885).

20 Georges Beaujon, *Un Critique neuchâtelois au XVIIIe siècle. Henri-David de Chaillet, 1751–1824* (Basel, 1894), and Charly Guyot, *Henri-David de Chaillet, critique littéraire, 1751–1823* (Neufchâtel, 1946).

21 See the many autobiographical statements scattered through Buchoz's periodical, *La Nature considérée,* in particular the issue for July 14–15, 1781.

22 Cited in Zeek, *Louis de Boissy,* pp. 20–1.

23 Alexandre Deleyre, *Eloge de Monsier Roux* (Amsterdam, 1777), and Charles Ira Rosenberg, "A Critical Analysis of Pierre Clément's 'Les Cinq Années littéraires'" (Ph.D. diss., Northwestern University, 1959).

24 Cioranescu, *Bibliographie,* 3: 991.

25 Pierre Sue, *Mémoire historique, littéraire et critique sur la vie et les ouvrages tant imprimés que manuscrits de Jean Goulin* (Paris, 1800).

26 Alfred Collison Hunter, *J.-B.-A. Suard. Un Introducteur de la littérature anglaise en France* (Paris, 1925).

27 Balcou, *Fréron*; Sgard, *Dictionnaire des journalistes*, p. 17; and René Moulinas, *L'Imprimerie, la librairie et la presse à Avignon au XVIIIe siècle* (Grenoble, 1974), pp. 295–300.
28 Jeremy Popkin, *News and Politics*, pp. 15–23.
29 See Sgard, *Dictionnaire des journaux*, pp. 79–84, which includes substantial bibliography on Joyneau-Desloges.
30 Lucien Lemaire, "Joseph Paris de l'Epinard, journaliste à Lille. Son Arrestation sous la Terreur," *Bulletin de comité flammand de France* (1921): 1–32.
31 Jean Quéniart, *L'Imprimerie et la librairie à Rouen au XVIIIe siècle* (Paris, 1969).
32 Louis Trénard, *Lyon, de l'Encyclopédie au préromantisme, histoire sociale des idées* (Paris, 1958), pp. 55-86.
33 Camusat, *Histoire critique*.
34 In the Revolution, journalists raised their self-image. For example, see Pierre Rétat, "Le Journaliste révolutionnaire comme 'Ecrivain patriote,'" *Il Confronto Letterario*, no. 15 suppl. (c. 1992), pp. 111–120.
35 A substantial literature exists for both German and English eighteenth-century periodicals. For a survey of each, see Joachim Kirchner, *Das Deutsche Zeitschriften*, 2 vols. (Wiesbaden, 1958), and the many entries in Katherine Kirtley Weed and Richmond Pugh Bond, *Studies of British Newspapers and Periodicals from Their Beginning to 1800: A Bibliography* (Chapel Hill, 1946). For the role of ministers in intellectual life, consult Walter Bruford, *Germany in the Eighteenth Century: The Social Background of the Literary Revival* (Cambridge, Mass., 1976); Alan Heimert, *Religion and the American Mind, from the Great Awakening to the Revolution* (Cambridge, Mass., 1966); and Henry May, *The Enlightenment in America* (New York, 1976).

5 THE FRENCH GOVERNMENT AND THE PERIODICAL

1 John Woodbridge, "Censure royale et censure épiscopale. Le Conflit de 1702," *Dix-huitième siècle*, 8 (1976): 333–55.
2 Bibliothèque nationale fonds français (hereafter BNFF), volume (v) 22133, folio (f.) 24, printed in Jean Balcou, ed., *Le Dossier Fréron. Correspondances et documents* (Geneva and Saint Brienc, 1975), document (doc.) 157.
3 Jeremy D. Popkin. *News and Politics in the Age of Revolution: Jean Luzac's "Gazette de Leyde"* (Ithaca, 1989), pp. 27–55.
4 Darline Gay Levy, *The Ideas and Career of Simon-Nicolas-Henri Linguet: A Study in Eighteenth-Century French Politics* (Urbana, 1980), pp. 172–239; and Raymond F. Birn, *Pierre Rousseau and the Philosophes of Bouillon* (Geneva, 1964), pp. 35–77.
5 René Moulinas, *L'Imprimiere, la librairie et la presse à Avignon au XVIIIe siècle* (Grenoble, 1974), pp. 372-9.
6 Bibliothèque nationale, nouvelle acquisitions françaises (BN, n.a.f.), v. 3347, f. 267.
7 *Archives de la Bastille*, v. 11,593, ff. 406–7 in Balcou, *Le Dossier Fréron*, doc. 9.
8 Claude Bellanger *et al.*, *Histoire générale de la presse française*, 3 vols., vol. 1, *Des Origines à 1814* (Paris, 1969), p. 161.
9 For more on the materialists, see Chapter 3.
10 Occasionally payoffs supplemented other efforts. See Georges Weill, *Le Journal. Origines, évolution et rôle de la presse périodique* (Paris, 1934), p. 116; and Eugène Hatin, *Histoire politique et littéraire de la presse en France*, 8 vols. (Paris, 1859–61), 3: 426–7.
11 Raymond Birn, *"Le Journal des savants sous l'ancien régime" Journal des savants* (1965): 27–31.

12 Bibliothèque de l'Arsenal, mss. 10297.
13 Howard Solomon, *Public Welfare, Science and Propaganda in Seventeenth Century France: The Innovations of Théophraste Renaudot* (Princeton, 1972), pp. 148–54.
14 Bellanger, *Histoire générale*, 1: 104–8.
15 Archives des affaires étrangères (AAE), Mémoires et documents français (Mem. et doc.), volume (v.) 1377, folios (ff.) 8–14.
16 *Ibid.*
17 AAE, Mem. et doc., v. 582, ff. 224–5.
18 Solomon, *Public Welfare*, pp. 144–56.
19 Bellanger, *Histoire générale*, 1: 190–1.
20 *Ibid.*
21 Bernard Faÿ, *The Revolutionary Spirit in France and America*, trans. Ramon Guthrie (New York, 1927), pp. 54–6, 87–91.
22 Jean Ehrard and Jacques Roger, "Deux Périodiques français au 18e siècle: *le Journal des savants* et *les Mémoires de Trévoux*. Essai d'une étude quantitative." in G. Bollème *et al.*, *Livre et société dans la France du XVIIIe siècle* (Paris, 1965), pp. 33–59.
23 Birn, "*Le Journal des savants*," pp. 27–31.
24 See BNFF, v. 32133, ff. 63–5 and 69.
25 BNFF, v. 32133, f. 80.
26 On the conservatism of the *Journal des savants*, consult Cyril B. O'Keefe, *Contemporary Reactions to the Enlightenment (1728–1762): A Study of Three Critical Journals: The Jesuit "Journal de Trévoux," the Jansenist "Nouvelles Ecclésiastiques" and the Secular "Journal des savants"* (Geneva, 1974).
27 BNFF, v. 22191, ff. 12–15.
28 Gilles Feyel, *La "Gazette" en province à travers ses réimpressions, 1631–1752* (Amsterdam, 1982), pp. 177–81.
29 Bellanger, *Histoire générale*, 1: 137–43; and Suzanne Tucoo-Chala, *Charles-Joseph Panckoucke & la librairie française, 1731–1798* (Paris, 1977), p. 211; and Denise Aimé-Azam, "Le Ministère des affaires étrangères et la presse à la fin de l'ancien régime." *Cahiers de la presse* (1938): 432.
30 Françoise Souchet, "Gazettes et journaux face à l'actualité," in Henri Duranton *et al.*, eds., *Les Gazettes européennes de langue française (XVIIe-XVIIIe siècles)* (St.-Etienne, 1992), pp. 205–12.
31 Tucoo-Chala, *Panckoucke*, pp. 213–14.
32 BN, n.a.f., v. 3347, f. 248.
33 AAE, Mem. et doc., v. 582, ff. 224–5.
34 Tucoo-Chala, p. 214.
35 *Ibid.*, p. 206.
36 Hatin, *Histoire de la presse*, vol. 2, p. 153.
37 M. Grimm and D. Diderot, *Correspondance littéraire philosophique et critique de France depuis 1753 jusqu'à 1790* 16 vols. (Paris, 1829), 3: 264–5.
38 Thelma Morris, *L'Abbé Desfontaines et son rôle dans la littérature de son temps* (Geneva, 1961); and Birn, "*Le Journal des savants*." Marianne Constance Couperus, *Un Périodique français en Hollande. Le Glaneur historique* (The Hague, 1971) gives insights into the struggle between the Versailles government and the foreign press.
39 BNFF, v. 22135, f. 135.
40 BNFF, v. 22133, f. 123.
41 *Ibid.*
42 Nina Rattner Gelbart, *Feminine and Opposition Journalism in Old Regime France: "Le Journal des dames"* (Berkeley, 1987), pp. 46–49.

43 BNFF, v. 22151, ff. 54, 55, and 57.
44 BNFF, v. 22084, f. 77.
45 BNFF, v. 22134, f. 141.
46 See, for example, the exchanges between Malesherbes and the Duchesse de Bourbon, *ibid.* v. 22134, ff. 142–56.
47 BNFF, v. 22135, f. 134.
48 BNFF, v. 22135, f. 135.
49 BNFF, v. 22135, f. 154.
50 BNFF, v. 22135, ff. 138–9 and 141.
51 BNFF, v. 22135, f. 142.
52 BNFF, v. 22135, ff. 146–50.
53 BNFF, v. 22135, f. 144.
54 BNFF, v. 22135, f. 145.
55 BNFF, v. 22135, f. 151.
56 BNFF, v. 22135, f. 152.
57 Jean Sgard, ed., *Dictionnaire des journaux, 1600–1789*, 2 vols. (Paris, 1991).
58 BNFF, v. 22134, f. 197.
59 BNFF, v. 22135, f. 68.
60 BNFF, v. 22142, f. 6.
61 BNFF, v. 22133, f. 45
62 BNFF, v. 22133, ff. 123–38.
63 BNFF, v. 22133, f. 123.
64 BNFF, v. 22133, ff. 123–38.
65 *Ibid.* See also BNFF, v. 22133, f. 140.
66 BNFF, v. 22133, f. 162.
67 Bellanger, *Histoire générale*, pp. 162.
68 Balcou, *Le Dossier Fréron*, p. 150.
69 BN, n.a.f., v. 3531, f. 61 and f. 45, printed in Balcou, *Le Dossier Fréron*, docs. 70 and 72.
70 BN, n.a.f., v. 3531, ff. 56–7, printed in Balcou, *Le Dossier Fréron*, doc. 72.
71 BN, n.a.f., v. 3531, ff. 58–60, printed in Balcou, *Le Dossier Fréron*, doc. 73.
72 BN, n.a.f., v. 3531, f. 41, printed in Balcou, *Le Dossier Fréron*, doc. 75.
73 BN, n.a.f., v. 3531, f. 53, printed in Balcou, *Le Dossier Fréron*, doc. 76.
74 BN, n.a.f., v. 3531, ff. 48–9, printed in Balcou, *Le Dossier Fréron*, doc. 79.
75 See in particular, Catherine Blangonnet, "Recherches sur les censeurs royaux et leur place dans la société au temps de Malesherbes [1750–1763]" (Thèse de l'école de Chartres, Paris, 1974).
76 BNFF, v. 22134, ff. 151–2.
77 BNFF, v. 22134, ff. 221–5.
78 BNFF, v. 22133, ff. 42–3.
79 Gelbart, *Feminine and Opposition Journalism*, p. 116.
80 BN, n.a.f., v. 3531, ff. 16–17, printed in Balcou, *Le Dossier Fréron*, doc. 68.
81 BN, n.a.f., v. 3531, ff. 20–1, printed in Balcou, *Le Dossier Fréron*, doc. 65.
82 BNFF, v. 22191, ff. 271 and 277.
83 Pierre Grosclaude, *Malesherbes. Témoin et interprète de son temps* (Paris, 1961), p. 258; BNFF, v. 22135, f. 130; and BNFF, v. 22191, f. 276.
84 BN, n.a.f., v. 3531, ff. 65–6, printed in Balcou, *Le Dossier Fréron*, doc. 65–6.
85 Grosclaude, *Malesherbes*, p. 158; BNFF, v. 22135, f. 130; and BNFF, v. 22191, f. 276.
86 BNFF, v. 22191, f. 281.
87 BN, n.a.f., v. 22191, f. 134 and BN, n.a.f., v. 3531, f. 62, printed in Balcou, *Le Dossier Fréron*, doc. 85–6.
88 BN, n.a.f., v. 3531, f. 88, printed in Balcou, *Le Dossier Fréron*, doc. 20.

89 BNFF, v. 22191, f. 276.

90 BNFF, v. 22133, f. 24, printed in Balcou, *Le Dossier Fréron*, doc. 157. For a similar, but not so well-known case, see Malesherbes's reply to Daniel Magenes on June 20, 1760, BNFF, v. 22135, f. 131.

91 BN, n.a.f., v. 3531, ff. 129–30, printed in Balcou, *Le Dossier Fréron*, doc. 159.

92 For more on this, see Nina Gelbart, *Feminine and Opposition Journalism*, especially pp. 170–206 and Jeremy Popkin, "The Prerevolutionary Origins of Political Journalism," in Keith Michael Baker, ed., *The French Revolution and the Creation of Modern Political Culture*, Vol. 1, *The Political Culture of the Old Regime* (Oxford, 1987), pp. 216–20.

93 Jean Balcou, *Fréron contre les philosophes* (Geneva, 1975), pp. 30–1.

94 BN, n.a.f., v. 3531, ff. 129–30, printed in Balcou, *Le Dossier Fréron*, doc. 159.

95 BN, n.a.f., v. 3531, ff. 90–2, 98–106, and 108–10, printed in Balcou, *Le Dossier Fréron*, docs. 121–30.

96 See below, pp. 165-7, for a view of Malesherbes's efforts in this regard.

97 Birn, *Pierre Rousseau*, pp. 121–30. When the foreign journalist Rousseau was given a censor in 1774, it was an innovation. It appears characteristic of more restrictive regimes, and, as far as may be understood by silences, many other foreign publishers never mentioned this as a possibility.

98 The memorists of the eighteenth century treated these suppressions frequently and reacted as though they were successful at denying access. For some examples, see Louis Petit de Bachaumont, *Mémoires secrets pour servir à l'histoire de la république des lettres en France depuis MDCCLXII jusqu'à nos jours. Ou Journal d'un observateur* 36 vols. (London, 1778), 10: 29, 222, 241; 11: 229; 17: 265; and 23: 18; Fr. Metra, *Correspondance secrète, politique & littéraire. Ou Mémoires pour servir à l'histoire des cours, des sociétés & de la littérature en France depuis la mort de Louis XV*, 16 vols. (London, 1987), 11: 319; and Siméon-Prosper Hardy, *Mes Loisirs. Journal d'événements tels qu'ils parviennent à ma connaissance* (Paris, 1912), pp. 202–3.

99 BNFF, v. 22133, f. 14.

100 BNFF, v. 22133, f. 15.

101 BNFF, v. 22133, ff. 16–17.

102 *Ibid.*

103 *Ibid.*; and Birn, *Pierre Rousseau*, p. 61.

104 BNFF, v. 22133, f. 20.

105 BNFF, v. 22134, f. 228; and Grosclaude, *Malesherbes*, pp. 71–3.

106 Pierre Rétat, "Les Gazetiers de Hollande et les puissances politiques au 18e siècle. Une Difficile Collaboration," *Dix-Huitième Siècle* no. 25 (1993), 319–33.

107 *Ibid.*

108 *Ibid.*

109 For an example of these anti-popular attitudes, see Popkin, *News and Politics*, passim.

110 Rétat, "Les Gazetiers de Hollande."

111 These conjectures about the strength and weaknesses of the spread of the news depend in large part on Charles Aubertin, *L'Esprit public au XVIIIe siècle* (Paris, 1889); Frantz Funck-Brentano, *Les Nouvellistes* (Paris, 1905); Christopher Todd, *Political Bias, Censorship and the Dissolution of the "Official" Press in Eighteenth-Century France* (Lewiston, N.Y., 1991), pp. 157–8; and Hatin, *Les Gazettes de Hollande et la presse clandestine aux XVIIe et XVIIIe siècles* (Paris, 1865), pp. 24–5.

112 Gilles Feyel, "La Diffusion des gazettes étrangères en France et la révolution postale des années 1750," in Duranton, *Les Gazettes européennes*, pp. 81–98.

113 René Moulinas, "Le Rôle de la poste royale comme moyen de contrôle financier sur la diffusion des gazettes en France au XVIIIe siècle," in *Modèles et moyens de la réflexion politique au XVIIIe siècle* (Lille, 1973), pp. 392.

114 Jean Sgard, ed., *Dictionnaire des journalistes (1600–1789)* (Grenoble, 1976), pp. 386–7.

115 Feyel, "La Diffusion des gazettes," pp. 95–6. The situation of the *Courrier d'Avignon* suggests another factor in royal policy toward the gazettes. As Chapter 1 described, the special circumstances, especially French governmental pressure, regarding the *Courrier d'Avignon* made it tame. Political factors also played into the calculations of every other gazette, and depending on their situation, they either tended to refrain from taking full advantage or to flout the rules. But it would seem that the main effect of all these considerations, while surely nuancing overall policy, was the *Courrier d'Avignon* and its role in dampening all periods of governmental openness. Indeed, Versailles seemed somewhat to recognize this in the way it singled out the *Courrier* for special encouragement.

116 Moulinas, "Du Rôle de la poste royale."

117 For the pricing of the *Gazette de France*, see Gilles Feyel, "La *Gazette* au début de la guerre de Sept Ans. Son Administration, sa diffusion (1751–1758)," in Hans Bots, ed., *La Diffusion et la lecture des journaux de langue française sous l'Ancien Régime* (Amsterdam, 1988), pp. 101–16.

118 Gelbart, *Feminine and Opposition Journalism*, p. 168. See, for the Enlightenment view of the same matter, Harry C. Payne, *The Philosophes and the People* (New Haven, 1976).

119 Birn, *Pierre Rousseau*, p. 61.

120 Feyel, "La Diffusion des gazettes," pp. 89–98. More unsystematically Choiseul may have also loosened up procedures on new domestic literary periodicals. See Hatin, *Histoire de la presse*, 3: 9.

121 AAE, correspondance politique [corr. pol.], Hollande, v. 520, f. 89.

122 AAE, corr. pol., Hollande, v. 520, f. 90.

123 AAE, corr. pol., Hollande, v. 520, f. 287. See also AAE, corr. pol., Hollande, v. 518, f. 309.

124 AAE, corr. pol., Hollande, v. 516, f. 214.

125 AAE, corr. pol., Hollande, v. 516, ff. 225, 227–8.

126 Bachaumont, *Mémoires secrets*, vol. 3, p. 311.

127 BN, n.a.f., v. 3347, f. 267.

128 BN, n.a.f., v. 3347, ff. 275–7.

129 BN, n.a.f., v. 3347, ff. 279–80.

130 BN, n.a.f., v. 3347, ff. 285–6.

131 *Ibid.*; and BN, n.a.f., v. 3347, f. 287.

132 BN, n.a.f., v. 3347, f. 287.

133 BN, n.a.f., v. 3347, ff. 285–6.

134 For more evidence of Malesherbes' stringency in these matters, consult Sgard, *Dictionnaire des journaux*, p. 353.

135 Madeline Fabre, "Edme-Jacque Genet," in Jean Sgard, ed., *Dictionnaire des journalistes (1600–1789)*, Anne-Marie Chouillet and François Moureau, eds., *Supplément II* (Grenoble, 1983), pp. 80–6.

136 Grimm, *Correspondance littéraire*, 5: 317; Bachaumont, *Mémoires secrets*, 1: 8–9, 127, 233–4, and 241–2; 2: 18 and 30.

137 Sgard, *Dictionnaire des journaux*, p. 517.

138 Feyel, "La Diffusion des gazettes," pp. 95–6, on the continued support for the *Courrier d'Avignon*.

139 For a study of an early escape from shackles, see Carroll Joynes, "The *Gazette de Leyde*: The Opposition Press and French Politics," in Jack R. Censer and

Jeremy D. Popkin, eds., *Press and Politics in Pre-revolutionary France* (Berkeley, 1987), pp. 133–69.

140 Fréron's use of "personalities" reached an apogee at this point with plenty of response from the philosophes. Balcou, *Fréron*, pp. 331–69.

141 Bachaumont, *Mémoires secrets*, 27: 278–9.

142 Gelbart, *Feminine and Opposition Journalism*, p. 172.

143 *Ibid.*, pp. 122–3.

144 See Chapter 1.

145 AAE, corr. pol., Hollande, v. 521, ff. 257–60.

146 *Ibid.*

147 *Ibid.*

148 *Ibid.*

149 *Ibid.*

150 AAE, corr. pol., Hollande, v. 523, ff. 262 and 277.

151 Popkin, *News and Politics*, p. 140.

152 AAE, corr. pol., Hollande, v. 524, ff. 94 and 106.

153 AAE, corr. pol., Hollande, v. 524, f. 139.

154 AAE, corr. pol., Hollande, v. 524, f. 140.

155 AAE, corr. pol., Hollande, v. 524, f. 141.

156 AAE, corr. pol., Hollande, v. 524, f. 142.

157 AAE, corr. pol., Hollande, v. 524, ff. 142bis and 159.

158 AAE, corr. pol., Hollande, v. 524, ff. 179–80.

159 AAE, corr. pol., Hollande, v. 524, f. 185.

160 AAE, corr. pol., Hollande, v. 525, ff. 61–2.

161 *Ibid.*

162 AAE, corr. pol., Hollande, v. 525, f. 63.

163 One exception was an openness that might be granted when a newspaper attacked the parlement. Hatin, *Histoire de la presse*, 3: 153–5.

164 Tucoo-Chala, *Panckoucke*, pp. 195–7.

165 *Ibid.*, pp. 207 and 209.

166 Hatin, *Histoire de la presse*, 3: 235.

167 AAE, corr. pol., Hollande, v. 526, ff. 144 and 153.

168 AAE, corr. pol., Hollande, v. 526, ff. 191–2.

169 AAE, corr. pol., Hollande, v. 526, f. 259.

170 AAE, corr. pol., Hollande, v. 527, ff. 13–14.

171 AAE, corr. pol., Hollande, v. 527, f. 20.

172 Gelbart, *Feminine and Opposition Journalism*, p. 227.

173 *Ibid.*

174 See Fréron's continued attacks on pp.154–7.

175 Faÿ, *The Revolutionary Spirit*, pp. 54–6, 81–2.

176 Considerable diversity reigned within the press despite Vergennes's desire. See Jean-Louis Lecercle, "L'Amérique et la guerre d'Indépendence," in Paule Jansen *et al.*, *L'Année 1778 à travers la presse traitée par ordinateur* (Paris, 1982), pp. 17–42.

177 Gelbart, *Feminine and Opposition Journalism*, pp. 283–7.

178 Tucoo-Chala, *Panckoucke*, p. 232.

179 For an interesting case, see Sgard, *Dictionnaire des journalistes*, pp. 622–3.

180 Gelbart, *Feminine and Opposition Journalism*, p. 168.

181 *Ibid.*, pp. 207–47.

182 Popkin, *News and Politics*, pp. 149–50. See also Sgard, *Dictionnaire des journalistes*, p. 487.

183 Although forbidden in the press, problematic news did circulate to a degree. See Hatin, *Les Gazettes de Hollande*, pp. 172–4 and 329. Jeremy Popkin, *News*

and Politics, p. 150, also gives testimony to the vitality of these sources as well as some governmental success at closing the door.

184 Sgard, *Dictionnaire des journalistes*, pp. 702–3.
185 See Peter Ascoli, "The French Press and the American Revolution: The Battle of Saratoga," in *Proceedings of the Fifth Annual Meeting of the Western Society for French History*, ed. Joyce Duncan Falk (Santa Barbara, Calif., 1977), pp. 46–55, and *idem.*, "American Propaganda in the French Language Press during the American Revolution" (unpublished paper, 1977).
186 This analysis depends on the wealth of information provided in Gunnar von Proschwitz and Mavis von Proschwitz, *Beaumarchais et le "Courrier de l'Europe,"* 2 vols. (Oxford, 1990).
187 On the openness of the press, consult Sgard, *Dictionnaire des journalistes*, p. 33. Still personalities were barred: *ibid.*, p. 624; and Hatin, *Histoire de la presse*, 2: 44, 47–50; and von Proschwitz, *Beaumarchais*, 1: 1.
188 Bachaumont, *Mémoires secrets*, vol. 10, p. 222.
189 Bellanger, *Histoire générale*, pp. 309–11; and Popkin, *News and Politics*, pp. 54–6.
190 This analysis of Linguet's thought relies very heavily on the excellent analysis of Levy, *Linguet*, pp. 180–5.
191 *Ibid.*, p. 193.
192 *Ibid.*, pp. 192–3.
193 *Correspondance secrète*, 9: 6.
194 Levy, *Linguet*, pp. 190–1.
195 *Ibid.*, pp. 200–2.
196 *Ibid.*, p. 225.
197 Jeremy Popkin, "Un Journaliste face au marché des périodiques à la fin du dix-huitième siècle. Linguet et ses *Annales politiques*," in Bots, *La Diffusion et la lecture*, pp. 11–19.
198 Popkin, "The *Gazette de Leyde* under Louis XVI," in Censer and Popkin, *Press and Politics*, pp. 98–132.
199 For information on the general relationship between the government and the *Mercure de France*, consult the Bibliothèque de l'Institüt, v. 1271, ff. 57–60, 64, 66–8, and 75; Tucoo-Chala, *Panckoucke*, pp. 205–6; and Frances Acomb, *Mallet du Pan (1749–1800): A Career in Political Journalism* (Durham, N.C., 1973), pp. 158–209.
200 Gilles Feyel, "La Presse provinciale sous l'ancien régime," in Jean Sgard, ed., *La Presse provinciale au XVIIIe siècle* (Grenoble, 1983), pp. 6–7.
201 *Ibid.*, pp. 8–9; and BNFF, v. 22134, ff. 124, 126, 133–6 and v. 22135, f. 158.
202 Feyel, "La Presse provinciale sous l'ancien régime," in Sgard, *Presse provinciale*, p. 44.
203 *Ibid.*, p. 5.
204 For interesting detail, consult Sgard, *Dictionnaire des journalistes*, p. 122.
205 *Ibid.*, p. 43.
206 Sarah Maza, *Private Lives and Public Affairs: The "Causes Célèbres" of Pre-revolutionary France* (Berkeley, 1993).
207 Carla Hesse, *Publishing and Cultural Politics in Revolutionary Paris, 1789–1810* (Berkeley, 1991), pp. 40–3.

6 THE READERSHIP

1 The search for quantitative data on reading and readers generally in the eighteenth century owes a tremendous debt to Daniel Mornet's *Les Origines intellectuelles de la révolution française* (Paris, 1933). Although little interested

the press, he produced the earliest analysis of a list of subscribers (see Table 6–4). Although a founder of many areas, Mornet had few offspring in this field until very recently. The search for information on readers gained more success in the last two decades, beginning with material on the revolutionary press. A very notable breakthrough occurred in Jeremy Popkin, *The Right-Wing Press in France, 1792–1800* (Chapel Hill, 1980), pp. 68–74. For an earlier important article, consult Max Fajn, "The Circulation of the French Press during the French Revolution," *English Historical Review* 87 (1972): 100–5. See more recently, Hugh Gough, *The Newspaper Press in the French Revolution* (Chicago, 1988). Materials on this subject have come slower for the Old Regime press but see especially Suzanne Tucoo-Chala, *Charles-Joseph Panckoucke & la librairie française, 1736–1798* (Paris, 1975); Gilles Feyel, *La Gazette en province, 1631–1752, à travers ses réimpressions* (Amsterdam, 1982); Hans Bots, ed., *La Diffusion et la lecture des journaux de langue française sous l'ancien régime* (Amsterdam, 1987); and Chapters 1 and 6 in Harvey Chisick, *The Production, Distribution and Readership of a Conservative Journal of the Early Revolution: The "Ami du Roi" of the Abbé Royou* (Philadelphia, 1992).

2 Most scholars credit Rolf Engelsing, *Der Burger als Leser, Lesergeschichte in Deutschland 1500-1800* (Stuttgart, 1974), as the publication that did most to encourage the study of reading habits. There has been an explosion of work, although as yet not many agreed upon lines of inquiry, on the subject in eighteenth-century France. Most of the effort, when not theoretical, has concentrated upon books. See, for a sampler of what is available: Roger Chartier, *The Cultural Uses of Print in Early Modern France*, trans. Lydia G. Cochrane (Princeton, 1987); Daniel Roche, "Urban Reading Habits during the French Enlightenment," *British Journal for Eighteenth-Century Studies* 2 (1979): 138–49, 221–31; Roger Chartier and Daniel Roche, "Les Pratiques urbaines de l'imprimé"; Anne Sauvy, "Le livre aux changes," in Henri-Jean Martin and Roger Chartier, *Histoire de l'édition française*, vol. 2, *Le livre triomphant, 1660–1830* (Paris, 1984), pp. 402–43; and Robert Darnton, *The Great Cat Massacre* (New York, 1984), chapter 7. Only very recently have scholars begun to transfer this work into the history of the press. See the section "Du Côté des lecteurs," in Bots, *La Diffusion*, pp. 129–201; and Jeremy Popkin, *News and Politics in the Age of Revolution: Jean Luzac's "Gazette de Leyde"* (Ithaca, 1989), pp.126–36.

3 Nina Rattner Gelbart, *Feminine and Opposition Journalism in Old Regime France* (Berkeley and Los Angeles, 1987); Susanna Van Dijk, *Traces des femmes: Présence féminine dans le journalisme français du XVIIIe siècle* (Amsterdam and Maarssen, 1988).

4 For these estimates, see Albert Soboul, *La France à la veille de la Révolution*, vol. 1, *Economie et société* (Paris, 1966); and Guy Chaussinand-Nogaret, *La Noblesse au XVIIIe siècle* (Paris, 1976). Robert Forster kindly assisted me in these calculations.

5 Also useful would be information on the very early revolutionary press, but little is so far available. See Chisick, *The "Ami du Roi,"* pp. 208–21.

6 For support for this speculation, consult Michel Marion, "Dix Ans des affiches, annonces, et avis divers (1752–1761), " in Jacques Godechot, ed., *Regards sur l'histoire de la presse et de l'information. Mélanges offerts à Jean Prinet* (St. Julien du Saolt, 1980), p. 25.

7 For family budgets in Paris, where workers likely had much more substantial incomes, consult Daniel Roche, *The People of Paris: An Essay in Popular Culture in the 18th Century*, trans. Marie Evans (Berkeley, 1987), pp. 97–194.

8 *Ibid.*, pp. 197–233.

9 For Germany, see Hans Erich Bödeker, "The Coffee House as an Institution of Communicative Sociability," (unpublished paper); and for England, see John Money, "Taverns, Coffee Houses and Clubs: Local Politics and Popular Articulacy in the Birmingham Area in the Age of the American Revolution," *Historical Journal*, 14 (1971): 15–47.

10 Chisick, *"The Ami du Roi,"* Chapter 6. This is not to say that French cafés totally failed in this regard, as there was some stocking of papers. See Christopher Todd, *Political Bias, Censorship and the Dissolution of the "Official" Press in Eighteenth-Century France* (Lewiston, N.Y., 1991), p. 25. The case made here is one of relative availability.

11 Charles de Ribbé, *Un Journal et un journaliste à Aix avant la Révolution. Etude de moeurs sur la ville d'Aix vers la fin du XVIIIe siècle* (Aix, 1859), pp. 12–13; and Paul Benhamou, "Essai d'inventaire des instruments de lecture publique des gazettes," in Henri Duranton *et al.*, *Les Gazettes européennes de langue française (XVII–XVIIIe siècles)* (St. Etienne, 1992), pp. 121–9. Exceptionally, entrance could be quite inexpensive, as little as three sous per admission. Eugène Hatin, *Histoire politique et littéraire de la presse en France*, 8 vols. (Paris, 1859) 3: 318.

12 See, for example, the structure of sociability at the top in Lenard R. Berlanstein, *The Barristers of Toulouse in the Eighteenth Century (1740–1793)* (Baltimore, 1975).

13 For discussion of this, see Gilles Feyel, "La *Gazette* au début de la guerre de Sept Ans. Son Administration, sa diffusion (1751–1758), " in Bots, *La Diffusion*, pp. 110–11; and Gilles Feyel, "La Diffusion des gazettes étrangères en France, et la révolution postale des années 1750," in Duranton, *Les Gazettes européennes*, pp. 93–4.

14 See Panckoucke's strategic limits when it came to finding new social groups in Robert Darnton, *The Business of Enlightenment: A Publishing History of the "Encyclopédie," 1775–1800* (Cambridge, Mass., 1979). Although this work plots Panckoucke's efforts regarding books, nothing in his press undertakings seems more aggressive as documented in Tucoo-Chala, *Panckoucke*, pp. 191-251. See for the revolutionary contrast, Carla Hesse, *Publishing and Cultural Politics in Revolutionary Paris, 1789–1810* (Berkeley and Los Angeles, 1991).

15 The main locations for these documents proved to be the Bibliothèque nationale (Paris); the Newberry Library (Chicago); and university libraries at Harvard, Yale and Princeton.

16 Claude Bellanger *et al.*, *Histoire générale de la presse française*, vol. 1, *Des origines à 1814* (Paris, 1969).

17 *Journal de Bruxelles* (1774); *Courrier de l'Europe* (1777).

18 For such promises, see an early example in the *Bibliothèque britannique* (1733).

19 For such claims to farmers and businessmen, see the *Affiches de Picardie* (1774), and the *Journal économique* (1781); for science, consult the *Bibliothèque des sciences* (1754) and the *Journal encyclopédique* (n.d.); on style, see the *Journal encyclopédique* and the *Affiches de Toulouse* (1782); on patriotism, see the *Affiches de Picardie* (1775) and the *Affiches de Toulouse*; on the explanation of complex problems, see *Gazette du commerce* (1763), and *Avant-coureur* (1773).

20 *Courrier de l'Europe* (1777).

21 See especially the 1778 prospectus of the *Annonces, affiches divers de l'Orléanais*.

22 *Journal des dames*, prospectuses for 1759, 1761, 1762, c. 1763, 1765, 1766, January 1774 and November 1774.

23 Others have, indeed, focused on the journalists' assertions of autonomy. See Henri Duranton, "Un Usage singulier des gazettes. La Stratégie voltarienne

lors de la parution de *l'Abrégé d'histoire universelle* (1753–1754)," in Bots, *La Diffusion*, pp. 31–8; Jeroom Vercruysse, "La Réception politique des journaux de Hollande, une lecture diplomatique," in Bots, *La Diffusion*, pp. 35–47; and Uta Janssens, *Matthieu Maty and the "Journal britannique:" A French View of English Literature in the Middle of the Eighteenth Century* (Amsterdam, 1975), pp. 43–8.

24 Darnton, *The Great Cat Massacre*, Chapter 7.

CONCLUSION

1 Even though editors and readers emerged largely from the same social class, religious differences could have caused a considerable gap, especially in the subjects handled in the discussion press. This was, however, not the case. See François Moureau, "Les Journalistes de langue française dans l'Allemagne des lumières. Essai de typologie," *Studies on Voltaire and the Eighteenth Century*, 216 (1983).

2 For the disaffection of the elite, see among many other possibilities, William Doyle, *Origins of the French Revolution* (Oxford, 1980), pp. 78–95 and Simon Schama, *Citizens: A Chronicle of the French Revolution* (New York, 1989), pp. 19–200.

3 Two other interesting, though probably more limited problems deserve some attention. Why did foreign gazettes cover the French monarchy at all in those periods when they were so limited in what they could say? Here intervenes the general commitment to broad coverage. Denial of one area did not preclude discussing the rest. A second query concerns the failure to manipulate significantly the content of the few Dutch papers circulating in France before Choiseul. This approach may relate to the view that their very high price would keep them out of the hands of undesirables. But the irrationalities of governing may have to suffice.

4 On the parlements, see Bailey Stone, *The Parlement of Paris, 1774–1789* (Chapel Hill, 1981), especially p. 180. More generally, consult Jeffrey Merrick, *The Desacralization of the French Monarchy in the Eighteenth Century* (Baton Rouge, 1990). In this work, notice how the evidence on desacralization tends to omit the Vergennes era. Also see Jeremy Popkin, *News and Politics in the Age of Revolution: Jean Luzac's "Gazette de Leyde"* (Ithaca, 1989), p. 150, on the activities of pamphleteers.

5 On pornographic materials, consult Robert Darnton, "The High Enlightenment and the Low-Life of Literature," in *The Literary Underground of the Old Regime* (Cambridge, Mass., 1982), pp. 1–40. On the economic debate, consult John Bosher, *French Finances, 1770–1795: From Business to Bureaucracy* (Cambridge, 1970).

6 For the general permeation of advanced social notions, consult first and foremost Daniel Roche, *Le Siècle des lumières en province. Académies et académiciens provinciaux 1680–1789* (Paris, 1978). For an interesting example of a conservative group flirting with radical notions, see Lenard R. Berlanstein, "Lawyers in Pre-revolutionary France" in Wilfrid Prest, ed., *Lawyers in Early Modern Europe and America* (London, 1981), pp. 164–80. For another interesting approach to this subject see Jacqueline de la Harpe, *Le "Journal des savants" et l'Angleterre, 1702–1789*, University of California Publications in Modern Philology (Berkeley, 1941), *passim*.

7 For the ability to accept advanced social ideas while fearing the working classes, see Harvey Chisick, *The Limits of Reform in the Enlightenment: Attitudes toward the Education of the Lower Classes in Eighteenth-Century France* (Prin-

ceton, 1981); and Harry C. Payne, *The Philosophes and the People* (New Haven, 1976). Of course, the actual social distance may even have exceeded the indifferent attitudes felt by the dominant classes. For a view of the entire social structure, consult Pierre Goubert and Daniel Roche, *Les Français et l'ancien régime*, vol. 1, *La Société et l'état* (Paris, 1984), pp. 29–185.

8 For the more ambiguous way that the elite mixed the old and new, but in the end seemed to emphasize traditional social goals, see Robert Forster, *Merchants, Landlords, Magistrates: The Depont Family in Eighteenth Century France* (Baltimore, 1980); and Lenard R. Berlanstein, *The Barristers of Toulouse in the Eighteenth Century (1740–1793)* (Baltimore, 1975).

9 The analysis here focuses on which issues concerned the discussion press. Why, however, were commonwealthman theory and parlementary Jansenism all but ignored and materialism and frondeur ideology little covered? For domestic papers an answer seems forthcoming. The last two issues were omitted simply because they were too hot to handle. Parlementary ideology shared a similar fate, probably because it was seen as integrally involved in current political struggles, as an area clearly off limits to the discussion press. Also, this ideology clearly opposed the monarchy's position. Finally, while commonwealthman theory may have exercised great impact in everyday life, traces of it are less easy to detect in written culture. This part of the press was closely tied to covering what was already in print, and thus overlooked other cultural manifestations. What remains more difficult to understand is the failure for foreign publications to capitalize at all upon the greater laxity available to them. Even though they could have published most anything, they did not. Doubtless, for the same reason as the domestic press, they eschewed commonwealthman theory which was relatively less discussed in print on the continent. But the reason other areas were ignored likely relates to the sensitivities of host governments. Willing to tolerate negative political reporting of other countries, these states doubtless feared abstract discussion of radical beliefs. Even parlementary Jansenism, acceptable in a report of French politics, would take on a new, more generalized guise in the discussion press. While the French government would probably have preferred those over the gazettes' treatment, it was exactly reversed for foreign authorities.

10 For the general spread of the various forms of the Enlightenment throughout France, see Daniel Mornet, *Les Origines intellectuelles de la révolution française, 1715–1787* (Paris, 1967).

11 Pierre Grosclaude, *Malesherbes. Témoin et interprète de son temps* (Paris, 1961), pp. 101–38; and Robert R. Palmer, *Catholics and Unbelievers in Eighteenth Century France* (Princeton, 1939, *passim.*

12 Jürgen Habermas, *The Structural Transformation of the Public Sphere*, trans. Thomas Burger (Cambridge, Mass., 1989) pp. 51–6. There is a rapidly expanding literature on Habermas. See among other articles: Alan Williams, "The State and the Family in Eighteenth-Century Paris: Toward a Sociology of Spheres" (Paper presented at the 1990 meeting of the Western Society for French History); Anthony J. La Vopa, "Conceiving a Public: Ideas and Society in Eighteenth-Century Europe," *Journal of Modern History* 64 (1992): 79–116; James H. Johnson, "Musical Experience and the Formation of a French Musical Public, "*Journal of Modern History* 64 (1992); 191-226; Jeremy Popkin, "The Concept of Public Opinion in the Historiography of the French Revolution: A Critique" *Storia della Storiografia* 20 (1991): 77–92; Benjamin Nathans, "Habermas's 'Public sphere' in the Era of the French Revolution," *French Historical Studies* 16 (Spring 1990): 620–44; and the forum, "The Public Sphere

in the Eighteenth Century," containing articles by Daniel Gordon, David A. Bell and Sarah Maza in *French Historical Studies*, 17 (Fall 1992): 882–956.

13 See for example Guy Chaussinand-Nogaret, *La Noblesse au XVIIIe siècle. De la Féodalité aux lumières* (Paris, 1976). This is not to say no differences existed between wealthy commoners and the nobility, but that gaps on intellectual subjects are not highly significant. Even defenders of the social differences between nobility and the upper middle class find friction, not vast separation. See Colin Lucas, "Nobles, Bourgeois, and the Origins of the French Revolution, "*Past and Present*, 60 (1973): 84–126. For an important exception that seeks to define a noble/bourgeois division on intellectual matters, consult Jean Quéniart, *Culture et société urbaine dans la France de l'Ouest au XVIIIe siècle* (Paris, 1978). But even this book seems to differentiate, mostly between merchants and their social superiors, not among the components of this still more upper crust.

14 For the most relevant works of François Furet and colleagues associated with him, see François Furet, *Interpreting the French Revolution*, trans. Elborg Forster (Cambridge, 1981) pp. 36–50 and 70–1; Mona Ozouf, "L'Opinion publique, " *The French Revolution and the Creation of Modern Political Culture*, vol. 1, Keith Michael Baker, ed., *The Political Culture of the Old Regime* (Oxford, 1987), pp. 419–34; Keith Michael Baker, *Inventing the French Revolution: Essays on French Political Culture in the Eighteenth Century* (Cambridge, 1989); and Ran Halévi, *Les Loges maçonniques dans la France d'ancien régime. Aux Origines de la sociabilité* (Paris, 1984).

15 François Furet and Ran Halévi, "The Year of 1789" in Jack Censer, T. Daniel Shumate and Josephine Pacheco, eds., *An International Perspective on Human Rights* (Fairfax, Va., 1992), pp. 47–80, and François Furet, "A Commentary," *French Historical Studies* 16 (1990): 792–802.

16 Furet and Halévi, "The Year of 1789," pp. 47–80. See also Marcel Gauchet, "Rights of Man," in François Furet and Mona Ozouf, eds., *Critical Dictionary of the French Revolution*, trans. Arthur Goldhammer (Cambridge, Mass., 1989), pp. 818–28.

17 Georges Lefebvre, *The Coming of the French Revolution*, trans. R. R. Palmer (Princeton, 1947).

18 Robert Forster and Jack P. Greene, *Preconditions of Revolution in Early Modern Europe* (Baltimore, 1970).

19 *The Cultural Origins of the French Revolution*, trans. Lydia G. Cochrane (Durham, N.C., 1991), pp. 169–92 depends on Lawrence Stone's use of the paradigm in *The Causes of the English Revolution, 1529–1642* (New York, 1972).

20 Claude Labrosse and Pierre Rétat, *L'Instrument périodique. La Fonction de la presse au XVIIIe siècle* (Lyons, 1985), pp. 139–78.

21 Of course, papers still existed for the less committed and their journalists spouted a commitment to objective, unbiased reporting. Perhaps such a claim remained a watchword in part because of the conditioning by the Old Regime press which overall tended to understatement. For the array of revolutionary papers, see Jeremy D. Popkin, *Revolutionary News: The Press in France, 1789–99* (Durham, N.C., 1990). One example of a paper promising objectivity was the *Mercure national*. See Jack Richard Censer, *Prelude to Power* (Baltimore, 1976), pp. 13–17.

22 Michael Schudson, *Discovering the News: A Social History of American Newspapers* (New York, 1978).

APPENDIX I

1 Jean Sgard has already summarized most of this sort of available data. Unless otherwise noted, see his "Les Souscripteurs du *Journal étranger*," in Hans Bots, ed., *La Diffusion et la lecture des journaux de langue française sous l'ancien régime* (Amsterdam, 1988), pp. 97–8. For these numbers on the *Gazette de France*, see also Gilles Feyel, "La *Gazette* au début de la guerre de Sept Ans. Son Administration, sa diffusion," in Bots, *La Diffusion*, pp. 101–16.

2 Jean Sgard, ed., *Dictionnaire des journaux (1600–1789)*, 2 vols. (Paris, 1991), p. 446.

3 Gilles Feyel, "La Diffusion des gazettes étrangères en France et la révolution postale des années 1750" in Henri Duranton, Claude Labrosse, and Pierre Rétat, eds., *Les Gazettes européennes de langue française (XVIIe–XVIIIe siècles)* (St. Etienne, 1992), pp. 81–98.

4 See Suzanne Tucoo-Chala, *Charles-Joseph Panckoucke & la librairie française, 1736–1798* (Pau, 1975), p. 209. This magazine also had a literary section.

5 Denise Aimé-Azam, "Le Ministère des affaires étrangères et la presse à la fin de l'Ancien régime," *Cahiers de la presse*, 1 (1938): 435.

6 This journal had a literary section.

7 This periodical took up literary news.

8 Jeremy D. Popkin, *News and Politics in the Age of Revolution: Jean Luzac's "Gazette de Leyde"* (Ithaca, 1989), pp. 120–22.

9 Uta Janssens, *Matthieu Maty and the "Journal Britannique," 1750–55: A French View of English Literature in the Middle of the Eighteenth Century* (Amsterdam, 1975), p. 58.

10 See also Raymond F. Birn, *Pierre Rousseau and the Philosophes of Bouillon* (Geneva, 1964), p. 151.

11 See Harvey Chisick, *The Production, Distribution and Readership of a Conservative Journal of the Early Revolution: The "Ami du Roi" of the Abbé Royou* (Philadephia, 1992), p. 19.

12 Nina Gelbart, "The *Journal des dames* and Its Female Editors: Politics, Censorship and Feminism in the Old Régime Press," in Jack R. Censer and Jeremy D. Popkin, eds., *Press and Politics in Pre-Revolutionary France* (Berkeley, 1987), p. 20.

13 Sgard, *Dictionnaire des journaux*, p. 355.

14 See also Michel Schlup, "Diffusion et lecture du *Journal helvétique* au temps de la Société typographique de Neuchâtel, 1769–1782," in Bots, *La Diffusion*, pp. 59–70.

15 Sgard, *Dictionnaire des journaux*, p. 678.

16 Tucoo-Chala, *Panckoucke*, p. 197.

17 Hervé Guenot, "Les Lecteurs des *Nouvelles de la république des lettres et des arts*," in Bots, *La Diffusion*, pp. 73–80.

18 Eugène Hatin, *Histoire politique et littéraire de la presse en France*, 8 vols. (Paris, 1859–61), 3: 209–11.

19 Sgard, *Dictionnaire des journaux*, p. 616.

20 *Ibid.*, p. 28.

INDEX